REVOLUTION IN LAW

REVOLUTION IN LAW

Contributions to the Development of Soviet Legal Theory, 1917-1938

Edited by Piers Beirne

Routledge
Taylor & Francis Group
LONDON AND NEW YORK

First published 1990 by M.E. Sharpe

Published 2015 by Routledge
2 Park Square, Milton Park, Abingdon, Oxon OX14 4RN
605 Third Avenue, New York, NY 10017

Routledge is an imprint of the Taylor & Francis Group, an informa business

Library of Congress Cataloging-in-Publication Data

Revolution in law: contributions to the development of soviet legal theory, 1917–1938 / Piers Beirne, editor.
p. cm.
Includes bibliographical references.
ISBN 0-87332-560-5 :
1. Law—Soviet Union—History and criticism. 2. Law and socialism—History. I. Beirne, Piers.
LAW
349.47—dc20
[344.7] 89-29816
CIP

ISBN 13: 978-0-87332-560-8 (hbk)

Contents

Preface and Acknowledgments

The current period of *glasnost'* has clearly opened up something other than yet another phase in the seemingly endless Soviet process of purging and rehabilitation. Soviet legal scholars are now attempting to reassess the significance of the mass repression of the 1930s, and they are doing so with a measure of candor not seen since the 1920s. *Revolution in Law: Contributions to the Development of Soviet Legal Theory, 1917–1938* is a collection of recently published and original work by Western scholars that seeks to facilitate reassessment of the history of Soviet law from the October revolution to the year of the great show trials. A companion volume will cover the period from 1938 to the present.

A collaborative work like this incurs a multitude of debts. Bob Sharlet, Steve Redhead, David Trubek, and Zig Zile will each know why I wish to acknowledge their respective kindnesses first. In various ways Maureen Cain, Alan Hunt, Gene Huskey, Bob Kidder, and Peter Solomon made this a better collection than it otherwise would have been. Sundry electronic tricks were performed by Wanda M. Gilpatrick, Dennis Patterson, and Peter Lehman. Rosy Miller, Elaine Shuman, and Martha Lippa valiantly performed much of the time-consuming work of checking and updating the references for several chapters in this collection that, for one reason or another, Soviet legal theorists failed to do themselves. Susan Corrente has gracefully shown me that the "withering away of law" is neither so realistic nor so desirable an objective as I once imagined.

I wish also to thank the National Endowment for the Humanities, which generously provided the opportunity for my initial collaboration with Robert Sharlet and Peter Maggs nearly a decade ago. The University of Southern Maine assisted me in various ways, and I am most appreciative of the administrative kindnesses of Patricia Plante and Dave Davis.

Editor's Introduction

Piers Beirne

In late 1917, after the sudden collapse of the Russian Provisional Government, the Bolsheviks found themselves altogether lacking in theoretical direction for the role of law during the transitional period between capitalism and communism. For Bolshevik theorists of state and law the several strands of existing legal theory presented, in concert, a formidable obstacle to the development of a Marxist theory of law.

Russian jurisprudence was dominated, until approximately the end of the civil war, by foreign, non-Marxist theories about the origins and purposes of law. Neither the legal positivism of Hans Kelsen nor the social functionalism of the Austrian jurist Karl Renner (although both were popular and widely read) afforded much of a basis for the development of a Marxist theory of law. Alongside these was the pervasive influence of German philosophical idealism; its ambassadors were numerous, but the names of Jhering, Laband, Jellinek, Windsheid, and Dernburg constantly recur as authoritative sources in Russian juristic treatises of the time. Following from the inauguration of the Pandektist Civil Code and the *Methodenstreit* debates within philosophical idealism, the legacy of late-nineteenth-century German social theory was the view that the core of the social universe was the individual, volitional agent whose rights and obligations were expressed in legal rules. This atomistic legacy of the idealist literature was most prominently received in the psychologism of Leon Petrazhitsky, a supporter of the conservative Russian Kadet party. Its message was dismissed as legalistic poppycock by the Bolsheviks, who chose instead to discover in any and all legal discourse the simple reflections of the material and ideological relations of social classes.

Nor did the writings of Marx or Engels seem to offer much beyond a paralyzing legal nihilism. While Marx himself had written extensively about the complex articulation of law within different modes of production, his writings on law and socialism were sparse, polemical, and always utopian. Marx's well-known statements to the effect that the state was "but the executive committee for managing the common affairs of the whole bourgeoisie" and that only under communism could "the narrow horizon of bourgeois law be crossed in its entirety" offered considerable inspiration but little practical guidance for those entrusted with the pressing dictates of socialist construction. The nihilism of this confused vacuum was exacerbated by the view, forcefully insisted on by Engels, that because law was the *world view* of the bourgeoisie it was only the most backward sections of the socialist movement that voiced their demands in legalistic terms.

Moreover, there was no indigenous Marxist tradition in Russian legal theory. The People's Will movement had been destroyed by 1887, and the Social Democratic writings of authors such as Kistiakovsky and Struve had been rejected by Lenin and castigated as reformist some twenty years before the 1917 revolution. The reception of classical Marxism in Russia had been strongly influenced by the lengthy, tragic tradition of Russian anarchism, which was opposed to state and legal power in any and in all of its institutional forms. It was the anarchist Mikhail Bakunin, a bitter foe of Marx, who translated the first Russian edition of *The Communist Manifesto.*

Those unfamiliar with Soviet legal history will not be surprised to learn that, despite the theoretical vacuum which confronted the Bolsheviks at the onset of the 1917 revolution, or perhaps precisely because of it, the next decade was an enormously fertile period for Marxist theories of law. This decade provides a wonderful illustration of the mutual penetration of politics, theory, and law. Questions about the appropriate form and content of the regulation of social relations were an important aspect of Bolshevik discussion and debate from the very beginning of the revolution. What relationship ought to exist between the tsarist legal system and the new forms of Bolshevik power? Which aspects of social relations should be regulated by law, which by simple coercion, and which by propaganda and exhortation? Should the technical expertise of tsarist lawyers be relied upon until a coherent system of proletarian law was enacted? When and under what conditions would proletarian law—when would *all* law—wither away?

To none of these questions did Bolshevik legal theorists have any ready-made answers. Nonetheless, developed communism demanded the withering away of law and the Bolsheviks therefore set themselves the task of trying to identify temporary, democratic, and accessible legal structures appropriate to a transitional period of socialist construction. Some very able (and some not so able) theorists committed their energies to this complex task, including Stuchka, Pashukanis, Lenin, Vyshinsky, and Krylenko. Their labors are the focus of this book.

Of the seven authors whose work appears in this collection one is an historian, two are lawyers, three are political scientists, and one is a sociologist. The diversity of the authors' backgrounds notwithstanding, the eight chapters have considerable theoretical consistency. Each of them takes seriously the notion that the complex intellectual and political history of Soviet law in the 1920s and 1930s must be understood at a number of different levels: the theoretical, the personal, the bureaucratic, and the political. In concert, the essays cover both the major themes of Soviet legal theory between 1917 and 1938 and also the major theorists who articulated them.

Chapter 1 (Susan Heuman, "Perspectives on Legal Culture in Prerevolutionary Russia"), written for this volume, outlines the social and political context of the jurisprudential ideas that developed in Russia after the 1864 legal reforms. These ideas inhabited a spectrum ranging from legal nihilism to legal idealism, and from liberalism to rule-of-law socialism. None of these ideas, however, seemed seriously to compromise the political absolutism of the tsarist state. The chapter paints with a broad brush the varieties of legal culture to be found in Russia on the eve of the 1917 revolution. It implicitly suggests that the failure of liberal Russian legal culture to exert any decisive effects, when combined with the virtual absence of a Marxist tradition in law, led to the institutional and theoretical vacuum into which the Bolsheviks were immediately plunged in October 1917.

Chapter 2 (Piers Beirne and Robert Sharlet, "Toward a General Theory of Law and Marxism: E. B. Pashukanis") documents the intellectual and political history of E. B. Pashukanis's seminal book *The General Theory of Law and Marxism*. First published in 1924 as an introduction to the problems of constructing a general theory of law, *The General Theory* contains without doubt the most creative attempt to develop a Marxist theory of law. Why is it, asked Pashukanis, that under certain conditions the regulation of social relationships assumes a *legal* character? The chapter describes how Pashukanis's answer to this question was the basis for his commodity exchange theory of law, and how it led unerringly to the demand for "the withering away of law" (*otmiranie prava*). This anarchic agenda, however, became increasingly incompatible with the new political and economic priorities of Stalinism. After several lukewarm self-criticisms, Pashukanis disappeared in early 1937, a victim of Stalinism.

Chapter 3 (Robert Sharlet, Peter B. Maggs, and Piers Beirne, "P. I. Stuchka and Soviet Law") outlines the contribution to Soviet legal theory of the Latvian-born theorist P. I. Stuchka, a jurist who is generally recognized as one of the principal architects of modern Soviet legal theory and of the Soviet legal system itself. Stuchka was the prodigious author and editor of many treatises, textbooks, symposia, and a Marxist encyclopedia of state and law. In addition, he published an extraordinary number of essays, articles, and reviews in which his contribution to the Marxist theory of law in the 1920s was largely contained. This chapter is intended to illustrate both the development of Stuchka's thought on Soviet law and Marxism and also the practical labors of a theorist who, for a tumultuous decade, was chairman of the Supreme Court of the Russian Republic in Moscow.

Chapter 4 (Piers Beirne and Alan Hunt, "Law and the Constitution of Soviet Society: The Case of Comrade Lenin") investigates a largely unrecognized but nevertheless important saga in the legal and political history of Soviet Marxism: the simultaneously coherent and contradictory theoretical tendencies in Lenin's pronouncements about law, legality, and delegalization ("the withering away of law") during the socialist transition. These tendencies are identified and discussed as they unfold against the historical background of the Russian revolution. The chapter argues that Lenin's political and theoretical objections to legal formalism greatly contributed to the tragic neglect of constitutional mechanisms needed to secure the radical democratic motives of the revolutionary process.

Chapter 5 (Piers Beirne and Alan Hunt, "Lenin, Crime, and Penal Politics, 1917–1924"), previously unpublished, investigates Lenin's influential pronouncements on crime and penality during the critical period of early Bolshevik power between October 1917 and his death in mid-1924. Three key elements in this discourse are identified: (1) a largely positivist view of criminality in socialist and communist societies; (2) support for various neoclassical strategies in Bolshevik penality; and, (3) a simultaneously coherent and contradictory fusion, within the penal complex, of strategies of law and terror. The chapter suggests that, like his view of the constitution of Soviet society, Lenin's view of penality stemmed from the complex interplay of authoritarian and libertarian tendencies in his political theory. These tendencies, both progressive and reactionary, are identified and discussed as they unfolded in the early years of Bolshevik power.

Chapter 6 (Robert Sharlet and Piers Beirne, "In Search of Vyshinsky: The Paradox of Law and Terror") is an intellectual biography of the infamous Procurator General A. Ia. Vyshinsky. It begins with Vyshinsky's anti-Bolshevik careerism before 1917, and concludes with his prosecution of Bukharin in the great show trial of 1938. The chapter shows that in between these years Vyshinsky the political activist and erstwhile theorist of Soviet law played a visible, albeit secondary, role in the commodity exchange school of law. By 1927 a clear gulf had emerged between Vyshinsky and this school: at a time when the withering away of law was openly espoused by Pashukanis and radical colleagues, Vyshinsky's incipient Stalinism was revealed in his insistence that Soviet law was a class law used simply to thwart all class enemies. In the late 1930s, Vyshinsky—the principal architect of the fusion of law and terror—ordered that designated percentages of the population in different parts of the country be arrested and purged, while at the same time trying to foster the growth of new Soviet law schools. During this period he presided over the demise of the commodity exchange school and the disappearance of its principal adherents.

Chapter 7 (Donald D. Barry, "Nikolai Vasil′evich Krylenko: A Reevaluation") outlines the changing political fortunes of N. V. Krylenko, a well-rounded figure of "revolutionary vengeance incarnate" known also for his extralegal interests, which included chess, mountain-climbing, hunting, and tourism. It describes Krylenko's early activities as head of the revolutionary tribunals in 1918, as an ineffective commissar of military affairs (just prior to Trotsky's appointment), and as commissar of justice at both the RSFSR and USSR levels. Krylenko is better known as the leading prosecutor in a series of important political trials in the late 1920s and 1930s in which he played the part of the tough, relentless accuser. These trials included the Shakhty trial of 1928, the "Industrial Party" trial of 1930, and the 1931 case of the Menshevik "Union Bureau." During the famous trials of the

Old Bolsheviks in the late 1930s, however, Krylenko's mantle was assumed by Vyshinsky. The chapter provides additional perspective for the evaluation of Krylenko as a legal functionary by examining the Soviet hierarchy's changing perceptions of him from the time of his purge in 1938 to his rehabilitation in 1955.

Chapter 8 (Eugene Huskey, "Vyshinsky, Krylenko, and Soviet Penal Politics in the 1930s") draws together and extends some of the themes of the previous two chapters. Its starting point is that the rise of Stalinism in the early 1930s settled the question of who would wield power, but not how that power was to be exercised. In the domain of law the terms of the ensuing political dispute were epitomized, to a certain extent, by the respective positions adopted by Krylenko and Vyshinsky. The chapter shows how in the 1930s, at least, Vyshinsky emerged as the exponent of a moderate position opposed to the alleged leftist errors of the legal nihilists. In his bitter public dispute with Krylenko, Vyshinsky opportunistically pressed for a return to the detailed precision of bourgeois legal codes and even to some of their procedural injunctions. Soon, however, Vyshinsky began to advance the ominous position that *any* legal principles and practices should be used provided that they served the interests of the proletariat.

By the late 1930s it therefore transpired that the dangerous vacuum created by the Bolsheviks' original legal nihilism was first displaced, ironically, by a Stalinist movement to restore and refetishize law, and then transformed, tragically, by the fusion of law and terror.

REVOLUTION IN LAW

Chapter 1

Perspectives on Legal Culture in Prerevolutionary Russia

Susan Eva Heuman

> Law? Natural law, state law, civil law, criminal law, catechetical law, law of war, international law, *das Recht*, *le Droit*, *pravo*. What does it mean, what is defined by this strange word?
>
> —Leo Tolstoy[1]

Historical Background

The traditional Russian attitude toward the law was ambivalent at best. From the time of Peter the Great the tsars established a governmental system designed to serve the will of the center.[2] Law was identified with the head of state rather than with legal precepts.[3] Although during each reign the failure to codify the law was recognized as a problem, the tsars drew back from permitting the establishment of an overarching theory of law. To acknowledge any principle of authority higher than the autocracy itself was unacceptable. Having refused to build a codified law based on a general theory of law (*pravo*), the autocracy resorted to the solution of issuing regulations (*zakony*) to deal with every problem. Thus Marc Raeff has described the nineteenth-century Russian Empire as a *Reglamentstaat*, with a multitude of separate written regulations.[4]

It was the tsarist ambivalence toward the law that ultimately undermined the great legal reforms of the 1860s. Introduced under Alexander II just after the emancipation of the serfs, the legal reforms of 1864 created an independent judiciary, jury trials, and a Bar (*advokatura*). By the turn of the century, judges were appointed for life and conducted public jury trials with substantial rights of appeal and attention to procedural rights for the defendants. Judges upheld the independent role of law, even abrogating executive administrative orders which they deemed illegal.[5]

Had legal institutions been successfully established throughout the empire during the reform period, a more powerful and resilient legal culture might have developed. As it happened, however, the government intervened whenever it felt threatened by the independence of judges and juries.[6] The courts had considerable autonomy in the area of political crimes until the Vera Zasulich case in 1878. Zasulich shot and wounded the St. Petersburg governor general as a retaliatory gesture for his having beaten a revolutionary prisoner named Bogoliubov. When Zasulich was acquitted to cheers in the courtroom, the regime intervened by taking many "political" trials out of the public realm of jury trials and remanding them to military courts-martial. During the trials of the People's Will in the 1880s, forty-two of the seventy-three cases were heard by military courts and seven by special Senate session. Only the least significant were heard in public jury trials. By 1906 about a thousand political prisoners had been executed during field courts-martial.

Estate and Class

It should be remembered, in any case, that the sophisticated legal system set up under the reforms of 1864 applied to only a small part of the population—about 10–15 percent. The great majority of the people were peasants emancipated from serfdom in 1861 and living in communes, under the jurisdiction of local custom. The land redemption payments and taxes imposed upon the communes as a condition for the emancipation made the actual freedom of the peasants impossible (they could not leave the commune) until their debts were erased by official decree during the Stolypin era.

In effect, the peasants were segregated into a separate estate within the realm where they were allowed to live according to their specific customary law (*obychnoe pravo*) or popular law (*narodnoe pravo*).[7] These unwritten rules were not always compatible with the realm of the written laws—laws for the upper classes, town dwellers, and educated society. The commune had its own method of regulating relations and settling disputes between peasants and nonpeasants. Much like other developing societies, the Russian Empire in the postreform era was a dual society. The peasants were freed from the landlords' control, but they were separated from the rest of society by their own laws and courts as well as by communal land tenure and the world of the commune. In modern terms, peasant Russia was a vast South African–style "homeland." This patriarchal, legal apartheid was justified by the separate world of peasant laws.[8]

The legal status of all persons in the Russian Empire was theoretically determined by their social position as classified by legal estates in the *soslovie* system. The first estate was the nobility, then came the clergy, and there were separate estates for town dwellers, peasants, and others in society. Each of the estates had its own legally defined rights and obligations.[9] Though class relations were changing, the state reacted to the increase in social and political unrest by trying to reinforce the status quo.[10] But new class groups such as workers, professionals, and the intelligentsia had no place in the antiquated *soslovie* system. The state recognized only an amorphous category called the *raznochintsy* (people of various origins who no longer belonged to a traditional group). Because the *soslovie* system was so closely tied to the state, it became difficult to decipher in legal or social terms. This dependence on the state and bureaucratic structure made the Russian estate system less autonomous than the sort of estate that had existed in France before the French revolution.

By the turn of the century, the social classifications of legal status were so ill-defined that some scholars have noted the existence of two distinct worlds in Russia. One was the heritage of the collective *soslovie* system of the arbitrary autocracy, the landowning nobility, and the rural world; the "other world represented an underdeveloped but emerging civil society of classes, defended by a reformist bureaucracy willing to face a modern world that traditional Russia preferred to ignore."[11]

After the 1905 revolution, a clear opposition to the *soslovie* system was articulated during debates in the First and Second Dumas in 1906 and 1907. On the day before the Stolypin *coup d'état* of June 3, 1907 a proposal for the abolition of the *soslovie* system stated:

> For the full development of the principle of legal equality and individual freedom in the state, it is necessary to abolish the *soslovie* system, that is, the division of the population into groups solely according to the principle of common origin, as a result of which members of *soslovie* corporations possess political and other rights (established by law and transmitted by heredity), which are unequal for various groups.[12]

But for the tsarist regime, the very idea of formulating a legal system that would fully encompass the multifaceted worlds of the prerevolutionary Russian Empire was an awesome, if not impossible, task. The disparate elements of their complex society had to be revealed and defined, and then integrated into one legal order that would make civil society cohesive. This was complicated by the fact that the society was an incongruous mixture of impressive capital cities and a growing number of industrial complexes, all set against the vast backdrop of the overwhelming majority—the peasantry—and a growing working class.

The autocracy dealt with the population as subjects who were granted certain rights and privileges based on their social and economic status. To transform the legal and political system in the Russian Empire would necessitate a change in the relationship between the individual and the state. But the tradition of the French Enlightenment did not have the impact on the Russian Empire that it had in Western Europe, where it produced a sense of natural rights. Natural rights might have given birth to a concept of civil rights that were independent of the bureaucratic state and its ideological framework.

The Rejection of Liberal Values

The individual was far from the center of the theory of law in the Russian Empire. The dominant orientation was the analytical school which considered law to be the body of norms safeguarded by the power of the state.[13]

Basically, the analytical school held to a positivistic approach to law that tried to find connections and similarities between scientific laws and juridical norms. Those theorists who tried to escape the positivistic approach placed law in the context of a general, often metaphysical, philosophy of man and of values; thereby, they hoped to find an independent criterion for judging the value of positive laws. Progressive Russian legal theorists such as the lawyer and sociologist B. A. Kistiakovsky (1868–1920) fought against metaphysical notions of abstract logic and tried to develop the idea of individual rights, hoping that this would limit political power—the power of the ruler and even that of the majority.

In 1909 Kistiakovsky wrote for the volume *Vekhi* (Landmarks) his essay "In Defense of Law."[14] This was an insightful historical review of the failure of the Russian intelligentsia to acquire a respect for legal institutions. Kistiakovsky lamented the fact that in Russia political concerns had always taken precedence over the proper functioning of the judiciary. He considered illusory the widespread notion that the Russian people would instinctively develop a type of social organization that would be superior to one constructed on the values of a legal order. This view, he argued, was only a justification for Russian suspicions of the West. Indeed, the *soslovie* system reinforced the Slavophile ideal of a *Gemeinschaft* (community) and an organic, communal-familial, collective approach to society and law, while the Western-oriented liberals supported the idea of a *Gesellschaft* (society) and an approach to law based on protection of the inviolable rights of the individual.[15]

Alexander Herzen had another explanation for the negative Russian attitute to law:

> Complete inequality before the law has killed any trace of respect for legality in the Russian people. The Russian, whatever his station, breaks the law wherever he can do so with impunity; the government acts in the same way.[16]

The distrust and rejection of law which is part of the Russian nihilist and anarchist tradition is best characterized by the thought of Mikhail Bakunin (1814–1876) and Prince Peter Kropotkin (1842–1921). Bakunin attacked law on the grounds that it was an instrument of ruling class oppression, the antithesis to human freedom. In the wake of the 1848 revolution in France, Bakunin asserted:

> I believe neither in constitutions nor in laws; the best constitution possible would not satisfy me. We need nothing less than to burst out into the life of a new world, lawless and therefore free.[17]

Individual freedom was central to the anarchists, though it was not dependent on man-made laws in their conception of the ideal society. In their view, freedom was independence from society; it was spontaneous, and compatible only with natural laws of collective life. Bakunin rejected all forms of dependence on control by human will. Instead, he accepted natural laws which he considered involuntary and inevitable:

> These natural laws must be distinguished from the authoritarian, arbitrary, political, religious, criminal, and civil laws that the privileged classes have established over the course of history, always for the sole purpose of exploiting the labor of the working masses and muzzling their freedom—laws which, under the pretext of a fictitious morality, have always been the source of the lowest immorality.[18]

Kropotkin attacked the "religion of law" in his essay "Law and Authority." Law was a product of the modern world which served to obscure the age-old world of customary law that was traditionally unwritten. Kropotkin's two worlds were divided into the organic, communal spirit of mutual aid and the authoritarian world created by written laws characteristic of capitalism.[19]

Similarly, Leo Tolstoy held the view that law was an instrument wielded by the state. In his "Letter to a student concerning law" (1909), addressed to a student of L. I. Petrazhitsky, Tolstoy answered the question posed in the epigraph to this essay: What is law?

> If we are thinking not in accordance with "science" . . . but in accordance with universal common sense, then the answer to this question is very simple and clear: for those in power law means the authorization, which they have given themselves, to do everything which is advantageous to themselves while for those subject to them law means permission to do whatever is not forbidden to them. Civil law is the right of some to own land, even tens of thousands of *desiatinas*, as well as other means of production, while for those who are deprived of land and other means of production it is the right to sell (upon threat of dying of poverty and hunger) their labor and their lives to the owners of land and capital. Criminal law is the right of some to send others into penal servitude, . . . while for those who are subject to penal servitude, imprisonment or execution, it is only their right to avoid these things until those who are in power decide otherwise.[20]

Tolstoy's letter exemplified the anarchist rejection of all forms of man-made laws. Of course, Tolstoy was an artist and not a political or legal analyst, but he articulated a view that was widely held not only by nihilists and anarchists but also by Marxists: Law was an expression of class power, an instrument to shape society in a manner that was advantageous to those who were in power.[21]

The Liberal Struggle to Create a Legal Culture

Turn-of-the-century liberal legal theorists including Kistiakovsky, Petrazhitsky (1867–1931), and P. I. Novgorodtsev (1866–1924) regarded the institution of the rule of law as critical for guaranteeing the rights of the individual and making those rights the basis of a modern constitutional government. Some went beyond civil rights to a view of human rights encompassing a combination of political and economic rights. But rather than exclusively reproducing Western models, these liberals attempted to build a theory of their own that would adapt Western concepts to the socioeconomic conditions of their own society. They sought the sources of the law in the social, economic, and even psychological fabric of Russian society.

The liberals and moderates hoped for a constitutional state or a rule-of-law state to replace the personal rule of the tsar. From the time of the Great Reforms of the 1860s to the 1890s, the liberal gentry tended to advocate gradual change by legal and nonrevolutionary opposition. Boris Chicherin (1828–1904), an aristocrat and a *zemstvo* leader who was an ardent Hegelian and a prolific writer on legal theory, advocated a *Rechtstaat*. But his conception of the *Rechtstaat* was of the Bismarckian Junker variety, founded on laws and legality but not on parliamentary (or popular) sovereignty. He was clearly antirevolutionary, for he considered socialist attacks on private property a threat to the idea of civil rights and freedom. However, Chicherin was consistent in his belief that Russia should strive for a constitutionally based system like those in Western Europe—with civil freedoms, legal order, and eventually, a constitutional order based on individual political rights.[22]

In his (1909) criticism of the lack of legal consciousness in Russia, Kistiakovsky argued that ideas about law could not simply be borrowed from the West:

> Borrowing is not enough—it is necessary to be seized by ideas at a certain moment in life. However old an idea may be, it is always new for the person experiencing it for the first time. It performs creative work in the consciousness as it is assimilated and transformed by the other elements present.[23]

For Petrazhitsky, Novgorodtsev, and Kistiakovsky, individual freedoms had to become the primary, not the secondary goal of society. As Kistiakovsky noted, in Western constitutional regimes individual rights were supposed to be the priority, but in fact,

> all individual and social freedoms or rights were not primary rights but only traces of legal principles: all that was not forbidden was allowed. As expressed in legal terminology, individual and social freeedoms were reflections of objective laws.[24]

In the wake of the Great Reforms a new sociological approach to law was pursued as a means of making law an instrument of social integration and social change. The antipositivist legal theorists looked to law as a means of welding the fragmented and diverse Russian society into one national and social community.

The founder of a sociological approach to law in Russia was S. A. Muromtsev (1850–1910), a leading voice in the Moscow Juridical Society, the first professional organization for lawyers, which was created in 1863. A professor of law at Moscow University from 1877 to 1884, his academic career was interrupted when the minister of education dismissed him for his political activities. One of these activities was Muromtsev's participation with nineteen other Moscow residents in writing and sending a memorandum to M. T. Loris Melikov, the head of the Commission for Safeguarding State Order and Social Peace (introduced in 1880). The memorandum suggested that, in light of the growing opposition to the government, an independent meeting of *zemstvo* representatives be invited to take part in government activities for the purpose of "guaranteeing the rights of the individual to the freedom of thought and expression."[25] Because of this type of activity, Muromtsev lost his post in Moscow University. By 1892 pressure from the government censors caused the juridical society to stop publishing its journal, *Iuridicheskii vestnik* (Juridical Messenger). In 1899 the Moscow Juridical Society was officially closed by government order.[26]

Muromtsev argued that the law required a general theory so that there would be a framework for empirical legal studies. He hoped that legal studies would seek universal attributes as well as the specific legal formations in individual societies.[27] Law was for him a system of social relations; legal norms were to be deciphered through conflict resolution between various groups. The government's successful efforts to censor the sociological study of law and the quest for a general theory of law forced the legal community to reconsider law as a reified abstract category that remained aloof from social and political issues. Through Muromtsev's influence, a group of jurists embarked on detailed studies of the social and political aspects of Russian law. There developed two types of jurisprudence: (1) theoretical jurisprudence dedicated to the development of law, and (2) applied jurisprudence which was dedicated to practical applications of the law for social progress.[28]

The legal theorists Petrazhitsky and Novgorodtsev, who were members of the Constitutional Democratic (Kadet) Party Central Committee, and Kistiakovsky, a member of *Osvobozhdenie* (Liberation), sought a foundation for the laws in social, psychological, and philosophical worlds that would come to terms with the Russian political and social order. They hoped for a system of "*Rechtstaat* Liberalism" based on popular sovereignty, in which the individual and individual rights would become the central element. For that to happen individuals had to be transformed from subjects into citizens; that is, individuals had to be legally defined as having basic (natural) rights and to conceive of themselves as individuals—not exclusively as part of an estate (*soslovie*) or a class.

In addressing the crisis of legal ideas in Russia, the liberal theorists recognized the dangers of legal positivism. For legal positivists, law was to be separate from moral values—a separation that could allow the content of the laws to express authoritarian ideas. It was precisely in recognition of this danger that the liberal theorists parted company with the positivists, for they identified the latter's theory of law as one which put political authority above the law; if the "sovereign" was above the law, then tyranny might ensue. Accordingly, the liberal theorists tried to establish individual liberties as the foundation for the system that would eventually express the power of a democratic majority. Their goal was to build a legal culture that would remain independent of the machinations of the autocracy.

As noted above, Kistiakovsky joined the other authors of *Vekhi* (Berdyaev, Bulgakov, Gershenzon, Izgoev, Struve, and Frank) in condemning the intelligentsia's devotion to revolutionary change because these educated social activists and theorists did not adequately consider what would replace the existing government. The *Vekhi* authors were most concerned with values in society, and they urged the intelligentsia to strive to modify the existing social order and change it into a system based on morality, law, and justice.

Another respected champion of the individual as the creator and center of legal relations was L. I. Petrazhitsky, a founder of the newspaper *Pravo.* A Kadet elected to the First Duma, Petrazhitsky openly involved himself with the opposition and even signed the Vyborg manifesto to protest the closing of the Duma by the tsar. His political activities caused him to lose his academic chair and the deanship at St. Petersburg University. Petrazhitsky was ordered to sign a promise that he would refrain from further political involvement, but he regained his post at the university even though he refused to sign the document.

Petrazhitsky was a major advocate for the cause of a liberal *Rechtstaat* in Russia. He rejected positive law as did the neo-Kantians (Kistiakovsky and Novgorodtsev, among others), but based on his psychological orientation in legal thought. Petrazhitsky's theory of law was based on the premise that law is an "internal" phenomenon—that its foundations are in the consciousness of individuals and groups. He considered intuitive law to be the foundation of all legal orders, not positive law, which depends on external authority. Positive law, in his view, was imposed on the individual by the state and its institutions; in fact, the state should have been created by the law instead of being a creator of laws.

Legal reformers were faced with the lack of legal consciousness that resulted from the autocracy's failure to allow its subjects to become citizens. As subjects, the people had servile souls and waited to be directed by their tsar father. Thus Petrazhitsky wrote in his *Theory of State and Law* (1909) that ideally the law

> communicates the firmness and the confidence, the energy and initiative essential for life. A child brought up in an atmosphere of arbitrary caprice (however beneficent and gracious), with no definite assignment to him of a particular sphere of rights (although of a modest and childish character), will not be trained to construct and carry out the plans of life with assurance. In the economic field, particularly, he will be deficient in confidence, boldness, and initiative: he will be apathetic, act at random, and procrastinate in the hope of favourable "chances," help from another, alms, gifts, and the like.[29]

Petrazhitsky's concept of intuitive law was conceived of as a complementary set of ideas to socialism and Marxism. Unlike those Marxists who assigned law to the coercive power of the state and assumed that law would disappear when the state withered away, Petrazhitsky urged that the law should be used in the struggle against bourgeois legal consciousness. Actually, there is a remarkable similarity between his approach to the class nature of legal consciousness and that of Marx. He wrote that differences in law as a psychic phenomenon

> may be connected with the class structure of a population—the typical domestic law prevailing in the well-to-do and rich strata is distinguished from the same law in the spheres of those who are not well-to-do and of proletarians, while the typical domestic law of the peasants is different from that of the businessman and the aristocrat.[30]

Petrazhitsky's conception of socialism was that of a centralized organ for production; it was a quasi-militaristic view that would program people to work in accord with the rules of a given society and also the economic needs that had to be satisfied for survival. This conception opposed the democratic basis for socialism envisioned by Herzen and Lavrov, who thought of federations of self-governing communes;[31] it also opposed the socialist idea of constitutionalism that Kistiakovsky hoped to develop—a democratic vision of a socialist constitutional system that was based on a socialist individualism. Petrazhitsky's vision of a socialist economic order presupposed that individual rights were secondary to the goals of building the society. However, Petrazhitsky's theory of law was important for the Russian constitutionalist movement; he hoped it would be enacted by representative legislative bodies.[32]

Those who looked to the normative approach as well as to the sociological approach to legal theory and jurisprudence were best represented in the writings of Kistiakovsky. Kistiakovsky considered normatism the combination of positivism and neo-Kantianism.[33] Both Novgorodtsev and Kistiakovsky were leading neo-Kantians, though Novgorodtsev was openly opposed to the sociological approach to the law that Kistiakovsky advocated. Influenced by the German neo-Kantians in Marburg and Heidelberg, Novgorodtsev and Kistiakovsky also rejected the idea of positive law that attempted to have no relationship to human values and morality. In fact, Novgorodtsev was important in the revival of natural law which, in its modern incarnation, was to be free of transcendental and metaphysical elements. Only in that way could it be useful to modern theories of jurisprudence, for it is through the universal values of natural law that the atmosphere would be generated for the creation of legal norms.[34]

Kistiakovsky spent some time in Germany nearly every year after his doctoral studies there. He participated in the neo-Kantian discussions with Rickert, Simmel, Windelband, and Max Weber. He considered the law to be a social fact that could be discerned through a multifaceted study of the society combined with the values of the individual. Though he was originally a political activist in the Marxist wing of the Ukrainian national movement, he had become a neo-Kantian who insisted that individual value judgments were an integral part of the process of creating legal norms from extensive social, psychological, normative, and economic analyses. Along with his predecessor Muromtsev and his colleague Petrazhitsky, Kistiakovsky sought the sources of the law in society and he hoped that through such an approach the peasant world of customary law would become an integral part of the legal system for all parts of the population. The society had to be analyzed so that the laws were a combined reflection of the ideals of those enacting them and of the social and political conditions from which legal ideas were developed.[35]

Kistiakovsky was a proponent of socialist constitutionalism, or rule-of-law socialism. He did not abandon his earlier dedication to the socialist ideals for an egalitarian society. Thus he argued that there was no reason to believe that constitutionalism and socialism were incompatible. On the contrary, he argued that socialism and constitutionalism (a state based on law) could only be fully developed if they became part and parcel of the same society.

> A rule-of-law state is often called bourgeois as contrasted with socialist. . . . It is clear that when a rule-of-law state is called bourgeois, this reflects the socio-economic structure while in fact a rule-of-law state actually refers to the juridical character of the government. . . . But many confuse the two, and the legal or juridical nature of a socialist government is neglected.[36]

For Kistiakovsky, constitutionalism and socialism were interdependent concepts. But for a government to function effectively, its legal framework had to be clearly articulated. A socialist state could only reach its fullest form if it was governed by a constitutional government, and a constitutional government could only be completely developed if it existed within a socialist system. He explained that just as capitalism is the preparatory stage for the development of socialism, so a government based on law is the preparatory stage for a government that would translate social justice into reality.[37]

Furthermore, Kistiakovsky argued that to establish a new socialist order did not necessarily mean that individual liberties could not be respected. Perceptively, he pinpointed some of the popular fears associated with the authoritarian measures that might be used to build the new socialist order:

> It is often claimed that a socialist state, having been turned into the only and universal employer, will turn into a despotic state and that it would destroy individual freedom according to its needs as if it were not organized democratically. Some even call it a future slavery and think that it will turn into some kind of a military settlement or barracks.[38]

On the contrary, Kistiakovsky foresaw the possibility of increasing the forum for self-determination; once private property was abolished, the individual would be able to participate directly in the government, take more initiative in economic life, and contribute to the cultural life of the country. In this context, the individual would be an active self-determining individual, not an object subjected to rules proclaimed by those in power or oppressed by gross economic inequalities. Kistiakovsky argued that human rights are the essential interconnection between the definition of rights, on the one hand, and the social, economic, and political structure of a society on the other. He considered political and economic rights, i.e., human rights, as an integral part of a program for political and social transformation.

In 1905 Kistiakovsky recognized that these pronouncements should not be taken out of their legal and economic context.

> Law cannot be ranked with such spiritual values as scientific truth, moral perfection, and religious sanctity. It does not have the same absolute significance and its context is, in part, determined by changeable economic and social conditions.[39]

Law is a cultural phenomenon—it derives from the interaction between social realities and human ideals. For Kistiakovsky, individual political rights would remain nominal if they were imposed on a society without being reformulated to reflect the potential for exercising them in a particular social and economic structure. Kistiakovsky's definition of political and economic rights was distinctive in that it incorporated the social and economic base into the description of economic rights—which would theoretically become socialist rights in the context of a socialist society.[40] He hoped that the institutionalization of individual liberties and of a governmental system based on a constitution were the training ground for the eventual development of human rights in a functioning socialist society. The potential danger of collective or state dominance over individuals was for Kistiakovsky as crucial and perplexing a problem in a socialist society as it was in a capitalist society. Individuals had to understand their rights and duties. That meant that society had to provide institutions and personnel to teach them what those rights are and what each person must do to be able to enjoy them.

As editor of the journal of the Moscow Juridical Society, *Iuridicheskii vestnik*, which resumed publication in 1912, Kistiakovsky started openly to defend individual rights and to attack the policies of the autocracy. But during the war years he became estranged from the increasingly chauvinistic Russian liberals, especially his friend P. B. Struve, the Kadet activist, and he separated from his colleagues over the Ukrainian national question. Although a moderate and an antiseparatist, Kistiakovsky became a militant champion of the rights of minority nationalities.[41] For him, national cultural rights were an integral part of human rights.

Severed Roots

The liberal democratic roots of legal culture expressed in the work of Kistiakovsky and others were severed at the time of the 1917 revolution. These theorists had hoped for a system of "*Rechtstaat* Liberalism" based on individual rights and popular sovereignty. To put these ideas into practice, individuals had first to develop legal consciousness, to be transformed from subjects into citizens who had basic (natural) rights and who could see themselves as individuals—more than just part of an estate or a class. In addition, a proper juridical foundation for the state was essential to prevent the violation of individual rights and interests. For Kistiakovsky, individualism and socialism complemented rather than contradicted the effective functioning of the new order: "the participation of the people in the legislative process and governing of the country will be subsequently developed and broadened."[42]

After the October revolution, legal philosophers struggled to define the meaning and role of law in the new Soviet Russia.[43] Individual rights were dismissed as a bourgeois concept. They were subsumed in the whirlwind attempt to overcome the aftermath of the wars and revolutions, the problems of backwardness, and the building of a new socialist legal order, state, and society based on the notion of a proletarian class dictatorship.

On November 27, 1917, the Soviet "Decree No. 1 on the Court" abolished the institutions created by Alexander II's judicial reforms. However, it proved impossible to escape completely from the traditions of the Russian legal system. Courts resembling those eradicated by decree were established with similar functions. Again, there was resistance to copying the codified legal forms of Western European countries. And, of course, there was little experience with lawmaking in Russia. A plethora of decrees were issued which could be supplemented or rescinded as required. The result was reminiscent of the *Reglamentstaat* existing before the revolution, a government of multitudinous regulations. By late 1917, therefore, the development and systematization of a Soviet socialist legal system became an urgent issue.

Notes

1. Tolstoy, *Polnoe sobranie sochinenii*, 1st series, vol. 38 (Moscow, 1936), pp. 55–56, as translated in Andrzej Walicki, *Legal Philosophies of Russian Liberalism* (London: Oxford University Press, 1987), pp. 80–81.

2. Marc Raeff, *The Well-Ordered Police State* (New Haven: Yale University Press, 1983), p. 216.

3. Walicki, *Legal Philosophies of Russian Liberalism*, p. 21.

4. Marc Raeff, "The Bureaucratic Phenomenon of Imperial Russia," *American Historical Review* 84, 2 (1979): 403.

5. The Russian judiciary was not considered much inferior to the European judicial systems, though there was interference with the system on the part of the state. See Walicki, pp. 102–103; A. A. Goldenweiser, *V zashchitu prava* (New York: Chekhov Press, 1952), pp. 211–212.

6. See Samuel Kucherov, *Courts, Lawyers, and Trials under the Last Three Tsars* (Westport, Conn.: Greenwood Press, 1953); John Hazard, "The Courts and the Legal System," in Cyril Black, ed., *The Transformation of Russian Society* (Cambridge, Mass.:

Harvard University Press, 1960), pp. 148–50; A. F. Koni, *Sobranie sochinenii* (Moscow, 1966), vol. 2, pp. 171–73, 180–181; Richard Wortman, *The Development of a Russian Legal Consciousness* (Chicago: University of Chicago Press, 1976), pp. 282–83; and N. A. Troitskii, *"Narodnaia Volia" pered tsarskim sudom, 1880–1891 gg.* (Saratov, 1971), pp. 24–25.

7. David Macey, *Government and Peasant in Russia, 1861–1906* (DeKalb: Northern Illinois University Press, 1987), pp. 15–19.

8. Leonard Schapiro, "The Pre-Revolutionary Intelligentsia and the Legal Order," in *Russian Studies*, ed. by Ellen Dahrendorf (New York: Penguin Books, 1987), pp. 58–60.

9. Gregory Freeze, "The *Soslovie* (Estate) Paradigm and Russian Social History," *American Historical Review* 96, 1: 1–32; Macey, p. 339.

10. Freeze, p. 27.

11. Frank Wcislo, "Soslovie or Class? Bureaucratic Reformers and Provincial Gentry in Conflict, 1906–1908," *The Russian Review*, vol. 47, 1988, p. 23. See also Leopold Haimson, "Conclusion: Observations on the Politics of the Russian Countryside (1905–1914)," in *The Politics of Rural Russia* (Bloomington: Indiana University Press, 1979), pp. 261–300; Leopold Haimson, "The Parties and the State: The Evolution of Political Attitudes," in Cyril E. Black, ed., *The Tranformation of Russian Society* (Cambridge, Mass.: Harvard University Press, 1969); Roberta Manning, *The Crisis of the Old Order* (Princeton: Princeton University Press, 1982), ch. 14; V. S. D'iakin, *Samoderzhavie, Burzhuaziia i dvorianstvo v 1907–1911 gg.* (Leningrad, 1978).

12. Gosudarstvennaia duma, vtoroi sozyv, *Zakonodatel'nye materialy* (St. Petersburg, 1907), trans. in Freeze, p. 31.

13. B. A. Kistiakovskii, *Sotsial'nye nauki i pravo* (Moscow, 1912), p. 321.

14. B. A. Kistiakovskii, "V zashchitu Prava: Intelligentsia i pravosoznanie," in *Vekhi. Sbornik statei o intelligentsii* [Landmarks: A Collection of Essays about the Intelligentsia], (Moscow, 1909). I draw on the Marshall Schatz and Judith Zimmerman translation in *Canadian Slavic Studies*, 4 (Spring 1970): 36–59.

15. See Andrzej Walicki, "Personality and Society in the Ideology of Russian Slavophilism: A Study in the Sociology of Knowledge," *California Slavic Studies* 2 (1963): 7–8.

16. Alexander Herzen, "Du développement des idées révolutionnaires en Russie," *Collected Works in Thirty Volumes* (Moscow, 1956), VII, 121; as quoted by Kistiakovsky, p. 130. Cf. the Schatz and Zimmerman translation, p. 40.

17. M. A. Bakunin, *Sobranie sochinenii i pisem*, ed. by Iu. Steklov, 4 vols. (Moscow, 1934–1936), vol. 3, pp. 317–318, as cited in Mikhail Bakunin, *From Out of the Dustbin: Bakunin's Basic Writings, 1869–1871*, trans. by Robert Cutler (Ann Arbor: Ardis, 1985), pp. 210.

18. Ibid., p. 121.

19. Kropotkin considered these two worlds as opposed to one another as community (*Gemeinschaft*) and society (*Gesellschaft*). See P. Kropotkin, *The State, Its Historic Role* (London: 1943), p. 41.

20. Tolstoy, pp. 55–56.

21. Walicki, *Legal Philosophies of Russian Liberalism*, p. 81.

22. Ibid., pp. 130–37.

23. Kistiakovskii, "V zashchitu Prava," p. 129.

24. Kistiakovskii, "Prava cheloveka i grazhdanina," *Voprosy zhizni* 1 (January 1905): 121.

25. Sh. M. Levin, *Obshchestvennoe dvizhenie v Rossii v 60–70-e gody XIX veka* (Moscow, 1958), p. 499.

26. Later Muromtsev became chairman of the First State Duma based on his experi-

ence as a lawyer, a *zemstvo* activist, and a member of the central committee of the Constitutional Democratic (Kadet) Party. *Zapiski sotsial'no-ekonomichnogo viddilu*, 1 (Ukrainskaia Akademiia nauk, 1923), pp. viii–xii. See also Alexander Vucinich, *Social Thought in Tsarist Russia* (Chicago: University of Chicago Press, 1976), pp. 142–43.

27. Muromtsev did not write one integrated treatise on law but rather several works that contain his ideas: *Essays on the General Theory of Civil Law* (1877) and *Definition and Basic Divisions of Law* (1879). See also S. A. Muromtsev, "Pravo i spravedlivost'," *Sbornik pravovedeniia i ovshchestvennykh znanii* 2 (1893), pp. 1–12.

28. See Vucinich, pp. 140–42; and Kistiakovskii, *Sotsial'nye nauki i pravo*, pp. 353–54.

29. L. I. Petrazhitsky, "Teoriia gosudarstva i prava" (Moscow, 1909), in *Law and Morality*, trans. by H. W. Babb (Cambridge, Mass.: 1955), p. 99.

30. Ibid., p. 245; see Walicki, *Legal Philosophies of Russian Liberalism*, pp. 285–86.

31. Walicki, *Legal Philosophies of Russian Liberalism*, p. 276.

32. Kistiakovskii, *Sotsial'nye nauki i pravo*, pp. 265–66.

33. W. A. Tumanov, *Burzhuaznaia pravovaia ideologia* (Moscow, 1971), pp. 184–92.

34. Vucinich, p. 148; I. Novogorodtsev, "Pravo estestvennoe," *Entsiklopedicheskii slovar'*, Brokgaus-Efron, vol. 24 (St. Petersburg, 1898), pp. 885–90.

35. The problem of writing a constitution was one faced not only by the Russian Empire at the time of the revolution. Max Weber, among others, became deeply involved with the efforts to draft the Weimar Constitution after the First World War. Legitimacy and the principal elements of a given system had to be rethought and redrafted.

36. Kistiakovskii, "Gosudarstvo pravovoe i sotsialisticheskoe" *Voprosy filosofii i psikhologii* 85 (November-December 1906): 494–95.

37. Kistiakovskii, *Sotsial'nye nauki i pravo*, p. 574.

38. Ibid., p. 577.

39. Kistiakovskii, "V zashchitu prava," pp. 125.

40. Kistiakovskii, "Prava cheloveka i grazhdanina," *Voprosy zhizni* 1 (January 1905): 120; see also Susan Eva Heuman, "A Socialist Conception of Human Rights: A Model from Prerevolutionary Russia," in Adamantia Pollis and Peter Schwab, editors, *Human Rights: Cultural and Ideological Perspectives* (New York: Praeger, 1979), pp. 50–51.

41. He expressed his position in the pages of *Russkaia mysl'* and the short-lived journal *Natsional'nye problemy*, which existed for only a few months until the government forced it to shut down in 1915.

42. Kistiakovskii, *Sotsial'nye nauki i pravo*, p. 590.

43. John Hazard, *Settling Disputes in Soviet Society: The Formative Years of Legal Institutions* (New York: Columbia University Press, 1960).

Chapter 2

Toward a General Theory of Law and Marxism: E. B. Pashukanis

Piers Beirne and Robert Sharlet

Evgeny Bronislavovich Pashukanis (1891–1937) has been the only Soviet Marxist legal philosopher to have achieved significant scholarly recognition outside of the USSR.[1] The preeminent Soviet jurist of the 1920s and early 1930s, Pashukanis fell victim to the great purges of the late 1930s and was thereafter reviled as an "enemy of the people" until his posthumous legal rehabilitation in 1956.[2] As a student at the University of St. Petersburg before World War I, Pashukanis had been active in the Russian revolutionary movement and, as a result of his involvement, found it necessary to complete his education abroad at the University of Munich where he specialized in law and political economy. The available details on his early life are sketchy, but it is known that he joined the Bolsheviks in 1918, briefly served as a local and circuit judge in the Moscow region, and then for several years into the early 1920s worked as a legal adviser in the People's Commissariat of Foreign Affairs while, simultaneously, he cultivated a blossoming career in juristic scholarship.[3]

In 1924 Pashukanis emerged from relative obscurity with the publication of his major theoretical work, *The General Theory of Law and Marxism*,[4] which quickly placed him in the front ranks of the field of aspiring Soviet Marxist philosophers of law. He regarded this treatise primarily as an introduction to the problems of constructing a Marxist general theory of law and by no means as the definite statement on the subject. In this spirit, he appropriately subtitled his monograph *An Experiment in the Criticism of Basic Juridical Concepts*, emphasizing that he had written the book primarily for "self-clarification" with the hope that it might serve as a "stimulus and material for further discussion."[5]

Pashukanis's *General Theory* was warmly received by reviewers and went into

---

This chapter is an amended version of Piers Beirne and Robert Sharlet, "Editors' Introduction," pp. 1–36 in *Pashukanis: Selected Writings on Marxism and Law*, Peter B. Maggs, trans. (London: Academic Press, 1980). Reprinted by permission.

a second edition in 1926, followed by a third edition in 1927 which eventually encompassed three printings.[6] The originality of Pashukanis's theory of law—which was largely outlined in the first Russian edition of *The General Theory of Law and Marxism* in 1924, and successively revised in a number of works after 1927—lay in the contraposition of three notions with what Pashukanis took to be the modus operandi of Marx's *Capital.* From Hegel Pashukanis borrowed the familiar distinction between essence and appearance, and also the notion in *The Philosophy of Right* that the Roman *lex persona* was an insufficient basis for the universality of rights attached to individual agents under capitalist modes of production.[7] And from Pokrovsky, an Old Bolshevik and the leading Russian historian between 1910 and 1932, Pashukanis borrowed the assertion that the development of Russian capitalism must be understood in the context of the historical primacy of mercantile capital.[8]

Pashukanis saw that it was not accidental that Marx had begun his analysis of the inner dialectic of the capital-labor relationship (the production of surplus value) with a critique of the categories of bourgeois political economy. It was not simply that the categories of rent, interest, industrial profit, etc., mystified the essential qualities of this relationship. Rather, in order to apprehend the historically specific form of the relationship of capitalist exploitation, one had first to pierce the veil of appearances/semblances/forms which the real relationship inherently produced, and on which it routinely depended for its reproduction.

Pashukanis therefore inferred that had Marx actually written a coherent theory of state and law, as indeed he had twice promised,[9] then it would necessarily have proceeded along the same lines as his iconoclastic analysis of the categories of political economy and the social reality which they mysteriously yet inaccurately express and codify.

Pashukanis consistently argued that there is an homology between the logic of the commodity form and the logic of the legal form. Both are universal equivalents which in appearance equalize the manifestly unequal: respectively, different commodities and the labor which produced them, and different political citizens and the subjects of rights and obligations. The salience of this insight has only very recently been recovered by Marxists,[10] and there are now some healthy indications that the sterile dichotomy between instrumentalist and formalist approaches to law is likely to be transcended. If Pashukanis's main argument is correct, then it obliges us to ask two crucial questions. First, the *specific* content of legal imperatives does not explain why the interests of dominant classes are embodied in the legal form. Why, for example, are these interests not embodied in the form on which they episodically depend, namely, naked coercion? Second, if under capitalism the struggle between competing commodity producers assumes legal form through the principle of equivalence, then it follows that the class struggle between proletariat and bourgeoisie must also typically appear in the medium of the legal form.[11] And how, then, are we able to transform legal reformism into a revolutionary political practice?

By the late 1920s, as a result of his scholarly reputation, Pashukanis had become the *doyen* of Soviet Marxist jurisprudence, eclipsing even his juridical mentor, Piotr Stuchka (*infra*, chapter 3). However, after 1928 Pashukanis's theory as a Marxist critique of bourgeois jurisprudence became increasingly incompatible with the new political and economic priorities of the First Five-Year Plan, especially the necessity for a strong dictatorship of the proletariat and its ancillary, Soviet law, which, after 1937, would become socialist law.

In the ensuing ideological struggle on the "legal front" of Soviet society, Pashukanis made the first of his eventual three self-criticisms in late 1930.[12] After that experience his theory underwent substantial revision during the period of the First and Second Five-Year Plans (1928–1937), as Pashukanis became the principal spokesman for the Stalinist conception of the Soviet state, while simultaneously striving to maintain his political commitment to the Marxist concept of the withering away of law. However, as soon as Stalin's "revolution from above" subsided with the essential completion of collectivization and a new legal policy of stabilization was demanded, the intrinsic ambivalence of Pashukanis's dual commitment to the respective marxisms of Stalin and Marx became apparent. This contributed to his downfall in early 1937. Following Pashukanis's purge, his successor as legal *doyen*, Andrei Vyshinsky (*infra*, chapter 6), began the almost immediate demolition of the considerable structure of his predecessor's influence and, concomitantly, the systematic reconstruction of the Soviet legal system. Vyshinsky ushered in the era of the "Soviet socialist state and law" which has prevailed to this day in Soviet jurisprudence and legal practice.

Finally, in the process of destalinization after Stalin's death in 1953, Pashukanis's name was "cleared" of the politico-criminal charges which were the cause of his demise, and since then his status as a legal philosopher has been partially rehabilitated in the Soviet Union. Ironically, in the USSR today Pashukanis is posthumously honored as one of the founders of the jurisprudence of Soviet socialist state and law, a formulation whose full implications he had resisted almost to the eve of his arrest.

Marxism and Soviet Jurisprudence: From War Communism to the New Economic Policy

The *General Theory of Law and Marxism* was a theory of the historical specificity of the legal form, and Pashukanis ostensibly introduced his argument with a critique of three trends in bourgeois jurisprudence dominant in the USSR before 1921: Renner's social functionalism, Petrazhitsky's and Reisner's psychologism, and Kelsen's legal positivism. The reader quickly learns that the gist of this critique contains two observations directed against the consequences of economic reductionism. The first concerns the ontological nature of legal regulation as a specific form of ideological category. The second concerns those instrumental forms of economism which reduce law to the status of an epiphenomenon within the compass of the base/superstructure metaphor.

Pashukanis noted that, within the sphere of political economy, concepts such as commodity, value, and exchange value are indeed ideological categories, but that this assignation by no means signifies that they indicate *only* ideas and other subjective processes. They are ideological concepts principally because they obscure objective social relationships. Yet the ideological character of a concept does not nullify the material reality of the relationships that the concept expresses. Nor does the fact that they are ideological concepts excuse us from searching for the objective conditions which they express yet somehow wrap in mystery. What needs to be proved is not that juridic concepts can and do become integrated into the structure of ideological existence, but that these concepts have *more* than an ideological existence. Pashukanis therefore asserted that law is also a real form of social being, and in so doing he seems astutely to have avoided the troublesome charge that both social scientists and theorists of ideology, in the final reckoning, base their assertions on a positivist epistemology.

Pashukanis was equally concerned to rebut the view that law is capable of voluntaristic manipulation by dominant social classes. Stuchka, for example, one of the early RSFSR commissars of justice and the author of Decree No. 1 on the Court, had misconstrued the nature of law in his *Revolutionary Role of Law and State* as a "system of relationships which answers to the interests of the dominant class and which safeguards that class with organized force." Pashukanis retorted that such a definition[13] is useful both in disclosing the class content of legal forms and in asserting that law is a social relationship, but that it masks the real differences between the legal form and all other social relationships that involve regulative norms. Indeed, if law is seen simply as a form of social relationship, and if one asserts that law regulates social relationships, then one must engage the tautology that social relationships regulate themselves.

Pashukanis correctly averred that the social organization of collectivities as diverse as bees and primitive peoples require rules. But not all rules are legal rules: some rules are customary and traditional and may be based in moral, aesthetic, or utilitarian considerations. Further, not all social relationships are legal relationships; under certain conditions the *regulation* of social relationships *assumes a legal character* (1924:58). Marxist theory must investigate not merely the material content of legal regulation during definite historical periods, but must also provide a materialist explanation of legal regulation as a definite historical form. The crucial question therefore involves the elucidation of the social conditions in which the domination and regulation of social relationships assumes a legal character.

Pashukanis argued that the fundamental principle of legal regulation is the opposition of private interests. Human conduct can be regulated by the most complex rules, but the legal element in such regulation begins where the isolation and antithesis of interests begin. "A norm of law acquires its *differentia specifica* . . . ," he said, "because it presupposes a person endowed with a right and actively asserting it" (1924:72). Accordingly, and following some of Marx's Hegelian-inspired comments in *The Law on the Theft of Woods* (1842) and *On the*

Jewish Question (1843), Pashukanis distinguished between those rules which serve the universal interest and those which serve a particular interest. The former are technical rules and are based on unity of purpose; the latter are legal rules and are characterized by controversy. Thus, the technical rules of railroad movement presuppose a single purpose, for example the attainment of maximum haulage capacity, whereas the legal rules governing the responsibilities of railroads presuppose private claims and isolated interests. Again, the treatment of invalids presupposes a series of rules both for the patient and for the medical personnel, but inasmuch as these rules are established to achieve a single purpose—the restoration of the patient's health—they are of a technical character. But when the patient and the physician are regarded as isolated, antagonistic subjects, each of whom is the bearer of his own private interests, they then become the subjects of rights and obligations, and the rules that unite them become legal rules.

Pashukanis asserted that Marx himself had pointed to the basic conditions of existence of the legal form. Thus, Marx had indicated that the basic and most deeply-set stratum of the legal superstructure—property relations—is "so closely contiguous to the foundation that they are the very same relationships of production expressed in juridic language." Law is some specific social relationship and can be understood in the same sense as that in which Marx termed capital a social relationship. The search for the unique social relationship, whose inevitable reflection is the form of law, is to be located in the relationships between commodity owners. The logic of legal concepts corresponds with the logic of the social relationships of commodity production, and it is specifically in these relationships—not in the demands of domination, submission, or naked power—that the origin of law is to be sought. We might add that Lenin himself had said, in relation to the law of inheritance, ". . . [it] presumes the existence of private property, and the latter arises only with the existence of exchange. Its basis is in the already incipient specialization of social labor and the alienation of products in the market."[14]

The ascendant bourgeoisie's central antagonism with feudal property, Pashukanis recalled, resided not in its origin in violent seizure, but instead in its immobility in exchange and circulation. In particular, it was unable to become an object of mutual guarantees as it passed from one possessor to another in acquisition. Feudal property, or the property associated with the feudal order, violated the abstract and cardinal principle of capitalist societies—"the equal possibility of obtaining inequality" (1924:83).

At a certain stage of development (with the appearance of cities and city communes, markets, and fairs) the relationships of human beings are manifested in a form which is doubly mysterious: they appear as the relationships of objects which are also commodities, and as the volitional relationships of entities which are independent and equal *inter se*: juridic subjects. Law thus appears side by side with the mystical attributes of value and exchange value. Moreover, it is in the concrete personality of the egoistic, autonomous subject—the property owner and the bearer of private interests—that a juridic subject such as *persona* finds complete and adequate embodiment.[15]

The historically specific object of a commodity, for Pashukanis, finds its pure form in capitalist economies. The authority which the capitalist enjoys, as the personification of capital in the process of direct production, is essentially different from the authority which accompanies production through slaves or serfs. Only capital stands in stark, unhierarchical contrast to the mass of direct producers. Capitalist societies are first and foremost societies of commodity owners. Commodities have a dual and a contradictory character. On the one hand, a commodity is and represents a use-value. But commodities necessarily embody different use-values because the qualitatively distinct social needs which they fulfill, and the quality and quantity of labor expended in their production, are necessarily different and unequal. And, on the other hand, a commodity is and represents an exchange-value. One commodity may be exchanged for another commodity in a definite ratio. The values encountered in this exchange are expressed by and facilitated through the mediation of another commodity—money—as the form of universal economic equivalent.

The potential for commodity exchange assumes that qualitatively distinct commodities enter a formal relationship of equivalence, so that ultimately they appear as equal. The exchange of commodities thus obscures a double abstraction in which concrete labor and concrete commodities are equalized *inter se* and are reduced to abstract labor and abstract commodities. This abstraction in turn perpetuates the fetish that commodities themselves, including money, contain living powers: commodities thus dominate their very producers, human subjects.

Pashukanis illustrated how commodity fetishism complements legal fetishism. Exchange transactions based on the *vi et armis* principles of feudalism create a form of property which is too transient and too unstable for developed commodity exchange. De facto possession must be transformed into an absolute and constant right which adheres to a commodity during its circulatory process. Pashukanis noted that Marx had tersely stated, in *Capital I*, that "commodities cannot send themselves to a market and exchange themselves with one another. Accordingly we must turn to their custodian, to the commodity owner" (1924:75).

The legal form itself is therefore cast as both an essential part and simultaneously a consequence of the exchange of commodities under capitalism. At the very same time that the product of labor is assuming the quality of commodities and becoming the bearer of value, man acquires the quality of a juridic subject and becomes the bearer of a right. In the development of legal categories, the capacity to perfect exchange relationships is merely one of the concrete manifestations of the general attribute of legal capacity and the capacity to act. Historically, however, it was specifically the exchange arrangement which furnished the notion of a subject as the abstract bearer of all possible legal claims. Nor does the juridic form of property contradict the factual expropriation of the property of many citizens; the attribute of being a subject of rights is a purely formal attribute, qualifying all persons alike as "deserving" of property but in no sense making them property owners.

It is only under developed commodity exchange that the capacity to have a right in general is distinguished from specific legal claims. Indeed, a characteristic feature of capitalist societies is that general interests are segregated from and opposed to private interests. The constant transfer of rights in the market creates the notion of an immobile bearer of rights, and the possibility therefore occurs of abstracting from the specific differences between subjects and of bringing them within one generic concept. Concrete man is relegated to an abstract man who incorporates egoism, freedom, and the supreme value of personality; the capacity to be a subject of rights is finally disassociated from the specific living personality and becomes a purely social attribute. The legal subject is thus the abstract commodity owner elevated into the heavens (1924:81), and acquires his alter ego in the form of a representative while he himself becomes insignificant. The specific characteristics of each member of *Homo sapiens* are, therefore, dissolved in the abstract concept of man as a juridic subject.

In order for property to be exchanged and alienated there must be a contract or accord of independent wills. Contract is therefore one of the central concepts in law, and once it has arisen, the notion of contract seeks to acquire universal significance. In contradistinction to theorists of public and constitutional law, such as Leon Duguit, Pashukanis held that all law is necessarily private law in that it emanates from commodity exchange. The distinction between private law and public law is therefore a (false) ideological distinction and it reflects a real contradiction in capitalist societies between the individual and the social interest. This contradiction is embodied in "the real relationships of human subjects who can regard their own private struggles as social struggles only in the incongruous and mystifying form of the value of commodities" (1924:109).

Pashukanis argued that the political authority of the state appears to be disassociated from the economic domination and specific needs of the capitalist class in the market. He thus hypothesized that the capitalist state is a *dual* state: a political state and a legal state. Thus he says that

> the state as an organization of class domination, and as an organization for the conduct of external wars, does not require legal interpretation and in essence does not allow it. This is where . . . the principle of naked expediency rules. (1924:92)

Class dominance, i.e., the dominance of the bourgeoisie, is expressed in the state's dependence upon banks and capitalist sectors, and in the dependence of each worker upon his employer. But it should not be forgotten that in the political class struggle—most evidently, at its critical phases—the state is the authority for the organized violence of one class on another. The legal state, on the other hand, reflects the impersonal, abstract, and equivalent form of commodity exchange. The legal state is the third party that embodies the mutual guarantees which commodity owners, qua owners, give to each other.

The *leitmotif* of early Soviet Marxist thought on law at the time of the October revolution and immediately thereafter, was the imperative of implementing the Marxist concept of the withering away of law. This initial eliminationist approach to law was best exemplified by Stuchka (*infra*, chapter 3), a Bolshevik revolutionary and a jurist, who in the days following the seizure of power was assigned the task of taking physical and political possession of the premises and institution of the highest court of imperial Russia. On arriving at the court building in what is now Leningrad, Stuchka found that the judges had fled the scene leaving behind only a number of frightened and bewildered clerks and messengers. To put this group at ease, Stuchka reassured them that although previously the judges had occupied the chambers while they themselves had waited in the antechambers, from that time on the clerks and messengers would sit in the judges' chairs and their former occupants would be relegated to the antechambers.[16]

The first Soviet attempt to implement the process of the withering away of law began less than a month after the October revolution. The Bolsheviks' first legislation on the judiciary abolished the hierarchy of tsarist courts, which were soon after replaced by a much less complex dual system of local people's courts and revolutionary tribunals.[17] This initiated a process of simplification and popularization that in the immediate postrevolutionary days and months swept away most of the inherited tsarist legal system, including the Procuracy, the Bar, and all but those laws vital to the transitional period between capitalism and communism (e.g., the Decree Abolishing Classes and Civil Ranks, November 1917). Even the remaining legal minimum was subject to interpretation by a new type of judge, usually untrained in law. These new judges were encouraged to guide themselves by their "revolutionary consciousness" in applying the law. The Bolsheviks' objective was that even these remnants would ultimately become superfluous and wither away or disappear. Their vision was of a new society in which people would be able to settle their disputes "with simplicity, without elaborately organized tribunals, without legal representation, without complicated laws, and without a labyrinth of rules of procedure and evidence."[18] However, harsh reality quickly impinged upon this vision as civil war engulfed the country. Confronted with the exigencies of governance under the most difficult conditions, the Bolsheviks deferred this transformative process and, as early as 1918, as John Hazard has conclusively demonstrated, began the process of relegalization, which culminated in a fully articulated legal system based largely on foreign bourgeois models and perfected in the first federal constitution (1924) during the early years of the New Economic Policy (NEP).

Pashukanis concluded his argument in *The General Theory of Law and Marxism* by opposing those who would wish to construct a *proletarian* system of law after the 1917 revolution. Marx himself, especially in *The Critique of the Gotha Programme*, had grasped the profound inner connection between the commodity form and the legal form, and had conceived of the transition of the higher level of communism not as a transition to new legal forms, but as the dying out of the legal form in general. If law has its real origin in commodity exchange, and if socialism is seen as the abolition of commodity exchange and the construction of production for use, then proletarian or socialist law was a conceptual, and therefore a practical, absurdity. While the market bond between individual enterprises (either capitalist or socialist) remained in force, so also the legal form had to remain in force.

The purportedly proletarian system of law operative under NEP was, Pashukanis believed, mere bourgeois law. Even the new system of criminal administration contained in the RSFSR Criminal Code (1922) was bourgeois law. Pashukanis noted that although the Basic Principles of Criminal Legislation of the Soviet Union and Union Republics had substituted the concept of "measures of social defense" for the concept of guilt, crime, and punishment (1924:124), this was nevertheless a terminological change and not the abolition of the legal form. Law cannot assume the form of commodity exchange and be proletarian or "socialist" in content. Criminal law is a form of equivalence between egoistic and isolated subjects. Indeed, criminal law is the sphere where juridic intercourse attains its maximum intensity. As with the legal form in general, the actions of specific actors are dissolved into the actions of abstract parties—the state, as one party, imposes punishment according to the damage effected by the other party, the criminal.

Pashukanis pointed out that the Soviet Union of 1924 had two systems of economic regulation. On the one hand were the administrative-technical rules which governed the general economic plan. On the other were the legal rules (civil and commercial codes, courts, arbitration tribunals, etc.) which governed the commodity exchange that was NEP's essential feature. The victory of the former type of regulation would signify the demise of the latter, and only then would Marx's description of human emancipation be realized. Five years later, in "Economics and Legal Regulation," Pashukanis still clung precariously yet tenaciously to his dictum that "the problem of the withering away of law is the yardstick by which we measure the degree of proximity of a jurist to Marxism" (1929:268).

It must be stressed that *The General Theory of Law and Marxism* was written during NEP at a critical juncture in Soviet development. Pashukanis argued that in certain respects NEP had preserved market exchange and the form of value, and that this was a consequence of "proletarian state capitalism" (1924:89).[19] Lenin himself had fully appreciated the contradictory character of the different modes of production encouraged by NEP. The Supreme Economic Council, set up in 1917 with the explicit aim of introducing socialist methods of production into both industry and agriculture, had achieved such limited success that in May 1921 Lenin observed: "there is still hardly any evidence of the operation of an integrated state economic plan."[20] Arguing that there was much that could and must be learned from capitalist techniques (e.g., Taylorism), Lenin wrote in December 1921 that NEP marked "a retreat in order to make better preparations for a new offensive against capitalism."[21] The painful experiences of War Communism had indicated that socialism would not be attained overnight, and that unless the political domination of the proletariat was ensured, it would not be attained at all. The temporary solution was to allow the peasantry limited ownership of the agricultural means of production. But this was to be regulated retreat:

> The proletarian state may, without changing its own character, permit freedom to trade and the development of capitalism only within certain bounds, and only on the condition that the state regulates (supervises, controls, determines the form and methods of, etc.) private trade and capitalism.[22]

The general feeling among the Bolsheviks, then, was that NEP was a temporary, necessary, and regulated retreat: one step backward, and two steps forward. Lenin warned that "It will take us at least ten years to organize large-scale industry to produce a reserve and secure control of agriculture. . . . There will be a dictatorship of the proletariat. Then will come the classless society."[23] The seeds of this progression were already at hand, however, and in May 1921 he observed that "the manufactured goods made by socialist factories and exchanged for the foodstuffs produced by the peasants are not commodities in the politico-economic sense of the word; at any rate, they are not only commodities, they are no longer commodities, they are ceasing to be commodities."[24]

Under NEP Pashukanis's theoretical achievements earned him more than just the praise of his contemporaries. During the years 1924–1930, he assumed a number of important positions in the Soviet academic hierarchy and was named to the editorial boards of the most influential law and social science journals. Through these strategic positions and key editorial posts, Pashukanis extended and strengthened the influence of the commodity exchange school of law on Marxist jurisprudence.[25]

When *The General Theory of Law and Marxism* appeared in 1924, Pashukanis was a member of Stuchka's Section of Law and State, and of the Institute of Soviet Construction, both of the Communist Academy which he subsequently described as "the centre of Marxist thought."[26] Later, he was to become a member of the bureau of executive committee of the Institute and of the Section, as well as head of the latter's Subsection on the General Theory of Law and State.

During 1925, the Section of Law and State formally launched the "revolution of the law" with the publication of a collection of essays entitled *Revoliutsiia prava* (Revolution of Law). Pashukanis served as co-editor and contributed a major article on Lenin's understanding of law.

In 1926, the second edition of *General Theory* was published. During that year Pashukanis joined the law faculty of Moscow State University and the Institute of Red Professors, the graduate school of the Communist Academy. *Bol'shaia sovetskaia entsiklopediia* (The Great Soviet Encyclopedia) also began publication in 1926, and Pashukanis was named chief editor for law shortly afterwards.

The third edition of *General Theory* was issued in 1927, the year *Revoliutsiia prava* was established as the official journal of the Section of Law and State with Pashukanis as a co-editor. Beginning that year, the Section's periodic reports reflected Pashukanis's increasing predominance. His annual intellectual output in books, articles, essays, *doklady*, reviews, and reports was prodigious. Along with Stuchka, Pashukanis dominated the scholarly activity of the Section. As an indication of his growing impact on Soviet legal development, he was assigned the task of preparing a textbook on the general theory of law and state, and was chosen to represent the Communist Academy on the commission for drafting the fundamental principles of civil legislation, created by the USSR Council of People's Commissars.

During this period Pashukanis began to assume additional positions and editorships. He became Deputy Chairman of the Presidium of the Communist Academy, and a co-editor of *Vestnik kommunisticheskoi akademii* (Herald of the Communist Academy), the major Marxist social science journal. He had previously been named a founding editor of the journal *Revoliutsiia i kul'tura* (Revolution and Culture), a new publication designed to promote the cultural revolution. His co-editors on these publications were the most eminent Marxist social scientists, including Lunacharsky, Pokrovsky, and Deborin.

In "The Marxist Theory of Law and the Construction of Socialism,"[27] written in 1927, Pashukanis undertook two objectives. First, he once again warned of the political dangers involved in trying to erect proletarian or socialist legal forms, and he asserted that the dialectic of the withering away of law under socialism consists in "the contrast between the principle of socialist planning and the principle of equivalent exchange" (1927:193). Thus, he took issue with those such as Reisner[28] who saw Decree No. 1 on the Court, or the RSFSR Civil Code, as evidence that NEP utilized private property and commodity exchange to develop the forces of production. But this was to imply that in this context private property and commodity exchange had a "neutral" character. What was important, Pashukanis pointed out, was that one should understand the use of these forms not from the perspective of developing the forces of production, but from "the perspective of the victory of the socialist elements of our economy over the capitalist ones" (1927:192). Provided that remnants of the capitalist mode of production were in practice eliminated and that subsequent social rules in the USSR were of a technical-administrative nature, then Pashukanis could argue prescriptively and, possibly, descriptively, that law would disappear only with the disappearance of capitalism.

This 1927 article contains some interesting emendations to his *General Theory of Law and Marxism*. The most important of these, in response to Stuchka's "State and Law in the Period of Socialist Construction,"[29] is the admission of "the indisputable fact of the existence of feudal law" (Pashukanis, 1927:195). Pashukanis now indicates that we find "purchase and sale, with products and labor assuming the form of commodities, and with a general equivalent, i.e. money, throughout the entire feudal period" (1927:195). But although feudal and bourgeois law may have a common form, their content and class nature is essentially different. Feudal law is based on the will of the simple commodity owner, while bourgeois law is based on the will of the capitalist commodity owner. This is a most important concession because, although Pashukanis did not yet admit the primacy of production relations within historical materialism, it allowed him to posit the existence of what he refers to as "Soviet law, corresponding to a lower level of development than that which Marx envisioned in *The Critique of the Gotha Programme* . . . [and which] is fundamentally different from genuine bourgeois law" (1927:194).

In his 1929 article, "Economics and Legal Regulation," Pashukanis explicitly discussed the reflexive status of the legal form, a question that was only implicit in his analysis of ideological forms in *The General Theory of Law and Marxism.* He used two arguments to refute the criticism of Preobrazhensky, Rubin, and Bohm-Bawerk, that economic regulation under conditions of socialism (in the USSR) is, in certain respects, like the regulation exercised by capitalist states under conditions of monopoly capitalism and imperialism (chiefly in Germany and England).

Pashukanis argued, first, that these sorts of criticism tend to be based on the false polarity of base and superstructural forms. "The social," he retorted, ". . . is the *alter ego* of the economic" (1929:241). "In every antagonistic society," he continued, "class relationships find continuation and concretization in the sphere of political struggle, the state structure and the legal order . . . productive forces [are] decisive in the final analysis" (1929:244). Superstructural forms, in other words, are incomprehensible apart from those social relationships to which they initially owe their existence. This claim marked a crucial transition in Pashukanis's work. Even if he had as yet neither identified the proper place of the political within the complex of the social relationships of production, nor posited that the political has primacy in Marxist political economy, he had at the very least conceded that productive relationships are in some sense "determinant factors in the final analysis." Quite clearly, the *origin* of law could not now be explained by commodity exchange—primitive or generalized—and Pashukanis seems to have recognized the inferiority of his radical position in the debates with Stuchka that were contained within the Communist Academy and not made public until 1927.[30]

Pashukanis's second argument was a weak rebuttal of the assertion that, because NEP relationships in part conformed to the law of value, and also to the law of the proportional distribution of labor expenditures, therefore the primitive socialist economy contained capitalist contradictions. These notions, he replied, stem from a simplistic understanding of Engels's concern with the leap from the kingdom of necessity to the kingdom of freedom. To hold that the form of value exists in the USSR is to miss, as did Preobrazhensky, the crucial point that the USSR is a dynamic formation founded on "the economics of co-operation and collectivization" (Pashukanis, 1929:251), and "the union of the working class and the peasantry" (ibid., 254). What matters, concretely, is not where the USSR is, but where it will be. The USSR is in a necessary phase preparatory to Engels's quantum leap. Further, it is trivial to claim that the law of the proportional distribution of labor expenditures is effective in the USSR. This law is effective in all societies. What matters is how it is determined, and in the USSR it is determined by "the economic policy of the proletarian state" (1929:257).

The regulation of the national economy by the proletarian state under NEP, Pashukanis continued, is qualitatively distinct from the domestic economic intervention of capitalist states during the 1914–1918 war. In contradistinction to the latter's "57 varieties" of socialism represented by wartime state control, the proletarian state had three unique characteristics by which it would effectively realize the dialectical transformation of quantity into quality: the indissolubility of legislative and executive, extensive nationalization, and the firm regulation of production in the universal rather than the particular interest. The more these characteristics are actualized,

> the role of the purely legal superstructure—the role of law—declines, and from this can be derived the general rule that as [technical] regulation becomes more effective, the weaker and less significant the role of law and the legal superstructure in its pure form. (1929:271)

Pashukanis's responsibilities continued to multiply when he was appointed Prorector of the Institute of Red Professors, which was also known as the "theoretical staff of the Central Committee."[31] In 1929, the Institute started a journal for correspondence students with Pashukanis as chief editor. By this time, the influence of his commodity exchange theory of law on the syllabi for the Institute's law curriculum and correspondence courses was pronounced.

Finally, in 1929–1930, Pashukanis reached the apex of the Marxist school of jurisprudence and the Soviet legal profession. In a major reorganization, the Institute of Soviet Law was fully absorbed and its publication was abolished. All theoretical and practical work in the field of law was concentrated in the Communist Academy. In turn, the Section of Law and State and the Institute of Soviet Construction of the Communist Academy were merged, and the journal *Revoliutsiia prava* was reoriented and renamed. Pashukanis became director of the new Institute of the State, Law and Soviet Construction (soon renamed the Institute of Soviet Construction and Law); chief editor of its new journal, *Sovetskoe gosudarstvo i revoliutsiia prava* (Soviet Government and the Revolution of Law); and a co-editor of *Sovetskoe stroitel'stvo* (Socialist Construction), the journal of the USSR Central Executive Committee.

An indication of Pashukanis's influence on the Soviet legal profession was the gradual emergence of the commodity exchange orientation within the Marxist school of law. Just a few years after the appearance of the *General Theory of Law and Marxism*, the group of Marxist jurists working with Pashukanis in the Communist Academy became known as the commodity exchange school of law. This group, led by Pashukanis, dominated Marxist jurisprudence and was strongest in the general theory of law and in the branches of criminal law and civil-economic law. As the commodity exchange theory of law became identified with the Marxist theory of law, Pashukanis gradually assumed the unofficial leadership of the Marxist school of law. By 1930, the Communist Academy was bringing all Soviet legal scholarship and education under its control, and Pashukanis, as the preeminent Marxist theorist of law, was soon being acknowledged as the leader of the Soviet legal profession.

As Pashukanis's prestige soared in the late 1920s, a critical accompaniment, at first low-keyed but later swelling in volume, began to be heard. From 1925 to 1930, Pashukanis was criticized for overextending the commodity exchange concept of law, confusing a methodological concept with a general theory of law, ignoring the law's ideological character, and even for being an antinormativist. Other critics disagreed with Pashukanis's positions on feudal law, on public law, and on the readiness of the masses to participate in public administration. He was denounced by one critic as a "legal nihilist."

Nearly all of Pashukanis's critics were Marxists. Most were members of the Communist Academy. As the commodity exchange school of law became ascendant, the Communist Academy divided into two wings: the moderates and the radicals. All of Pashukanis's critics within the Communist Academy were associated with the moderate wing of the commodity exchange school. This group was led by Stuchka, and the radical wing was led by Pashukanis. Outside of the Communist Academy, A. A. Piontkovsky, at that time a member of the rival Institute of Soviet Law, was Pashukanis's major critic.[32]

Stuchka's criticism, which began to appear publicly in 1927, was by far the greatest challenge to Pashukanis. Basically, Stuchka, as a leader of the moderate wing of the commodity exchange school, criticized Pashukanis's overextension of the commodity exchange concept of law from civil law to other branches of law. Specifically, he criticized Pashukanis for overextending the notion of equivalence, insufficiently emphasizing the class content of law, reducing public law to private law, and denying the existence of either feudal law or Soviet law.

Stuchka apparently had been criticizing Pashukanis within the Communist Academy before the first publication of his criticism in 1927. In his article "State and Law in the Period of Socialist Construction," Stuchka footnoted his criticism of Pashukanis to the effect that their mutual opponents, presumably those outside the Communist Academy's legal circles, had been exaggerating the extent of their differences. Stuchka conceded that differences existed between him and Pashukanis and that, under the circumstances, it was best to bring them out into the open. In this article, however, he tended to minimize these differences.

Stuchka's contributions to building a Marxist theory of law were undisputed by his contemporaries. During the early 1920s he had, first, argued for a materialist conception of law and for a class concept of law against prevailing idealist conceptions. Second, he was responsible for the conception of a revolutionary role for Soviet law during the transitional period from capitalism to communism.[33] Perhaps Stuchka's greatest contribution to the development of the Soviet legal system was his insistence, which grew in intensity throughout the 1920s, on the necessity for "Soviet" law during the transition period, although he had no illusions about this body of law becoming a permanent feature of the Soviet system. In an article in early 1919, Stuchka clearly stated that "We can only speak of proletarian law as the *law of the transition period. . . .*" He underscored the temporary nature of proletarian law by characterizing it as "a simplification, a popularization of our new social system."[34] At the end of the decade Stuchka summarized his recognition of the importance of law as an agent of socioeconomic development in the foreword to his collected essays: "Revolution of the law is revolutionary legality in the service of furthering the socialist offensive and socialist construction."[35] In this context, Stuchka criticized Pashukanis's theory of law for its omissions, its one-sidedness insofar as it reduced all law to only the market, to only exchange as the instrumentalization of the relations of commodity producers—which means law in general is peculiar to bourgeois society.[36]

If Stuchka's criticism was sharp and constructive, then the criticism put forward by Piontkovsky was definitely hostile. Piontkovsky was a specialist in criminal law, an advocate of the development of a specifically Soviet legal system, and a member of the Institute of Soviet Law until its absorption by the Communist Academy. Piontkovsky's main and most effective criticism was that Pashukanis had mistaken an ideal-type concept, the commodity exchange concept, for a theory of law. He developed this in his book, *Marxism and Criminal Law*, which was published in two editions. Possibly because Piontkovsky was outside the legal circles of the Communist Academy, his criticism of Pashukanis's work was more explicit and much more blunt. He effectively incorporated into his own criticism the criticism of Pashukanis's colleagues, but without being subject to the restraints that they apparently imposed upon themselves in the interest of unity within the Communist Academy.

Piontkovsky valued Pashukanis's *General Theory of Law and Marxism*, but with definite reservations. He devoted a large part of his book to what he termed the "dangers" of Pashukanis's theory, while at the same time, in his second edition, he defended himself against counter-criticism from Pashukanis's followers. One of these had written that Piontkovsky's study had nothing in common with Marxism and by no means explained reality, to which Piontkovsky replied:

> Of course, our point of view has nothing in common with that Marxism that is limited only to the explanation of reality, but has . . . something in common with that Marxism . . . which is a "guide" to action.[37]

By the end of the decade, the volume of criticism of Pashukanis's radical version of the commodity exchange theory of law had grown considerably. It was no longer easy to distinguish whether the criticism emanated from inside or outside the Communist Academy. Stuchka's and Piontkovsky's criticism began to converge as the criticism took on an increasingly political tone in 1930. One critic observed that Pashukanis had repaired to the "enemy's territory" and had lapsed into "bourgeois legal individualism." Another critic, in a similar tone, characterized Pashukanis's commodity exchange theory of law as a "collection of mechanistic and formalistic perversions."[38]

The most salient aspects of these debates involved the fundamental questions concerning the role of state and law in the lower phase of communism. These questions indicated a certain dissatisfaction and uneasiness with the type of thought characteristic of Marxist legal circles during the 1920s. Most fundamental was Stuchka's question of the relationship of dictatorship to law. As he wrote, "We know Lenin's definition of dictatorship as 'a power basing itself on coercion and not connected with any kind of laws.' " But then Stuchka went on to ask, "What should be the relationship of the dictatorship of the proletariat *to its law* and to law in general as the means of administration?"[39]

The other important question, raised from outside the Communist Academy by Piontkovsky, involved the relationship of Pashukanis's general theory of law to the vital tasks of political and economic development in a society dominated by feudal social relationships. Piontkovsky pointed out that Pashukanis's theory of law was "not revolutionary" in the sense that it was not designated for a voluntarist approach to social change.[40]

"Revolution from Above" and the Struggle on the Legal Front

Despite growing criticism of Pashukanis's theory, the impact of his commodity exchange school of law on the withering away process became apparent in the late 1920s. Pashukanis and his colleagues assiduously devoted themselves to bringing about the realization of his prediction that private law and the legal state would gradually begin to wither away upon the elimination of the institutions of private property and the market. From their point of view, the prevailing political and economic trends were favorable. The doctrine of "socialism in one country," signaling the forthcoming end of the strategic retreat of the NEP, was first officially expressed in 1925 at the Fourteenth Party Conference. Later in the same year, the Fourteenth Party Congress adopted the policy of industrialization, which meant that substantial growth could be anticipated in the socialist sector of the economy. For the commodity exchange school of law, the imminent end of the NEP and the subsequent growth of the state sector meant a significant weakening of the juridical superstructure. In 1927 the Fifteenth Party Congress called for the construction of socialism, an objective that for Pashukanis and his colleagues required the gradual elimination of law. The growth of the socialist base, argued Estrin, meant "the simplification and contraction" of the "legal form" in other words, a withering away of the law.[41]

The revolutionaries of the law directed their main attacks against the NEP codes as the core of the real legal culture, and against the legal education system as the nexus between the real and ideal legal cultural patterns and the means by which they were transmitted and maintained. They reasoned that if the thicket of bourgeois laws could be gradually thinned out, the ground could eventually be cleared, with the remaining legal structures becoming increasingly superfluous and falling into disuse toward that time when they would be razed. Tactically, this meant the necessity of initially replacing the NEP codes with shorter, simpler models which would compress (and hence eliminate) the finer distinctions of bourgeois justice. The longer-term thrust was toward radically reforming legal education for the purpose of preparing cadres who would be socialized and trained to preside over the transition from the legal realities of NEP to a future without law. Their primary target was the notion of equivalence, which they regarded as the unifying theme of bourgeois legal culture and the factor most responsible for its cohesion. Against the symmetry of economic-legal equivalence, they opposed the asymmetrical principle of political expediency in their radical efforts to recodify NEP law and reform legal education during the First and Second Five-Year Plans.

Expediency as a principle of codification meant that the draft codes of the transitional legal culture were characterized by flexibility and simplicity, in opposition to the stability and formality of the NEP codes based on equivalence. Although only a few of the draft codes of the Pashukanis school were actually adopted (in the emerging Central Asian republics), their recodification efforts nevertheless had a subversive effect on the administration of civil and criminal justice during the first half of the 1930s. The draft codes were widely distributed in the legal profession, while their basic principles were constantly elaborated upon in the legal press and taught in the law schools. The revolution of the law appeared to be winning, creating what was subsequently called an atmosphere of legal nihilism.

In the legal transfer culture, criminal law became "criminal policy" (*ugolovnaia politika*), reflecting its extreme flexibility, while many of the procedural and substantive distinctions characteristic of bourgeois criminal jurisprudence were discarded in the interest of maximum simplicity. Similarly, the civil law of equivalent commodity exchange was supplanted by the new category of economic law, encompassing the economic relationships between production enterprises within the Five-Year Plans which were enforced as technical rules based on the criterion of planning expediency. All of this was taught in the law schools, where the legal cadres were being prepared to preside over the gradual withering away of the law.[42]

Although the second Soviet attempt to carry out the withering away of law progressed well into the 1930s, Pashukanis and the commodity exchange school, as advocates of his theory, collided with the process of Soviet rapid industrialization at the Sixteenth Party Congress in June 1930. The conflict between industrialization and withering away, which had been implicit since 1925, now clearly emerged. Until 1928, this implied conflict had been largely academic while NEP and the policy of economic recovery were still in effect. However, once large-scale industrialization and forced collectivization were underway, a collision was inevitable as it became apparent that the intervention and active support of strong and stable legal and political systems would be necessary in the USSR. Consequently, the commodity exchange school of law began its rapid decline in the late 1920s, culminating in 1930 as Marxist jurisprudence was brought into line with the "socialist offensive along the whole front."

Stalin, as General Secretary, in his address before the Central Committee Plenum of April 1929, warned against promoting hostile and antagonistic attitudes toward law and state among the masses. He argued instead that the intensification of the class struggle by the kulaks required the strengthening, rather than the weakening, of the dictatorship of the proletariat.[43] This tendency culminated at the Sixteenth Party Congress in the rejection of the concept of the gradual withering away of law and state. On that occasion Stalin reconceptualized this process:

> We are for the withering away of the state, while at the same time we stand for strengthening the dictatorship of the proletariat which represents the most potent and mighty authority of all the state authorities that have existed down to this time. The highest development of state authority to the end of making ready the conditions for the withering away of state authority: there you have the Marxist formula. Is this "contradictory"? Yes, it is "contradictory." But it is a living, vital contradiction and it completely reflects Marxist dialectics.[44]

The Communist Party's rejection of the gradualist notion of withering away made it necessary, therefore, to redefine the transitional role of law and state, and it seriously undermined the theoretical foundations of the commodity exchange school of law.

In 1932, in his *Doctrine of State and Law*, Pashukanis recognized that he should not have equated law as an historical phenomenon with the equivalent exchange of commodities. In class societies every relationship of production has a specific form in which surplus labor is extracted from the direct producers, and he now argued that "the nature of the bond between the producer and the means of production is the key to understanding the specificity of socio-economic formations" (1932). The factor that determines the typical features of a given legal system is therefore the form of exploitation. We might add that by now Pashukanis himself must seriously have wondered whether the primacy of the individual subject within his theory of law had its origins not in the legacies of Hegel, Marx, and Pokrovsky, but rather in that subjectivist epistemology represented in bourgeois jurisprudence by Jhering, Laband, Jellinek, and possibly Max Weber—all of whom he would undoubtedly have read during his studies at the University of Munich.

Sensitive to the political dangers which he detected in his own earlier work, in Stuchka, and in the Second International, Pashukanis raised the delicate question of whether social relationships which are not relationships of production or exchange can enter into the content of law. He asserted that law in bourgeois society does not serve only the facilitation of commodity exchange, and bourgeois property is not exhausted by the relationships between commodity owners. To argue that law is reducible simply to economic relationships is in the end to identify it with economic relationships, which in turn both excludes all but property and contract law, and denies the reflexive effect of the legal superstructure on economic relationships. And to hold to this latter argument would clearly be inappropriate in the context of the end of the First Five-Year Plan and the beginning of the Second. Pashukanis argued that law cannot be understood unless we consider it as the basic form of the policy of the ruling class. "A legal relationship is a *form* of production relationship," he claimed, "because the active influence of the class organization of the ruling class transforms the factual relationship into a legal one, gives it a new quality, and thus includes it in the construction of the legal superstructure" (Pashukanis, 1932:297).

Accordingly, Pashukanis reformulated his definition of law provided in the *General Theory of Law and Marxism* as "*the form of regulation and consolidation of production relationships and also of other social relationships of class society*" (1932:287). He added that this definition is incomplete without reference to a coercive apparatus (the state) which guarantees the functioning of the legal superstructure. But the dependence of law on the state does not signify that the state creates the legal superstructure. The state is itself "only a more or less complex reflection of the economic needs of the dominant class in production" (1932:291). To emphasize the primacy of the state would be to miss the distinction, so crucial for the working class in its struggle with capitalism, between the various forms of rule (democracy, dictatorship, etc.)[45] and the class essence of all states. Bourgeois theorists of the state "conflate characteristics relating to the form of government and characteristics relating to the class nature of the state" (ibid., 280). Following Lenin, Pashukanis stressed that the techniques of legal domination are less important than the goals to which they are directed. In each of its stages, Soviet law therefore naturally differed from the law of capitalist states. Further,

> . . . law in the conditions of the proletarian dictatorship has always had the goal of protecting the interest of the working majority, the suppression of class elements hostile to the proletariat, and the defence of socialist construction. . . . As such it is radically different from bourgeois law despite the formal resemblance of individual statutes. (1932:293)

In the course of the "revolution from above" of forced collectivization and rapid industrialization, a politically chastened but still theoretically active Pashukanis tried unsuccessfully, as it transpired, to redefine his concept of the state during the transitional period. In effect, Pashukanis superimposed the Stalinist concept of the state in Soviet socioeconomic development onto the remnants of his original theory of law. Then by simultaneously presiding over the theoretical articulation of the Stalinist state as well as the practical process of the withering away of criminal law, Pashukanis inevitably contributed to the growth of a jurisprudence of terror. As bourgeois criminal law and procedure were superseded in application by a simplistically vague and highly flexible "Soviet criminal policy"—shaped by Pashukanis and his associate Nikolai Krylenko (*infra*, chapters 7 and 8) through several proposed draft codes—legal forms were co-opted for extralegal purposes, judicial process was subordinated to political ends, and law itself was used to legitimate and rationalize terror. The jurisprudence of terror institutionalized and routinized political terror within the context of formal legalism. In effect, terror was legalized and the criminal process overtly politicized. Through the legalization of terror, the concomitant criminalization of a wide range of political (and even social) behavior, and the politicization of the co-opted administration of justice, the jurisprudence of terror became a highly effective instrument of party policy. Speaking in late 1930, Pashukanis expressed the basic premise of the jurisprudence of terror which he seemed to recognize as an inevitable stage on the road to communism and the ultimate withering away of the law. Rejecting the notion of a stable system of law, he argued for "political elasticity" and the imperative that Soviet "legislation possess maximum elasticity" since "for us revolutionary legality is a problem which is 99 per cent political."[46]

The inherent contradiction between the ideas of a strong state and weak criminal law did not become fully evident until the waning of the revolution from above was embodied in the Seventeenth Party Congress's (1934) policy emphasis on the need for greater legal formality and stability in Soviet jurisprudence as a means of consolidating the gains of the previous turbulent years. Paradoxically, it was Vyshinsky (*infra*, chapter 6), the Procurator General of the USSR and soon to become prosecutor of the major purge victims, who became the spearhead of Stalinist criticism of the adverse effect of Pashukanis's and Krylenko's legal nihilism on the administration of ordinary ("nonpolitical") criminal justice.[47]

Similarly, Pashukanis and another associate, Leonid Gintsburg, exercised an equally strong influence on civil jurisprudence through their concept of economic law. John Hazard, then an American student at Pashukanis's Moscow Institute of Soviet Law, subsequently reported:

> Law concerning the rights of the individual was relegated to a few hours at the end of the course in economic-administrative law and given apologetically as an unwelcome necessity for a few years due to the fact that capitalist relationships and bourgeois psychology had not yet been wholly eliminated.[48]

The brilliant insights of *The General Theory of Law and Marxism* had become quite emasculated after the Sixteenth Party Congress and the introduction of the Second Five-Year Plan. It is at this point that we no longer need to speculate on whether the intellectual revisions to the main thrust of Pashukanis's work were induced by strictly political and opportunist pressures. In the *Course on Soviet*

Economic Law, written with Gintsburg and published in 1935, Pashukanis offered a lengthy, simplistic, and functionalist account of the nature of Soviet economic law under the transitional conditions of socialism. Conceived within the manifest constraints to conform with the Stalinist interpretation of Marx's and Engels's brief and unsatisfactory analyses of the period transitional between capitalism and the higher phase of communism, the *Course* defines Soviet economic law as "*a special (specific) form of the policy of the proletarian state in the area of the organization of socialist production and Soviet commerce*" (Pashukanis and Gintsburg, 1935:306).[49] Bourgeois law serves the interests of the capitalist class in capitalist production; Soviet law serves the interests of the proletariat organized as the ruling class under socialism. The special nature of the production policies (i.e., planning) of the proletarian state are revealed through the concept of socialist (revolutionary) legality. Bourgeois legality, according to Pashukanis and Gintsburg,

> is the will of the ruling class . . . directed at the support of the basic conditions of the capitalist mode of production. Socialist (revolutionary) legality expresses the will of the last of the exploited classes which has taken power, of the proletariat. (1935:314)

Just as criminal policy came to be regarded as counterproductive after the Seventeenth Party Congress, so too economic law during the Second Five-Year Plan began to encounter muted criticism from the direction of a countervailing tendency toward the need to return to the concept of contract (albeit a *planned* contract) as a method of stabilizing and more effectively managing the planning process. Pashukanis, as the principal theoretical exponent of both criminal policy and economic law, became increasingly politically vulnerable in the mid-1930s.

In "State and Law under Socialism," published on the eve of the new Constitution of 1936, Pashukanis weakly confronted the most serious criticism that the commodity exchange theory of law had always explicitly invited—that it was a left communist, or perhaps anarchist, theory which, if implemented, would greatly impede the construction and reproduction of socialist relations of production in the USSR. Pashukanis apologetically quotes Lenin's *State and Revolution* to the effect that

> we want a socialist revolution with people as they are now—with people who cannot do without subordination, without supervision, without "overseers and auditors" . . . it is inconceivable that people will immediately learn to work without any legal norms after the overthrow of capitalism. (1936:349)

Stalinism and Soviet Jurisprudence

The demand for greater contractual discipline within the planned economy, the revival and strengthening of Soviet family law so long submerged within economic law, and, above all, the publication of the draft of a new constitution in June 1936, all clearly foreshadowed an impending major change in Soviet legal policy. The new constitutional right of ownership of personal property and the provisions for the first all-union civil and criminal codes implied the reinforcement rather than the withering away of the law. Stalin's famous remark later that year that "stability of the laws is necessary for us now more than ever" signaled the new legal policy, and the promulgation of the Stalin Constitution a few weeks later, in December 1936, formally opened the Stalinist era in the development of Soviet legal culture.[50]

As the symbol of the defeated revolution of the law, Pashukanis was arrested, and disappeared in January 1937. The purging of Pashukanis and his associates cleared the way for the rearticulation of the dormant Romanist legal ideas of stability, formality, and professionalism. The process of rebuilding Soviet legal culture began immediately under the aegis of Vyshinsky, Pashukanis's successor as *doyen* of the legal profession. While Pashukanis had been the theorist of NEP legal culture, explaining its rise and predicting its demise, Vyshinsky, the practitioner, was its consolidator by reinforcing and converting it into the Soviet legal culture.[51]

Vyshinsky's onslaught against Pashukanis involved an intellectual contortionism replete with invective-laden and often self-contradictory statements.[52] Vyshinsky argued that law is neither a system of social relationships nor a form of production relationships. "Law," he stressed, "is the aggregate of rules of conductor norms; yet not of norms alone, but also of customs and rules of community living confirmed by state authority and coercively protected by that authority."[53]

Soviet socialist law, Vyshinsky continued, is radically unique in both form and content because

> it is the will of our people elevated to the rank of a statute. In capitalist society, allusions to the will of the people served as a screen which veiled the exploiting nature of the bourgeois state. In the conditions of our country, the matter is different in principle: there has been formulated among us, a single and indestructible will of the Soviet people—manifested in the unparalleled unanimity with which the people vote at the elections to the Supreme Soviet of the USSR and the Supreme Soviets of the union and autonomous republics. . . .[54]
>
> The specific mark of Soviet law . . . is that it serves, in the true and actual sense of the word, the people—society. . . . In the USSR for the first time in history the people—the toiling national masses themselves—are the masters of their fate, themselves ruling their state with no exploiters, no landlords, no capitalists.[55]

Law was now to be viewed as a set of normative prescriptions, enforced by the state (whose own character is unproblematic), in accord with Stalin's conception of the character and duration of the transitional phase. The conditions for the existence of Soviet socialist law are the necessity "to finish off the remnants of the dying classes and to organize defence against capitalist encirclement.''[56] Soviet socialist law must incorporate and instill revolutionary legality and stability. ''Why is stability of statutes essential? Because it reinforces the stability of the state order and of the state discipline, and multiplies tenfold the powers of socialism. . . .''[57]

Ignoring the internal class contradictions of the new Soviet state, Vyshinsky applauded Stalin's teaching that ''the withering away of the state will come not through a weakening of the state authority but through its maximum intensification.''[58] The process of withering away is of necessity postponed until

> all will learn to get along without special rules defining the conduct of people under the threat of punishment and with the aid of constraint; when people are so accustomed to observe the fundamental rules of community life that they will fulfill them without constraint of any sort.[59]

The legal culture of NEP along with the statutory legislation of the intervening years, so long castigated as bourgeois, was redefined as a socialist legal culture. The need to systematize the legal culture, so long obstructed as inconsistent with its withering away, became the new agenda for the legal profession. Jurists, driven by the revolution of the law from the law schools, the research institutes, and the legal press, reappeared as participants in the reconstruction of legal education and research. Disciplines banished from the law curriculum by the radical jurists were reintroduced beginning in the spring term of 1937. New course syllabi and textbooks for every branch of law—especially those eliminated or suppressed by the legal transfer culture—began to appear with great rapidity. New editions of earlier texts were purged of Pashukanis's influence and quickly reissued. Carrying out the mandate of Article 14 of the Stalin Constitution, numerous jurists were mobilized to prepare drafts for the all-union civil and criminal codes. Finally, a vulgar neopositivist jurisprudence, based on ''class relations'' and largely derived from the Stalin Constitution and even the *Short Course*, replaced the tradition of revolutionary legal theory epitomized by Pashukanis.[60]

* * *

By way of conclusion, we must briefly outline the importance of a question confronted but unanswered in Pashukanis's project that is also unanswered, and unfortunately unaddressed, in our own time. How, precisely, are we to understand the historical configuration of state and law in social formations where capitalist property has been abolished but where communism has by no means yet been achieved? How are we to resolve the apparent paradox that the legal practices of most, if not all, social formations dominated by the political rule of the proletariat have included the form, and very often the content, of the legal rules typically associated with capitalist modes of production?

To explain this question, as did Stalinism, in terms of capitalist encirclement and the construction of socialism in one country, is to avoid the issue. This is so for at least two reasons. First, as Marx always and Lenin usually argued, under socialism the proletarian dictatorship has two features which radically demarcate it from all other state *dictatures*: the extent of its powers and the duration of its domination must be limited, and these must ultimately inhere in the consent of its citizens. These features are structural preconditions of socialism, and without wishing to lapse into utopianism or idealism, they seem necessary irrespective of the specific economic, political, or ideological histories of a given social formation. This would therefore exclude that common explanation of the intensity and longevity of the Soviet polity which pointed to the essential continuity of pre- and postrevolutionary political practices. Further, these qualities of the proletarian dictatorship—clearly discernible as the early Roman, and not the post-Reformation concept of dictatorship[61]—must dialectically contain the capacity for self-transformation. State and legal forms, even while they are actively utilized by the proletariat or by the party which genuinely represents it, must simultaneously be in the process of immanent transformation. As Lenin himself put it in 1919, "The communist organization of social labor, the first step towards which is socialism, rests, and will do so more and more as time goes on, on the free and conscious discipline of the working people themselves."[62] As such, we are convinced that only intellectual sophistry could assert that, at least since the late 1920s, the proletarian dictatorship in the USSR is a *dictatorship* (in the classical sense) of the *proletariat*.

The second reason in part involves the absence of the conditions necessary to the truth of the first. If the historical development of the USSR cannot be characterized as the development of the dictatorship of the proletariat, then how can it best be understood? If it is the case, as the 1936 Constitution proclaimed, that capitalist property relationships have been abolished and that they have been replaced by state property and collective farm property, then one must inquire how it is that the agencies of the proletarian dictatorship have been used not only to prevent the external threats posed by capitalist encirclement, but much more so to repress what are perceived as internal dangers? This, to us, can only be explained by the endemic existence of class contradictions within the USSR. At the very least, therefore, we must reject the mechanistic identification of transformations in legal forms of capitalist property with the abolition of exploiting classes.[63] What is needed is transformation in social relationships themselves. We are left with an ironic twist to Lenin's dictum, when applied to the USSR since his death, that the dictatorship of the proletariat is the continuation of the class struggle in new forms. This was the thrust of Pashukanis's own concern.

Notes and References

Authors' note: Unless otherwise indicated, all citations to works by Pashukanis refer to pages in Beirne and Sharlet, eds., and Peter B. Maggs, trans., *Pashukanis: Selected Writings on Marxism and Law*, (London: Academic Press, 1980).

1. His major treatise was *Obshchaia teoriia prava i marksizm*, first published in Moscow in 1924 and subsequently translated into French, German, Japanese, Serbo-Croatian, and into English in its third edition of 1927 as *The General Theory of Law and Marxism*. In J. Hazard, ed., and H. Babb, trans., *Soviet Legal Philosophy* (Cambridge: Harvard University Press, 1951), pp. 111–225.

2. According to the official *spravka*, Pashukanis was legally rehabilitated by the Military Division of the RSFSR Supreme Court in March 1956. The editors wish to acknowledge the generosity of Professor Dietrich A. Loeber of the University of Kiel for sharing a copy of this document with them. The most recent evidence of Pashukanis's limited intellectual rehabilitation is contained in the Soviet collection of some of his early writings from the 1920s. These will appear under the entry E. B. Pashukanis, *Obschchaia teoriia prava i marksizm* (Moscow: Nauka).

3. The sources for this biographical information are Robert Sharlet's interview with the late L. Ia. Gintsburg in Moscow, 1974; and J. Hazard, *Settling Disputes in Soviet Society: The Formative Years of Legal Institutions* (New York: Columbia University Press, 1960), pp. 17–18. The English reader should see generally Eugene Kamenka and Alice Tay, "The Life and Afterlife of a Bolshevik Jurist," *Problems of Communism* (1970), vol. 19, no. 1.

4. See pp. 37–131, Beirne and Sharlet, *Pashukanis* (1980), for translation of the first Russian edition.

5. E. B. Pashukanis, "Predislovie" to *Obshchaia teoriia prava i marksizm* (Moscow, 1926; 2nd corrected and supplemented edition), p. 3.

6. See R. Sharlet, "Pashukanis and the Rise of Soviet Marxist Jurisprudence, 1924–1930," *Soviet Union* (1974) 1, 2, pp. 103–121, esp. pp. 103–112.

7. For Pashukanis's own account of his Hegelian heritage, see E. B. Pashukanis, "Hegel on State and Law," *Sovetskoe gosudarstvo* (1931), pp. 1–32.

8. See M. N. Pokrovsky, *History of Russia from the Earliest Times to the Rise of Commercial Capitalism* (1910–1912), translated and edited by J. D. Clarkson and M. R. M. Griffiths, (London: Martin Lawrence, n.d.). See further G. M. Enteen, *The Soviet Scholar-Bureaucrat: M. N. Pokrovskii and the Society of Marxist Historians* (Pennsylvania and London: Pennsylvania State University Press, 1978).

9. See K. Marx, "Letter to Weydemeyer" (February 1, 1859), in *Marx and Engels: Selected Correspondence* (New York: International Publishers, 1942), p. 119; and K. Marx, *The Grundrisse* (1857–1858), translated by M. Nicolaus (New York: Random House, 1973), p. 108.

10. For example, see A. Fraser, "Legal Theory and Legal Practice," *Arena*, no. 44–45 (1976), pp. 123–156; C. Arthur, "Towards a Materialist Theory of Law," *Critique* 7 (1976–1977), pp. 31–46; I. Balbus, "Commodity Form and Legal Form: An Essay on the 'Relative Autonomy' of the Law," *Law and Society Review* (1977), vol. 2, no. 3, pp. 571–588; J. Holloway and S. Picciotto, "Capital, Crisis and the State," *Capital and Class* (Summer 1977), no. 2, pp. 76–101; C. Arthur, Introduction to *Evgeny B. Pashukanis, Law and Marxism: A General Theory* (London: Ink Links, 1978), pp. 9–31, a translation from the German edition of *Allgemeine Rechtslehre und Marxismus: Versuch einer Kritik der juristischen Grundbegriffe*; S. Redhead, "The Discrete Charm of Bourgeois Law: A Note on Pashukanis," *Critique* 9 (1978), pp. 113–120; Bob Fine, *Democracy and the Rule of Law* (London: Pluto Press, 1984), pp. 155–169.

11. Other than in some of his early writings, such as *On the Jewish Question* (1843), Marx himself had very little to say on the importance of the legal form. But see F. Engels and K. Kautsky, "Juridical Socialism," *Politics and Society* (1977), vol. 7, no. 2, pp. 199–200.

12. See E. B. Pashukanis, "The Situation on the Legal Theory Front" (1930), trans-

lated in J. Hazard, ed., *Soviet Legal Philosophy* (1951), pp. 237–280. Pashukanis's second self-criticism appeared in 1934, his third—"State and Law under Socialism" (1936)—is fully translated in Beirne and Sharlet, *Pashukanis*, pp. 346–61.

13. This definition was officially adopted by the Commissariat of Justice in 1919, and incorporated into RSFSR *Laws* (1919). See also P. I. Stuchka, "Marksistskoe ponimanie prava," *Kommunisticheskaia revoliutsiia* (1922), no. 13–14, pp. 37–38; and "Zametki o klassovoi teoriia prava," *Sovetskoe pravo* (1922), no. 3.

14. V. I. Lenin, "What the 'Friends of the People' Are and How They Fight the Social Democrats" (1894), *LCW*, vol. 1, p. 153.

15. The concept of *persona* in Roman jurisprudence originally derived from the function of an actor's stage mask. The mask enabled the actor to conceal his real identity and to conform to the role written for him. Transposed into the legal realm, as a permanent condition, man must assume a legal mask in order to engage in the activities regulated by legal rules. See further, O. Gierke, *Associations and Law*, translated and edited by G. Heiman (Toronto: University of Toronto Press, 1977).

16. P. I. Stuchka, "Na ministerstvom kresle," in P. I. Stuchka, *13 let bor'by za revoliutsionno-marksistskuiu teoriiu prava* (Moscow, 1931).

17. See *Dekrety sovetskoi vlasti* (Moscow, 1957), vol. 1, pp. 124–126.

18. J. Hazard, *Settling Disputes in Soviet Society* (1960), p. vi.

19. In 1927 Pashukanis asserted that the term "proletarian state capitalism" was an error. See J. Hazard, ed., *Soviet Legal Philosophy* (1951), pp. 179f.

20. V. I. Lenin, "To Comrade Krzhizhanovsky: The Praesidium of the State Planning Commission" (May 1921), *LCW*, vol. 42, p. 371.

21. V. I. Lenin, "Draft Theses on the Role and Function of the Trade Unions under the New Economic Policy" (1922), *LCW*, vol. 33, p. 184.

22. Ibid., p. 185.

23. V. I. Lenin, "Report on Party Unity and the Anarcho-Syndicalist Deviation" (March 16, 1921), *LCW*, vol. 32, p. 251.

24. V. I. Lenin, "Instructions of the Council of Labour and Defence to Local Soviet Bodies" (May 1921), *LCW*, vol. 32, p. 384.

25. See R. Sharlet, "Pashukanis and the Rise of Soviet Marxist Jurisprudence," (cited note 6), pp. 112–115.

26. Pashukanis's phrase in "Disput k voprosu ob izuchenii prestupnosti," *Revoliutsiia prava* (1929), no. 3, p. 67.

27. E. B. Pashukanis, "Marksistskaia teoriia prava i stroitel'stvo sotsializma," *Revoliutsiia prava* (1927), no. 3, pp. 3–12, translated in Beirne and Sharlet (1980), *Pashukanis*, pp. 186–99.

28. M. A. Reisner, *Pravo, nashe pravo, chuzhoe pravo, obshchee pravo* (1925), Moscow, translated in J. Hazard, ed., *Soviet Legal Philosophy* (1951), pp. 83–109.

29. P. I. Stuchka, "Gosudarstvo i pravo v period sotsialisticheskogo stroitel'stva," *Revoliutsiia prava* (1927), no. 2. See also the criticism in S. I. Raevich, book review, *Sovetskoe pravo* (1928), no. 2 (32), p. 98.

30. Indeed, it is most likely that "Economics and Legal Regulation" was an indirect response to Stuchka's *Vvedenie v teoriiu grazhdanskogo prava* of 1927. Here Stuchka had reiterated that exchange must be subsumed within the concept of production because ". . . the distribution of the agents of production is itself only one of the aspects of production." See P. I. Stuchka, *Izbrannye proizvedeniia* (Riga, 1964), p. 565; and R. Sharlet, "Pashukanis and the Commodity Exchange Theory of Law, 1924–1930," unpub. Ph.D. diss., Indiana University, 1968, p. 210. The Communist Academy effected a compromise in 1929, in its first syllabus on the general theory of law. The concept of law was now rooted in the process of commodity production and exchange. See A. K.

Stal'gevich, *Programma po obshchei teoriia prava* (Moscow, 1929), p. 11;, and see R. Sharlet's 1968 dissertation, p. 210.

31. A. Avtorkhanov, *Stalin and the Soviet Communist Party* (New York, 1959), p. 21.

32. On the two wings of the commodity exchange school see R. Schlesinger, *Soviet Legal Theory* (London: Kegan Paul, 1945), pp. 153–156.

33. A. Vyshinsky, "Stuchka," *Malaia sovetskaia entsiklopediia* (1930), vol. 8, pp. 514–515.

34. P. I. Stuchka, "Proletarskoe pravo," in P. I. Stuchka, *13 let* . . . (1931), pp. 24, 34.

35. P. I. Stuchka, Foreword to *13 let* . . . (1931), p. 4.

36. P. I. Stuchka, *Vvedenie v teoriiu grazhdanskogo prava* (1927), in P. I. Stuchka, *Izbrannye proizvedeniia* (1964), pp. 563–564.

37. A. Piontkovsky, *Marksizm i ugolovnoe pravo: sbornik statei* (Moscow, 1929; 2nd ed.), pp. 32–33, 39.

38. Quoted in E. B. Pashukanis, "The Situation on the Legal Theory Front" (1930), in Hazard, *Soviet Legal Philosophy*, pp. 253, 250.

39. P. I. Stuchka, "Dvenadtsat' let revoliutsii gosudarstva i prava," in P. I. Stuchka, *13 let* . . . (1931), p. 189.

40. A. Piontkovsky, *Marksizm i ugolovnoe pravo* (1929), p. 87.

41. A. Ia. Estrin, "XVth Congress of the Party and Questions of Law," *Revoliutsiia prava* (1928), no. 2, p. 13. See also R. Sharlet, "Pashukanis and the Withering Away of Law in the USSR," in S. Fitzpatrick, ed., *Cultural Revolution in Russia, 1928–1931* (Bloomington: Indiana University Press, 1978), pp. 169–188.

42. See R. Sharlet, "Stalinism and Soviet Legal Culture," in R. C. Tucker, ed., *Stalinism* (New York: Norton, 1977), pp. 161–162.

43. J. Stalin, *Problems of Leninism* (Moscow: State Publishing House, 1947; 11th ed.), pp. 344–345.

44. J. Stalin, "Political Report of the Central (Party) Committee to the XVIth Congress, 1930," in J. Hazard, ed., *Soviet Legal Philosophy* (1951), p. 234.

45. Marx himself had first appreciated the salience of this distinction in *The Eighteenth Brumaire of Louis Bonaparte* and *The Civil War in France*.

46. E. B. Pashukanis, "The Situation on the Legal Theory Front" (1930), in Hazard, *Soviet Legal Philosophy*, pp. 278–280.

47. See R. Sharlet, "Stalinism and Soviet Legal Culture," in Tucker, ed., *Stalinism*, f49 and pp. 172–173.

48. J. Hazard, "Housecleaning in Soviet Law," *American Quarterly on the Soviet Union* (1938), vol. 1, no. 1, p. 15.

49. To Pashukanis's credit, he still refused to recognize the concept of "proletarian law." But even this incorporated somewhat of a major retreat, however, by his terminological nicety of the "class law of the proletariat" (1935:307).

50. See R. Sharlet, "Stalinism and Soviet Legal Culture," in Tucker, pp. 168–169.

51. Ibid., p. 169.

52. This critique is largely contained in four sources. See A. Ia. Vyshinsky, "The Fundamental Tasks of the Science of Soviet Socialist Law" (1938), in J. Hazard, ed., *Soviet Legal Philosophy* (1951), pp. 303–341; "The Marxist Theory of State and Law," *Bolshevik* (1938); "The Eighteenth Congress of the CPSU and the Tasks of the Theory of Socialist Law," *Sovetskoe gosudarstvo* (1939), no. 3; J. Hazard, ed., and H. Babb, trans., *The Law of the Soviet State* (New York: Macmillan, 1948).

53. A. Vyshinsky, "Fundamental Tasks of the Science of Soviet Socialist Law" (1938), in Hazard, *Soviet Legal Philosophy*, p. 337.

54. Ibid., p. 339.

55. A. Vyshinsky, *The Law of the Soviet State* (1948), p. 75.
56. Ibid., p. 62.
57. Ibid., p. 51.
58. Ibid., p. 62.
59. Ibid., p. 52.
60. Published in November 1938, *The History of the Communist Party of the Soviet Union (Bolshevik): Short Course* almost immediately became the Stalinist forerunner of Mao's *Little Red Book*, which would later be its functional equivalent in China.
61. See particularly, V. I. Lenin, "A Great Beginning" (1919), *LCW*, vol. 29, p. 420.
62. Ibid., p. 420.
63. Any distinction between economic and legal property faces the logical difficulty that economic property is usually conceptualized in legal terms (ownership, use, possession, etc.). This problem has recently been posed, unsatisfactorily, by several authors. See E. Balibar, *On the Dictatorship of the Proletariat* (London: New Left Books, 1977), pp. 66–77; C. Bettelheim, *Class Struggles in the USSR 1917–1923* (New York: Monthly Review Press, 1976), pp. 20–32; A. Glucksman "The Althusserian Theatre," *New Left Review* (1972), p. 68; N. Poulantzas, *Political Power and Social Classes* (London: New Left Books, 1973), p. 72. But, see the interesting and important reformulations contained in G. A. Cohen, *Karl Marx's Theory of History: A Defense* (Princeton: Princeton University Press, 1978); and P. Corrigan, H. Ramsay, and D. Sayer, *Socialist Construction and Marxist Theory* (New York and London: Monthly Review Press, 1978).

Chapter 3

P. I. Stuchka and Soviet Law

Robert Sharlet, Peter B. Maggs, and Piers Beirne

Introduction

Piotr Ivanovich Stuchka was born to a peasant family on July 27, 1865, near Riga in the Latvian province of the old Russian empire. Little has been recorded about his early years, but it is known that he completed the *Gymnasium* at Riga in 1884 and then entered the law department of St. Petersburg University. It was during his years at St. Petersburg that he began to immerse himself in the writings of the intellectual precursors of the Russian revolutionary movement, the writings of Marx and Engels, and those of the Russian Marxist Plekhanov. Stuchka received his law degree in 1888 and immediately began work as a political activist and a progressive journalist on liberal Latvian newspapers. During this period his recorded work on questions of law and politics consisted of not quite two dozen newspaper articles and polemical essays in socialist periodicals. These included specialized articles on such topics as labor legislation, the many problems of judicial and criminal law reform in the Baltic provinces, and various issues of tactics and strategy in the revolutionary movement.

For these activities Stuchka was exiled in 1897 to the Viatka Guberniia. In 1904 he founded the Latvian Social Democratic Party and led it into an alliance with the Russian Social Democrats (which, in 1914, was to merge with Lenin's Bolshevik faction). He took part in the 1905 revolution and, following the severe military repression after the revolution and his own move to St. Petersburg, he defended many revolutionaries in the tsarist courts. In 1906 he resigned from the Central Committee of the Latvian Social Democratic Workers' Party (Kalnins, 1972:136–39); his resignation doubtless stemmed both from his opposition to the Menshevik

This chapter is a revised and expanded version of our "Editors' Introduction," pp. ix-xxii in *P. I. Stuchka: Selected Writings on Soviet Law and Marxism*, edited, introduced, and translated by Robert Sharlet, Peter B. Maggs, and Piers Beirne (Armonk, N.Y.: M. E. Sharpe, 1988). Reprinted by permission.

dominance of Latvian socialism and also from his demands for stricter controls of Latvian anarchists. In 1907 he was appointed leader of the Latvian Bolsheviks.

Soviet historians record that Stuchka played a key role, during the disastrous Russian participation in the 1914–18 War, in politicizing the Latvian rifle regiments in the socialist cause. Indeed, these very troops later took an active part in the October 1917 revolution; because of their political reliability, they were used as a military vanguard by the Bolshevik leadership. Stuchka is known to have been a member of the Petrograd Committee of the Bolsheviks in February 1917, and then of the Bolshevik faction of the Petrograd Soviet. According to Leon Trotsky (1959:440; see also Daniels, 1967:190–91), Stuchka was one of seven Bolshevik candidates for the Presidium at the Congress of Soviets of October 25, 1917. He was appointed Commissar of Justice (Stuchka, 1922) in Lenin's first government of 1917 (he had been associated with Lenin as early as 1895) and took an active part in the drafting of the revolutionary decrees on the legal relations of the transitional period.[1] While working at the center of the revolution, Stuchka remained active in Latvian political affairs. Taking a leave of absence from his responsibilities in the administration of revolutionary justice, he returned to the Baltic region in late 1918 to provide direction to the emerging political developments there. Shortly after, the German army was finally driven out and Stuchka was proclaimed as the first prime minister of the ill-fated Latvian Soviet Republic. However, his incumbency was short-lived: in January 1920, his government was overthrown in the course of the Russian Civil War and foreign military intervention against the Bolsheviks.

Stuchka then returned to Moscow, the center of Bolshevik power, and resumed his legal work. His major contribution to the law was carried out in the 1920s, a decade that was an unusually fertile one for the development of Marxist legal theory in the USSR. During the period from the New Economic Policy (1922–27) to the emergence and consolidation of Stalinism around 1929–30, Stuchka held several positions in the Communist Academy, was a delegate to the Central Executive Committee of the Communist International, and leader of the latter's Latvian section (Sharlet, 1968:41). He was appointed to a senior justice office in 1921, an office from which he guided the programs of relegalization and recodification as the Bolsheviks were forced to "retreat" to the limited capitalism of the New Economic Policy. His book *The Revolutionary Role of Law and State* appeared in the same year, and the origins of the Soviet Marxist theory of law can properly be traced to it. In January 1923, Stuchka was appointed chairman of the Supreme Court of the Russian Republic (and a member of the Control Commission of the Communist International), a responsibility that he was to retain until his death. For his dedication to the revolutionary cause and for his immense achievements as a Marxist intellectual and public official, Stuchka was honored by the party and decorated by the government on the occasion of his sixty-fifth birthday in 1930. Upon his death (by natural causes) on January 25, 1932, his ashes were interred in the Kremlin Wall behind Lenin's Mausoleum on Red Square.

Stuchka adhered to the ill-fated "commodity exchange" school of legal theory, which took seriously the idea of "withering away of law," and thus in the late 1930s came into direct conflict with Stalin's and Vyshinsky's determination to expand the use of law for the enforcement of discipline and the creation of a stable incentive system. In common with Pashukanis and other members of the commodity exchange school of law, Stuchka's good name fell rapidly into disrepute. His efforts in legal theory came to be ignored and even vilified. According to Roy Medvedev, in 1937 Stuchka was declared "a propagator of harmful ideology and a deliberate wrecker in the field of jurisprudence" (1973:202).[2] State Prosecutor Vyshinsky referred to Stuchka as an adherent of "the Bukharinist perversions of Marxism-Leninism" (1938:53) and to his notion of the role of law in the transitional period as "a coarse perversion of the Marx-Engels-Lenin-Stalin theory of socialism" (ibid., 55; see further this book, chapter 6).

Not until the reforms of the post-Stalin era was Stuchka rehabilitated. Today, Stuchka is regarded in the USSR as one of the main architects of Soviet legal theory and of the Soviet legal system itself. His work and career are the objects of considerable scholarly attention (Strogovich, 1960; Kliava, *Introduction to Stuchka*, 1964; Plotnieks, 1978), and an extensive, albeit censored, collection of his writings has been issued (Stuchka, 1964). Indeed, a glowing tribute to Stuchka was published in 1986 in the leading Soviet legal journal (Skripilev and Grafskii, 1986:137–38; see also Smirnov, 1985:24).

However, Stuchka's intervention in Soviet legal theory is still relatively unheralded outside the USSR. In part this is because his contribution to legal theory lay less in the realm of erudite abstraction than that of pedagogy, of polemics, and of the practical dictates of the building of socialism. Only a very small part of Stuchka's work has been available to an English-language audience—the first four chapters of his *Revolutionary Role of Law and State* (Hazard, 1951:17–69), and a few pages of his voluminous essays (Jaworskyj, 1967:72–75, 87–92, 99, 240–243; Zile, 1977; Rosenberg, 1984:223–228, 249–260). This neglect persisted despite Stuchka's recognition several decades ago by prominent Western jurists (e.g., Schlesinger, 1945; Hazard, 1951; Kelsen, 1955), more recently by authors in the Federal Republic of Germany (e.g., Loeber, 1965; Reich, 1969) and, very occasionally, by Western Marxists (e.g., Poulantzas, 1964).

Our recent collection of Stuchka's writings, *P. I. Stuchka: Selected Writings on Soviet Law and Marxism*, was therefore intended to fill at least some of this void. Our translations there displayed the important themes of the three major periods into which the changing thrust of his work on law can be partitioned. These periods include (1) his critique of bourgeois jurisprudence; (2) his positions within the complicated Marxist debates in the 1920s and 1930s about the proper content and objectives of Soviet legal theory; and (3) his involvement in the actual practices of the Soviet state and Soviet law in the fifteen years immediately after the 1917 revolution.

Let us now comment on Stuchka's work during each of these three periods.

From "Bourgeois Law" to "Revolutionary Legality"

To our knowledge, there was no serious debate about law among Russian Marxists before 1919. According to Stuchka (1927:184–185) himself, in his essay "State and Law in the Period of Socialist Construction," there was no theoretical work on law from a revolutionary Marxist perspective before December 1919. It was at this date that the Collegium of the People's Commissariat of Justice—of which Stuchka had been Commissar since March 1919—provided the first official Soviet definition of the concept of law. This appeared in the "Basic Principles of the RSFSR Criminal Law," and declared that "law is the system or order of social relations corresponding to the interests of the ruling class and protected by the organized force of that class."

Much of Stuchka's writing in this early period displays his practical involvement with the creation of proletarian legal institutions, such as the people's courts. The central problem addressed by Stuchka in this period—for example, in his essays "A Class Court or a Democratic Court?" (1917) and "Proletarian Law" (1919)—was the relationship between the tsarist legal system and the new apparatuses of Bolshevik power. Because the former was bourgeois in both form and content it must be discarded, but with what proletarian institutions should it be replaced? In trying to steer a path between the errors of anarchism (to which he was always opposed) and those of legal formalism, Stuchka (1919:11) pointed to two types of rules in the old Code of Laws of the Russian Empire: on the one hand were rules, presumably of a more or less technical nature, that "did not contradict revolutionary legal consciousness" and, on the other, were rules determining the very essence and direction of activity of the old regime. The initial phase of the proletarian revolution should seek to promote policies that encourage the "burning" of the latter and the retention of the former. "In general," he argued, "the charter for judicial procedure will henceforth simply be no more than an institution, or a guide, or a manual" (ibid.).

At first Stuchka was greatly optimistic about the prospect of socialist construction, but at the same time frustrated with the tardiness with which it was proceeding. To a certain extent, in the very early phases of the revolution, the workers themselves had anticipated subsequent Bolshevik strategies. Immediately after the February revolution of 1917, in Kronstadt and in the Vyborg side of Petrograd for example, the workers had ignored the tsarist courts and began to set up their own revolutionary courts. Stuchka himself admitted that the revolution had acted very slowly with respect to the old bourgeois apparatuses of power. He complained, on the one hand, that courts remained bourgeois institutions in part because judges were not yet subject to democratic election and recall, and also because there still existed salary differentials based on such factors as the old division of members of the judicial magistracy. On the other hand, Stuchka reported, with seeming approval, that the provisional revolutionary courts were actually beginning the tasks of construction.

Stuchka (1919) reasserted his commitment to the democratization of the law of the transition period in his article "Proletarian Law." The composition of the courts, he insisted, should be "close" to the people or "coming from" the depths of the people. Ordinary civil relations should be equally comprehensible to the citizen and to the lawyer; indeed, the courses in revolutionary judicial procedure that Stuchka was now teaching at the Socialist Academy of Social Sciences, were open to judges in the people's courts. "Proletarian law," he argued, "is primarily a simplification, a popularization of our new social order" (ibid., 20). At the same time, he discussed various aspects of the actual content of the Soviet law of the transitional period. These laws included a mass of new decrees on the abolition of estate and civil hierarchies, the separation of the state and the schools from the church, the eight-hour working day, abolition of the means of production and the bourgeois freedom of contract, and new rules of "social law" to do with the family, divorce, and prostitution. Finally, he suggested that the time was now opportune for the publication of a compendium of proletarian law. This compendium—to be published in a technical version for lawyers, and a simpler version for citizens—needed to contain the laws of the new constitution, the rights and duties of the citizen, social law, property law, labor law, and international law.

Besides his prominent intervention in the practical aspects of socialist construction, Stuchka also played a weighty role in the early phase of Soviet Marxist legal theory. Tendentially, his work served, in an important but rather simplistic way, as the nexus between Marx's, Engels's, and Lenin's fragmentary writings on law and the sophisticated theoretical analysis of law engaged in by Pashukanis.

In 1921 Stuchka published the first edition of his noted text *The Revolutionary Role of Law and State*. Like many of his works, which were primarily produced either as primers and textbooks for pedagogical purposes or as treatises on specialized topics, this book was widely read in jurisprudential circles and was used in law courses as an introduction to Marxist analysis of law. At the level of general questions about the nature of legal rules, it was never Stuchka's intention to develop an integrated or coherent general theory of law. Rather, his intention seems to have been both to criticize the major schools of bourgeois legal theory (especially those that had adherents in the Soviet Union during the New Economic Policy) and also to develop some of the chief concepts of Marxist legal theory.

Serious Marxist debate about law began only with the publication of Stuchka's *The Revolutionary Role of Law and State*. Indeed, it is to this book that the apparent rupture with much of the earlier jurisprudence can be traced. While it is exceedingly difficult to summarize the contents of *The Revolutionary Role of Law and State*, we can identify three major arguments in it:

1. Law is the system or order of social relationships corresponding to the interests of the ruling class and protected by the organized force of that class. Law is of two types: (a) rules that stem from sectional, private interests, and (b) technical rules that are of a purely administrative nature.

2. Law is the product of class struggles. Class struggles occur in the processes of production and exchange.

3. Law has a vital role to perform in the transitional period between capitalism and communism. The law of the transitional period—"Soviet law"[3], or "proletarian law"[4]—is a temporary form of authority that primarily involves a simplification and a popularization of the new social order and which is supported by coercion and ideological persuasion.

Stuchka's concern with the transition from bourgeois to proletarian legal institutions was also evident in two other essays—"The Marxist Concept of Law" (1922) and "Notes on the Class Theory of Law" (1922a). These were written at the beginning of the New Economic Policy, and in them Stuchka articulated three themes. First, he stressed that it is important to remember Engels's dictum that law and legalism are the classical principles of bourgeois ideology. As such, a chief aspect of NEP was to be a principled struggle by communists against legal ideology. He therefore argued that the bourgeois-juridical perspective, with its notions of "blind justice" and the "nightwatchman state," must be rejected in favor of the recognition that law and state are essentially phenomena of class relations. However, as a second theme, Stuchka reminded his audience that revolutionary class struggle in part consists of "struggle around law." This is so precisely because the distribution of the means of production is expressed in and protected by the law of private property. Only under developed communism is it possible to dispense with law. Third, he attacked those who promulgated the slanderous view that the Bolsheviks were opposed to legality. On the contrary, Stuchka stressed, progress in the socialist transition must be based on revolutionary legality and class legal consciousness.

The Marxist Theory of Law

In the early 1920s, NEP mandated and accelerated full-scale restoration of law as a condition of economic recovery from the devastation of war and as a prelude to a concerted program of industrialization. Familiar legal institutions were revived. An elaborate program of codification was begun, based largely on foreign models. For the Bolshevik jurists, the restoration of law involved the need for a Marxist critique of the USSR's essentially bourgeois legal system in preparation for the time when the party could end the retreat and resume the process of the withering away of law. In this phase of the revolution, Stuchka pioneered the Marxist critique of bourgeois jurisprudence and of the branches of bourgeois law. His efforts in these respects must be assessed both as speculative and preliminary and also as an incipient alternative to the radical wing of the emergent commodity exchange school of law advanced by Pashukanis.

Stuchka's concern to develop a Marxist theory of law is the major theme of his essays "A Materialist or Idealist Concept of Law?" (1923) and "In Defense of the Revolutionary Marxist Concept of Class Law" (1923a).

In the former, published in the most prominent Soviet Marxist philosophical journal of the early and mid-1920s (*Pod znamenem Marksizma* [Under the Banner of Marxism]), Stuchka (1923) entered the lists against natural law philosophy, the historical school of law and, especially, the psychological theory of law of Petrazhitsky and his principal Soviet adherent, Reisner. Here Stuchka inveighed against those jurists who presume to find the origins of law in ideology, in the "heads of people," rather than in real, socioeconomic interactions or the material relationships of people. In searching for the source of law, he averred, "being" must take precedence over its "consciousness." He then explored the ideological formation of law by tracing transformations in the idealist notion of the origin of law in popular will—from the will of a deity, an absolute idea, the popular masses, the parties to a contract, the social collective, to the contemporary notion of the will of the individual. He attacked those (such as Kunow) who believed that the legal order is a purely mechanical adaptation between social structure and a given mode of production. Following Marx's first chapter in *Capital* ("On Commodities"), Stuchka suggests that law has dual forms. On the one hand, law is the concrete form of a social relation, and embodies a specific injunction; on the other, it is an abstract form of a social relation, the *legal* form of that relation. Addressing himself to the thorny problem of base and superstructure, Stuchka argued that the concrete forms of the property relation coincide with production relations. Finally, he claimed that law has a third aspect, namely, the intuitive form which "with respect to a given social relation, occurs within a person, his evaluation of this relation from the point of view of justice, internal legal consciousness, etc." (Stuchka, 1927:73).

In his "In Defense of the Revolutionary Marxist Concept of Class Law," Stuchka (1923a) criticized Reisner for attacking the materialist approach to law from the point of view of the psychological conception of law. In response, Stuchka recapitulated and clarified the fundamental positions taken thus far, and he delineated the differences between them and the Reisner-Petrazhitsky perspectives. This entailed making the following distinctions between (1) law as a material object and law as ideology; (2) class law and intuitive law; (3) social class as the source of law and the individual as the source of law; (4) the actual legal relationship and the form of law; and (5) law as a part of the base and law as a superstructural phenomenon. Stuchka reiterated that his little book *The Revolutionary Role of Law and State* merely intended to pose the correct questions about law from a Marxian perspective rather than to provide definitive answers. Hence, some new terrain was entered as he refined further the concept of "system" as the system of social relations grounded in the processes of production and commodity exchange.

By 1924 Stuchka had become a major figure in the Communist International. His various political and legal posts were the tumultuous external setting for an intellectual life devoted to the development of the Marxist theory of law. An early member of the Socialist (later Communist) Academy, Stuchka organized and led its section on the general theory of law which, in the early 1920s, became the cynosure of the emerging

Marxist school of jurisprudence and the spearhead of the "revolution of the law." He was also a professor of law at Moscow State University, a law lecturer in the Institute of Red Professors, and the first director of the Moscow Institute of Soviet Law. Through these strategic positions, Stuchka shaped the theoretical orientation of the new generation of emerging Soviet Marxist lawyers.

However, in 1924 Pashukanis published his *General Theory of Law and Marxism* (see chapter 2, *supra*). Much that happened in Soviet jurisprudence and legal education in the next few years must of course be understood as an extension of, or a reaction to, the themes of Pashukanis's book and of the sections of the commodity exchange school that adhered to it. It is clear that much of Pashukanis's argument in *General Theory of Law and Marxism* contradicted one of the pillars of Stuchka's theory of law, namely, that law is a class phenomenon. Indeed, at several places in his *General Theory*, Pashukanis explicitly took issue with Stuchka. For example, he pointed out (Pashukanis, 1924:61–62) that Stuchka's definition of law was indistinguishable from social relations in general, and that perhaps because it emerged from the People's Commissariat of Justice, Stuchka's definition stemmed from the needs of the practicing lawyer. It "shows the empirical limit which history always places upon legal logic, but it does not reveal the deep roots of this logic itself" (Pashukanis, 1924:62).[5] Stuchka's definition of law, in short, revealed the class content present in the legal form, but it failed to explain why this content appeared in such a form. Nevertheless, in the preface to the third edition of *Revolutionary Role of Law and State*, published in 1924, Stuchka noted the number of new works on the Marxist theory of state and law and identified Pashukanis's *General Theory* as the most outstanding. With a few reservations, he found Pashukanis's book "to the highest degree [to be] a valuable contribution to our Marxist theoretical literature on law and [that it] directly supplements my work, which provides only an incomplete and greatly inadequate general doctrine of law." Stuchka thus helped raise Pashukanis from academic obscurity to the forefront of the "revolution of law."

In 1925, the first issue of the journal *Revolution of the Law* appeared as a collection of essays under the editorship of Stuchka. The impressive list of contributors included Bukharin, Pashukanis, and the philosophers Adoratsky and Razumovsky. Stuchka's (1925; and see *infra*, chapter 4) own contribution on "Lenin and the Revolutionary Decree" was a combination of his personal recollections of Lenin and a brief excursion into the legal history of Soviet power just after the Bolshevik revolution. As such, it sought to impart—or to fabricate—a Leninist history to the Soviet Marxist theory of law. Stuchka set for himself here the task of reconciling Lenin's hostility to jurists with his own belief in the importance of law and legality for achieving revolutionary objectives. He provided a number of quotations from Lenin affirming his strong belief in the efficacy of law, and even suggested that Lenin had an "*excessive belief*" in governance by decree during the years of Civil War and the policy of War Communism. However, Stuchka then proceeded to soften his criticism by outlining, with approval, Lenin's pragmatic approach to the early Bolshevik decrees.

According to Stuchka, Lenin viewed the resort to law and even bourgeois parliamentarianism as appropriate instruments for revolutionaries, under certain circumstances. He also regarded the governmental decree as an essential legitimizing mechanism for statements about Bolshevik policy, a way of communicating policies to the masses in a more formal, politically secular and, hopefully, persuasive manner. Finally, Lenin saw the decree as a vital medium for the "translation" of abstract policy into the more practical language of implementation. In the course of sketching out Lenin's views, Stuchka provided a rare (for this period) albeit brief excursion into the legal history of early Bolshevik policy toward the judiciary, and some interesting glimpses into the struggles to enact Decree No. 1 on the Court.

By the mid-1920s, the ties between prerevolutionary Russian legal theory and bourgeois German and foreign jurisprudence had ostensibly been severed, and domestic juristic opponents had been bested in intellectual debate. Moreover, the adherents of the Marxist school were extending their critical work beyond the general theory of law into civil, criminal, and other branches of law. At this juncture, Stuchka launched a massive project: *The Encyclopedia of State and Law*. Stuchka served as chief editor of this two-year, three-volume undertaking and, in addition, he himself wrote most of the entries concerned with the principal concepts of Marxist legal theory. His contributions to the *Encyclopedia* represent not only his "mature" work but also the distillation and consolidation of his most influential work in the Marxist theory of law as it then existed. It is clear—surveying Stuchka's *Encyclopedia* essays on "bourgeois law" (1925–27), "jurisprudence" (1925–27a), "the state" (1925–27b), "revolutionary legality" (1925–27c), "law" (1925–27d), "the legal relationship" (1925–27e), "legal consciousness" (1925–27f), and the new concept of "Soviet law" (1927g)—that the theoretical offensive against the bourgeois juridical world view achieved its greatest intensity in this project, under the banner of the revolution of the law.

In the first two *Encyclopedia* entries ("Bourgeois Law" and "Jurisprudence"), Stuchka attempted to compare the hypocrisy of bourgeois jurisprudence with the new science of class law developed by Soviet jurists. Both essays seem, in retrospect, pedestrian, repetitive, and unenterprising—no doubt reflecting, by Stuchka's own admission, the lack of serious Marxist analysis either of legal history or of the history of ideas. In "The State," he inserted a brief discussion of the proletarian state into a summary of the historical forms of state power, on the one hand, and specific theories associated with specific states on the other. There are two small, albeit interesting and important, features of this essay. Firstly, Stuchka suggested that the concept of the proletarian state will only become unnecessary with "the uniting of the whole world in a *single* Union of Soviet Socialist Republics." It is tempting to regard this pithy statement as a rejection of the doctrine of socialism in one country; whether or not Stuchka subscribed to such a rejection, it is impossible to know. Certainly, the statement suggests a basis for Stalin's theory of the strengthening of the state as developed in the 1930s. Second, while reiterating his opposition to anarchism and to utopianism, Stuchka resigned himself—as, too, had Lenin on several occasions just before his death—to the fact that the project of socialist construction engaged in by the dictatorship of the proletariat was likely to be "extremely long." Aside from the fact that this wager proved historically accurate, it served later to insulate Stuchka from much of the Stalinist criticism of the leftist "red professors" of the radical wing of the commodity exchange school of law.

In "Revolutionary Legality" Stuchka disassociated "Soviet," or "socialist," or "revolutionary" legality from the legality of the *Rechtsstaat.* Legality in the latter Stuchka defined as "the self-limitation which a bourgeois state authority imposes upon itself" (1925–27c:139). Revolutionary legality, in contrast, involved not the limitation of state authority, but the observance of uniform enforcement of Soviet law from one end of the huge country to the other. Stuchka's definition was the forerunner of the current Soviet concept of socialist legality. But Stuchka tempered the extreme centralism inherent in his definition with a call to allow a reasonable amount of discretion for the officials actually enforcing the law.

In his entry "Law," Stuchka clearly differentiated the basis of his legal theory from that of the commodity exchange formulation adhered to by Pashukanis. Stuchka's theory of the class nature of law provided the necessary theoretical basis for the extensive use of law during the construction of socialism: the officially-decreed definition of law adopted in the 1940s basically flows from Stuchka's theory. Stuchka returned to his differences with Pashukanis in his *Encyclopedia* entry "Legal Relationship." Here, he again argued that the commodity exchange theory was unable adequately to explain legal relationships. Rather, one should seek a "class" explanation, and do so by looking at the class consciousness of those entering into legal relationships. In an approach that eventually became the orthodox one in the Soviet Union, Stuchka (1925–27e:157) argued that

> to become legal, or to be turned into a legal relation, a social relation must acquire a particular supplementary characteristic: *correspondence to the class interest and its protection by the organized authority of the ruling class.*

In addition, Stuchka (1925–27f) gave an historical interpretation to legal consciousness. He argued that, immediately following the revolution, social transformation was outpacing legislation. Thus, in accordance with Decree No. 1 on the Court, the Bolsheviks had declared that courts had to be guided by "revolutionary legal consciousness"—the understanding of the will of the victorious proletarian class. With the limited retreat to NEP and the accompanying development of detailed Soviet legislation and of instruments for enforcement, legal consciousness was replaced, for the law enforcement agencies, with "revolutionary legality."

Stuchka's article on "Soviet Law" is also of considerable importance. It was written for the third volume of the *Encyclopedia of State and Law*, and published in 1927, toward the end of the NEP period. In it Stuchka clearly articulated an ideological basis for considering the law in force in the USSR to be "Soviet law" and—against anarchists and ultraleftists—legitimate and worthy of respect. He defined Soviet law as the law of the transition period from class society to classless society. This view he contrasted with two other views. For one of these views, what was in force in the Soviet Union were remnants of bourgeois law, retained as a temporary measure until the eventual withering away of the state and law; for the other, bourgeois law and Soviet law coexisted, but the term *Soviet* law was limited to the law regulating peculiarly Soviet institutions. Because they termed part or all of the Soviet legal system as "bourgeois," both these views threatened its legitimacy. By terming the entire legal system "Soviet," Stuchka emphasized its legitimate, positive role in the carrying out of "class" (i.e., party) policy. In this, as in many other cases, Stuchka's practical views prevailed.

However, a major difficulty confronting Stuchka's definition of law was the well-known passage in Lenin's *State and Revolution* to the effect that postrevolutionary law would still be bourgeois law. Stuchka skipped over this passage quickly, and he seemed plainly uncomfortable with it. Justifying his own position, he claimed that the revolution had rapidly superseded the laws of the old regime, that Soviet law had placed strict legal limits on the degree of bourgeoisification of the law under NEP, and that an "attack in the direction of socialism" had begun.

For the extreme anarchist elements in the Bolshevik revolution, the phrase "Soviet law" must have appeared to be a contradiction in terms. For Pashukanis, the law of the Soviet state was merely a continuation of bourgeois law applied to the shrinking and doomed area of commodity exchange. Stuchka admitted that the idea of Soviet law arose only after the revolution, but that it had become an accomplished fact with the elaboration of detailed Soviet legislation in all areas. Once again, Stuchka provided the theory that by the mid-1930s would win out over that of Pashukanis and become an important part of the orthodox basis of Soviet legal theory. Very soon, it would be exceedingly difficult to muster ideological support for a law that was branded as "bourgeois" in nature.

In sum, although Stuchka's *Encyclopedia* entries were often cryptic and dogmatic, they served the important purpose of providing a basis for a theory of law capable of supporting the Soviet legal system not for the brief transition period envisioned by the more radical communists, but for decades, indeed for the indefinite future. Stuchka's logic in fact suggested the abandonment of the idea of the withering away of law altogether. In retrospect, therefore, the *Encyclopedia* project can be seen as an intellectual monument to the heady years of Marxist hopes for the withering away of law.

Socialist Construction and Soviet Legality

As part of the general "cultural revolution," the Marxist school of law, now based in the Communist Academy, launched its journal *Revoliutsiia prava* (Revolution of

Law) in 1927. This new periodical was intended to serve as a forum for the theoretical struggle against foreign bourgeois jurists and their domestic allies. However, within the Marxist school important intellectual and political cleavages were becoming apparent. Notable among these was the conflict between the radical and moderate wings of the commodity exchange school, respectively epitomized in the writings of Pashukanis and Stuchka. The common public front of the Marxist jurists was seriously ruptured by Stuchka's (1927) article "State and Law in the Period of Socialist Construction" that appeared in the second issue of the *Revoliutiia prava.*

While consistently praising the originality of Pashukanis's *General Theory of Law and Marxism*, Stuchka now felt the need to offer serious criticisms of it. First, he argued that Pashukanis was wrong to have identified the origin of law in the needs of commodity exchange, and that to do so was to engage in a species of economism. Law, he countered, originates both in the appropriation of land and in the class struggles in the processes of production. Law reflects not the exchange of commodities but the authority and the power of economically dominant classes.

Second, Stuchka suggested that although Pashukanis had correctly identified the similarity between economic fetishism and legal fetishism under capitalism, he had nevertheless erred in extending this parallel to law in general. For Stuchka, feudal law, bourgeois law, and Soviet law were basically different forms of law. Bourgeois law, for example, can itself be divided into two types. In the first period of capitalism, property law (the private ownership of the means of production) determines the distribution of products. With the advent of monopolistic imperialism the anarchy of production is replaced by trusts, by syndicates, and by state imperialism. In other words, capitalist development entails the "rationalization" of bourgeois law in the pursuit of profit for private capital. Moreover, precisely because Pashukanis had falsely equated bourgeois law with law in general, he had proceeded to commit himself to another error, namely, to the utopian belief that the process of the withering away of law involved a direct transition from bourgeois law to nonlaw.

Third, Stuchka urged—against Pashukanis—that Soviet law should have a creative role in the period of socialist construction. "Soviet law," he asserted, "must be the political economy of the transitional period, the *economic policy of Soviet power laid out in paragraphs*" (Stuchka, 1927:186). Although Soviet law was "in general a reprint of bourgeois law," it was nevertheless a law that existed without a bourgeoisie. Soviet law was a necessary, temporary feature of the proletarian dictatorship whose object was socialist planning and whose Soviet character was protected by the class state of the proletariat.

The Fifteenth Party Congress of 1927 called for the construction of socialism and the end of the strategic retreat of NEP, and urged the spread of a "cultural revolution" throughout Soviet society. Stuchka took up the party's call on behalf of the Marxist jurists in his article "Culture and Law" (1928). For Stuchka, the cultural revolution was an extension of the "revolution of the law" already underway since the mid-1920s. He synthesized both aspects of this revolutionary process into the "cultural revolution of the law" and criticized the two extreme interpretations—one for advocating the premature withering away of the law, and the other for urging excessive legal coercion. The task of Marxist jurists Stuchka saw as the need to supersede the bourgeois legal culture of NEP and to forge a Soviet legal culture. The struggle to attain the latter would entail the recognition of the apparent paradoxical logic of the revolution—there was, on the one hand, the need to construct new apparatuses of state and law, but, on the other, the commitment to their imminent withering away. Stuchka's interim solution to this paradox was to advocate the simplification of existing law as a gradual step toward its eventual elimination, while retaining its capacity for coercion during socialist construction.

In the spring of 1929 Stalin initiated the "revolution from above." The First Five-Year Plan was gaining momentum and collectivization had begun, with its crescendo of violence then only months away. Anticipating the Stalinist political tendencies that would emerge at the Sixteenth Party Congress a year hence, Stuchka (1929) advocated the strengthening of the state as the dialectical path to its ultimate withering away. At the same time, he lamented the increasing bureaucratism of the Soviet administrative system—this he considered to be an unwanted bourgeois legacy, and he therefore proposed to counter it with the expansion of mass political participation through the local soviets. Only mass participation in policy, he reasoned, could lay the essential groundwork for the eventual elimination of the state. But the prescription for the withering away of the state should not, according to Stuchka, be applied to law. Because law was then a vital mechanism for carrying out socialist construction in the countryside, he concluded that the decentralization of law was not the correct path. Instead, he advocated the continued simplification of the legal process, making it comprehensible and accessible to the Soviet masses. Indeed, given the flood of complex legislation that was beginning to inundate the Soviet system, Stuchka saw the simplification of law as an especially urgent task.

After investigating the forced collectivization campaign against the peasantry during the winter of 1929–30, Stalin himself criticized some of the worst excesses of the cadres in his famous "Dizzy with Success" speech of 1930. Stuchka's essay "Revolution and Revolutionary Legality" (1930) was a variation on Stalin's theme and was addressed especially to the juridical cadres in the collectivization drive, some of whom were now, retroactively, deemed guilty of overzealousness. He specifically attacked the nihilistic and immature tendencies that sought to eliminate law and revolutionary legality. Only to overzealous leftism did revolutionary legality seem a constraint to the success of the revolution. Quoting Stalin, Stuchka insisted, to the contrary, that a nexus existed between revolutionary legality and the objectives of socialist construction. These two concepts, far from being in conflict with each other, in practice were complementary. Revolutionary legality, far from being a bourgeois concept, was both a mechanism for eliminating oppressive social relations—such as the domestic subjugation of women in households and families—and also a form for the inculcation of order and strict social discipline. This discipline was to be directed from the center against local excesses.

Revolutionary legality, it thus transpired, was to operate as a crucial pivot for the continuation of the revolution, of forced collectivization, and of industrialization.

Although Stuchka had been one of the principal advocates of the cultural revolution of the law, he soon found himself besieged by the very process that he had helped to create. At a major conference of Marxist jurists, in 1930, a resolution was passed criticizing Stuchka for his "errors" on the legal front. In response Stuchka promised to undergo the obligatory "self-criticism." He replied in the form of a long essay, "My Journey and My Mistakes" (1931). However, instead of the usual self-deprecating exercise that was the standard fare for these times, Stuchka proceeded to a defense of his views which was defiant in tone and even contemptuous of his principal critic. The criticism of Stuchka during this conference came mainly from his erstwhile colleague Pashukanis and from a minor Stalinist apparatchik, Angarov. Ironically, part of the general thrust of criticism at the conference was that Stuchka had not been sufficiently critical of Pashukanis's theoretical errors—to which Stuchka responded by referring his critics to his 1927 essay on his differences with Pashukanis. At the conference, Pashukanis himself (who was also undergoing self-criticism) attacked Stuchka for his role in drafting The Fundamental Principles of Civil Legislation, and for his work as a civil jurist on the RSFSR Supreme Court. In his rebuttal, Stuchka defended his record with considerable skill, assailed Pashukanis in rather strong personal terms, and carried to its logical conclusion his own criticism of the latter's tendency to reduce all law to bourgeois civil law.

Soon after this article was published, Stuchka died a natural death. One can only speculate what would have happened to his defiant spirit had he survived into the era of the great purges of the late 1930s.

Notes

1. *Dekrety*, 1957–71.
2. See further, *Sovetskaia Latviia*, July 28, 1960.
3. See P. I. Stuchka (1921); p. 66 in Hazard (1951).
4. See also P. I. Stuchka, "Proletarskoe pravo" [Proletarian Law], pp. 210–220 in *Oktiabr'skii perevorot i diktatury proletariata: Sbornik statei* [The October Revolution and The Dictatorship of the Proletariat: A Collection of Articles] (Moscow, 1919), pp. 210–220.
5. Pashukanis reiterated this criticism in the second edition of his book: "the elements which provide the material for the development of the legal form can and should be segregated in the system of relationships which are responsive to the dominant class . . . ," quoted in Sharlet, "Pashukanis and the Commodity Exchange Theory of Law," pp. 69–70.

References

(1) Works by Stuchka

Stuchka, P. I. (1917). "A Class Court or a Democratic Court?" pp. 7–8 in Stuchka (1988).
——— (1919). "Proletarian Law," pp. 9–21 in Stuchka (1988).

——— (1921) (1951). *The Revolutionary Role of Law and State*, pp. 17–69 in Hazard (ed.), *Soviet Legal Philosophy.*

——— (1922). "The Marxist Concept of Law," pp. 22–37 in Stuchka (1988).

——— (1922a). "Notes on the Class Theory of Law," pp. 38–55 in Stuchka (1988).

——— (1922b). "Five Years of Revolution in Law," *Ezhenedel'nik sovetskoi iustitsii*, no. 44–45.

——— (1923). "A Materialist or Idealist Concept of Law," pp. 65–80 in Stuchka (1988).

——— (1923a). "In Defense of the Revolutionary Marxist Concept of Law," pp. 81–88 in Stuchka (1988).

——— (1924). "Foreword" to *Revoliutsionnaia rol' prava i gosudarstva.* 3rd edition. Moscow: Gosizdat.

——— (1925). "Lenin and the Revolutionary Decree," pp. 89–96 in Stuchka (1988).

——— (1925–27). "Bourgeois Law," pp. 97–100 in Stuchka (1988).

——— (1925–27a). "Jurisprudence," pp. 101–107 in Stuchka (1988).

——— (1925–27b). "The State," pp. 108–138 in Stuchka (1988).

——— (1925–27c). "Revolutionary Legality," pp. 139–142 in Stuchka (1988).

——— (1925–27d). "Law," pp. 143–154 in Stuchka (1988).

——— (1925–27e). "Legal Relationship," pp. 155–159 in Stuchka (1988).

——— (1925–27f). "Legal Consciousness," pp. 160–161 in Stuchka (1988).

——— (1925–27g). "Soviet Law," pp. 162–165 in Stuchka (1988).

——— (1927). "State and Law in the Period of Socialist Construction," pp. 173–194 in Stuchka (1988).

——— (1928). "Culture and Law," pp. 195–200 in Stuchka (1988).

——— (1929). "Revolutionary Legal Perspectives," pp. 201–208 in Stuchka (1988).

——— (1930). "The Revolution and Revolutionary Legality," pp. 209–218 in Stuchka (1988).

——— (1931). "My Journey and My Mistakes," pp. 219–251 in Stuchka (1988).

——— (1964). *Izbrannye proizvedeniia po marksistsko-leninskoi teorii prava.* Ed. G. Ia. Kliava. Riga: Latviiskoe gosudarstvennoe izdatel'stvo.

——— (1988). *Selected Writings on Soviet Law and Marxism* (edited and translated by Sharlet, Maggs, and Beirne). Armonk, N.Y.: M. E. Sharpe.

(2) Other Works

Arthur, Chris (1978). "Editor's Introduction," pp. 9–31 in *Law and Marxism: A General Theory (Evgeny B. Pashukanis).* Trans. Barbara Einhorn. London: Ink Links.

Beirne, Piers, and Robert Sharlet (1980). "Editors' Introduction," pp. 1–36 in *Pashukanis: Selected Writings on Marxism and Law.* Trans. Peter B. Maggs. London: Academic Press.

Daniels, Robert V. (1967). *Red October: The Bolshevik Revolution of 1917.* New York: Charles Scribner's Sons.

Engels, Friedrich (1878) (1975). *Anti-Dühring.* London: Lawrence & Wishart.

Hazard, John N. (ed.) (1951). *Soviet Legal Philosophy.* Trans. Hugh W. Babb. Cambridge: Harvard University Press.

Jaworskyj, Michael (ed.) (1967). *Soviet Political Thought: An Anthology.* Baltimore: Johns Hopkins University Press.

Kalnins, Bruno (1972). "The Social Democratic Movement in Latvia," in Alexander Rabinowitch, Janet Rabinowitch, and Ladis K. D. Kristof, *Revolution and Politics in Russia.* Bloomington, Ind.: Indiana University Press.

Kelsen, Hans (1955). *The Communist Theory of Law.* New York: Praeger.

Loeber, Dietrich A. (1965). "Unbewaltigte Vergangenheit im sowjetischen Zivilrecht zur Auseinandersetzung um das wissenschaftlichte Erbe von Peter I. Stuchka," pp. 129–150 in D. Frenzke and A. Uschakow (eds.), *Macht und Recht im kommunistischen Herrschaftssystem.* Cologne: Wissenschaft und Politik.

Marx, Karl (1875) (1970). "The Critique of the Gotha Programme," pp. 315–331 in *Marx/Engels Selected Works.* London: Lawrence & Wishart.

Marx, Karl, and Friedrich Engels (1848) (1973). "The Communist Manifesto," pp. 98–137 in *Marx/Engels Selected Works*, vol. 1. Moscow: Progress Publishers.

Medvedev, Roy A. (1973). *Let History Judge.* New York: Random House.

Pashukanis, E. B. (1924) (1980). "The General Theory of Law and Marxism," pp. 40–131 in Piers Beirne and Robert Sharlet (eds.), *Pashukanis: Selected Writings on Marxism and Law.* Trans. Peter B. Maggs. London: Academic Press.

——— (1927) (1980). "The Marxist Theory of Law and the Construction of Socialism," pp. 188–199 in Beirne and Sharlet (eds.).

Plotnieks, A. A. (1978). *Stanovlenie i razvitie marksistsko-leninskoi obshchei teorii prava v SSSR, 1917–1936.* Riga: Zinatne.

Rabinowitch, Alexander, Janet Rabinowitch, and Ladis K. D. Kristof (eds.) (1972). *Revolution and Politics in Russia.* Bloomington, Ind.: Indiana University Press.

Reich, Norbert (1969). "Introduction," pp. 7–55 in Peter I. Stuchka, *Die revolutionare Rolle von Recht und Staat.* Frankfurt am Main: Suhrkamp.

Rosenberg, William G. (ed.) (1984). *Bolshevik Visions: First Phase of the Cultural Revolution in Soviet Russia.* Ann Arbor: Ardis.

Schlesinger, Rudolf (1945). *Soviet Legal Theory: Its Social Background and Development.* London: K. Paul, Trench, Trubner & Co.

Sharlet, Robert (1968). "Pashukanis and the Commodity Exchange Theory of Law, 1924–1930." Ph.D. diss., Indiana University.

Skripilev, E. A., and B. G. Grafskii (1986). "P. I. Stuchka i aktual'nye voprosi metodologii nauki prava," *Sovetskoe gosudarstvo i pravo*, 6:137–38.

Smirnov, V. V. (1985). "Law, Culture, Politics: Theoretical Aspects," pp. 23–33 in W. E. Butler and V. N. Kudriavtsev (eds.), *Comparative Law and Legal System: Historical and Socio-Legal Perspectives.* New York: Oceana Publications.

Strogovich, M.S. (1960). "K voprosu o postanovke otdel'nykh problem v rabotakh P. I. Stuchki, N. V. Krylenko, E. B. Pashukanisa," in *Voprosy obshchei teorii sovetskogo prava.* Moscow: Gosiurizdat.

Trotsky, Leon (1959). *The Russian Revolution.* Garden City, New York: Doubleday.

Vyshinsky, A. Ia. (1938) (1948). *The Law of the Soviet State.* New York: Macmillan.

Zile, Zigurds L. (1977). *Ideas and Forces in Soviet Legal History.* 3rd ed. Madison, Wis.: College Printing.

Chapter 4

Law and the Constitution of Soviet Society: The Case of Comrade Lenin

Piers Beirne and Alan Hunt

I. Introduction

Much has been written in the last decade about law and socialist construction, and about the character and content of the approach of socialists to law.[1] The present essay is chiefly concerned with the role of law in the transitional period between capitalism and socialism and in the development from socialism to a future communist society.[2] We address this issue in the context of a very specific conjuncture, namely, Lenin's contribution to and understanding of the Bolshevik experience with the dictatorship of the proletariat (hereinafter DoP) and the "withering away of law." Although Lenin never analyzed law as a distinct theoretical object, his writings nevertheless contain many observations and comments pertinent to a socialist theory of law. His writings on law are diverse and include numerous polemical asides, occasional theoretical remarks, and some more sustained treatments of theoretico-political issues that bear directly upon law and legal phenomena. Notwithstanding several uncritical accounts by Soviet authors, there is no sustained treatment of Lenin's conception of law and legality in the transition from capitalism to communism.[3] Our first objective here, therefore, is to fill this gap. Moreover, some obvious silences in Lenin's writings can legitimately be replaced by examining his activities on such bodies as the Council of People's Commissars and his role in enacting a mass of legislation from November 1917, until his death in early 1924.

However, one of the many difficulties in an examination of early Soviet history is the temptation to confuse different levels of analysis. Analysis of the theoretical implications of Lenin's observations on the uses of law, for example, must be

This chapter was originally published in *Law & Society Review* 22, 3 (1988): 575–614. Reprinted by permission of the Law and Society Association.

distinguished from an historical focus on the particular development of Soviet legal institutions. Without this distinction we are drawn to a simplistic disjunction between Soviet "theory" and "practice" culminating in a fruitless "if only" discussion based on the conflation of different analytical levels: for example, "if only the civil war had not been so protracted, then the democratic soviets would have had a chance to develop"; or, "if only Bukharin's strictures about the growth of the bureaucracy had been heeded, then. . . ."[4] We do not posit some artificial disjunction between Leninist theory and the particulars of Soviet history. Instead, we conduct a theoretical enquiry into those aspects of Lenin's texts pertinent to the role of law in the socialist transition and the development of communism. In this context we must briefly comment on the discursive levels provided by Lenin's concept of the DoP.

The concept of the DoP, within the Marxism-Leninism that became the official credo of Stalinism, was used as an article of faith to separate revolutionaries from revisionists. Indeed, in *State and Revolution* Lenin (1917c:412; see also 1918h:231–242) was emphatic that "a Marxist is solely someone who extends the recognition of the class struggle to the recognition of the dictatorship of the proletariat." However, in Lenin's texts as a whole the concept of the DoP has a more complex history than such a passage suggests. Indeed, it is central to his thought in three related but distinct forms which have not previously been noted. First, the DoP was to be a necessary, rigorous, and rapid conquest of political power by the revolutionary forces so as to prevent the restoration of the old order. In this sense, it was to be an exceptional, temporary phase, quasi-military in nature, needed to secure the complete defeat of the previous regime but not in itself constitutive of the new socialist order. Second, the DoP was to involve Lenin's demand that the bourgeois state machinery be smashed. His key contention here was that the variety of state intitutions characteristic of capitalist societies is inappropriate for the objectives of the revolutionary classes on assuming political power.[5] Lenin never precisely identified how the bourgeois state was inappropriate for the tasks of the proletariat, although his position derived from the broader thesis that there must be a complete rupture between the whole historical period of capitalist society and that marking the advent of socialism.[6] Third, Lenin frequently referred to the DoP as a revolutionary period that actively promoted the institutions and social relations for the transition from socialism to communism. Previously, the transitions between the different forms of class society had certain institutional and political continuities because these were all dictatorships of a minority against the majority. In contrast, the socialist revolution was to be made by or on behalf of the great majority or both. The socialist revolution, therefore, was to differ from all previous revolutions in the principled importance it attached to the future. In this sense the DoP was less negative and coercive than active and educative in its quest for communism.

This theoretical grounding of Lenin's concept of the DoP provides a key for unlocking both the coherence and the contradiction of his views on the role of law in the socialist transition. The coherence of Lenin's views can be expressed in the form of five theses:

Thesis 1. Bourgeois law is inherently limited by the unequal relations on which it is founded. Yet during the bourgeois democratic revolution it provides a significant arena of struggle for securing universal political liberties—the cornerstone of bourgeois democracy—and in which democratic forces can secure concessions from the ruling classes.

Thesis 2. In the immediate context of the revolutionary seizure of power and the establishment of the proletarian dictatorship, law is a minor, but nevertheless useful, educative vehicle in the dissemination of the socialist program through the form of decrees and legislative enactments.

Thesis 3. The period of the DoP and beyond provides the conditions for the realization of the emancipatory capacity of the popular classes. One dimension of the process will be the emergence of the practices and values of "socialist legality." Socialist legality will be marked by informality, flexibility, and the explicit dominance of political objectives and will therefore directly contrast with the formalism of bourgeois law.

Thesis 4. The requirements of the revolutionary transition from capitalism to communism will involve, both in the short and the long run, a complete rupture with the political and legal institutions of bourgeois society (Parliament, bourgeois democracy, and law). The alternative requires the institutional form of soviets and the development of proletarian/socialist democracy.

Thesis 5. Communist society will be a nonlegal social order. Only the existence of classes and social inequality necessitates legal institutions and mechanisms. Because communism abolishes the conditions that produce law and also greatly simplifies and extends participation to all citizens, general requirements for legal regulations or processes are unnecessary.

In parts 2 and 3 of this paper we examine Lenin's view of law under divisions derived from the coherence of these five theses. However, it will be apparent that adjacent to and overriding this coherence is a serious tension, notably expressed in his *State and Revolution* (Lenin, 1917c), immanent in Lenin's repeated stress on the need for the disappearance of state and law under communism. We argue in part 4 that this tension led to and was part of an inadequate constitutionalism in his theory of the socialist transition, a requirement that must include the distribution of powers, checks, and supervision between state and political institutions. Although there is a certain coherence in Lenin's view of law, it fails to address adequately those problems which, in varying forms and with different intensity, will be experienced by all attempts to construct a socialist society.

II. Law, Constitution, and Russian Capitalism

Lenin's earliest and perhaps most substantial writings encompassed a major debate about the causes and dynamics of the development of Russian capitalism. For present purposes the economic history that these texts debated is less salient than the narrower question of the analysis of the role of law in the economic transformation of Russia at the turn of the century. Lenin's antagonists at this time were the Narodniks,[7] who were themselves influenced by Marxist economic theory. They argued that capitalism was an imported phenomenon whose penetration into the Russian economy was both limited and reversible. Politically, the Narodniks envisioned a socialist transition that built upon the communal features of the peasantry and that thereby obviated the need for capitalist development. Lenin was not concerned with debating abstractly the merits of a capitalist stage of development. Instead, he argued that capitalist relations were so deeply embedded in rural Russia that capitalism was not an import from Western Europe, even though importation had played a part in the more visible fact of capitalism, namely, the small number of large industrial enterprises recently established in St. Petersburg, Moscow, and other centers. The depth of capitalist penetration was revealed by the rapid spread of wage labor and commodity exchange in the countryside and by the resultant economic differentiation within the peasantry. Capitalism was for Lenin an indigenous, natural, and spontaneous economic development.

What role, then, did Lenin attribute to law in the development of Russian capitalism? Although he did not explicitly address this question, his answer would undoubtedly have been "very little," for he attributed little or no causal agency to law. Referring to the major legal restrictions upon the peasantry that remained long after the Emancipation Edict of 1861, he argued that "the whole process of the differentiation of the agricultural peasantry is one of real life evading these legal bounds" (Lenin, 1908a:103). For Lenin juridical classification was irrelevant in the analysis of economic relations; indeed, the multiplicity of legal forms of land tenure concealed the actual development of capitalist relations of production. In general, he attributed little significance to law: either it provided formal clothing for real economic and social relations or, in its material form as police and courts, it provided the mechanism of repression.

This lack of concern with the role of law is more significant than appears at first sight. There is a marked contrast between Lenin's account of the development of capitalism in Russia and that offered by Marx in *Capital*, where England was the major historical point of reference. Marx's (1867 [1975], vol. 1, chaps. 27–28) account stressed the creation of free labor as an essential precondition for capitalist development, and in it law and particular legislation played a central role. Whilst there is no suggestion that Russian economic development followed a pattern described by Marx, Lenin's voluminous account nevertheless omitted consideration of this theme. It can only be suggested that his general desire to stress the spontaneous nature of capitalist development in Russia resulted in this absence or omission.

Lenin never claimed either to have advanced or to have adopted a jurisprudential position. Yet woven throughout the great mass of his references and comments about law is a strong jurisprudence whose core is an uncompromising imperativeness. Thus he wrote: "A will, if it is the will of the state, must be expressed in the form of a *law* established by the *state*" (Lenin, 1917a:90); and "What is law? The expression of the will of the classes which have emerged victorious and hold the power of the state'' (Lenin, 1908b:327); and ''Laws are political measures, politics'' (Lenin, 1916a:48). He harnessed this imperativeness to a conceptual association among law, state, and class. Law he saw as the bearer and embodiment of class interests through the coercive capacity of the state. In this his primary focus was on the way in which law is the bearer of class interests in forms that, more or less hypocritically, misrepresent social reality. Thus, his frequently repeated criticism of bourgeois legality and democracy hinged on the issue of *formal* equality and ''the crying contradiction between the formal equality proclaimed by the 'democracy' of the capitalist and the thousands of *real* limitations and subterfuges which turn the proletariat into *wage slaves*'' (Lenin, 1917c:472).[8]

Lenin's critique of bourgeois legality was intimately linked with a distinctive feature of his analysis of democracy that had no obvious antecedent in Marx. He argued that, as the highest and final stage of capitalism, monopoly capitalism marks a shift from political democracy to political reaction. As a result the bourgeoisie is always prepared to abandon its own bourgeois democracy when its class interests are at stake: ''The more highly developed a democracy is, the more imminent are programs or civil war in connection with any profound political divergence which is dangerous to the bourgeoisie'' (Lenin, 1918h:245). Moreover, ''all of this legality *must* inevitably be cast to the four winds when the fundamental and cardinal question of the preservation of bourgeois property is affected'' (Lenin, 1910:306). In discussing the political situation before the 1914–1918 War, Lenin argued that this ''most stable constitutional legality, is now coming to a point where this legality, *their* legality, *will have to be* shattered so that the domination of the bourgeoisie may be preserved'' (1910:310–311). Thus, in the most general terms Lenin deferred to the historical contingency of legality and constitutionality within the framework of a political sociology that insisted upon a strict correlation between the intensification of class struggle and the shift to political reaction within the bourgeois democracies.[9]

Legality and democracy were for Lenin narrowly ideological in that they involved a more or less self-conscious deception by the bourgeoisie (and, even more so, by socialists who could not free themselves from the ideological influence of the bourgeoisie). However, he emphasized the practical importance of the democratic struggle as preparation for the struggle for socialism (Lenin, 1916:144) and stressed the educative and necessary character of the struggle for democracy (Lenin, 1916a:73). As we will see, much of the practical, agitational, and educational activity of the Bolsheviks stressed, on the one hand, the importance of demands for legal reforms and the winning of rights, and on the other, the inherent limitations of all legal and constitutional reforms.

The Struggle against Tsarism

Issues about law, legislation, legality, constitutions, courts, and related matters often confronted Lenin during the two decades of his political activity before

October 1917. While these topics were rarely his focal concerns, his writings on them were extensive. However, we will try to demonstrate that Lenin's discourse on these matters related closely to his central political and theoretical concerns.

Lenin was adamant that politics serve classes and that the state serves the dominant class. Accordingly, in discussing legal developments he focused upon what may be termed a "class" reading of law. This can be illustrated by his short article (Lenin, 1901e) "Objective Statistics." Here he analysed the ninety-one laws enacted by the government during the previous twelve months. Of these the majority (sixty) served the practical needs of the capitalists, and twenty-two dealt with the administration of the tsarist state—thus attesting to the "government's solicitude for itself" (ibid., 412). With heavy irony Lenin belittled any possible popular benefit that might accrue from the remaining minor edicts. In addition, one law extended the area of forests devoted to the development and improvement of His Imperial Majesty's hunting. He concluded, with nicely modulated irony, "Can there be any doubt whatever that such richly varied legislative and administrative activity will guarantee our country rapid and undeviating progress in the twentieth century?" (Lenin, 1908:413).

Similarly, Lenin wrote a number of articles and pamphlets exposing the brutality of the tsarist police. His intent was usually to deal polemically with the exposure of the repressive behavior of the tsarist police on the one hand, and on the other, to address party membership by giving illustration and instruction as to the necessary sort of public agitational work. In "Beat—But Not to Death" (Lenin, 1901), he related the fatal beating of a peasant and the subsequent trial of the police involved. Beyond the savage irony that the police would have been safe had they stopped short of their victim's death, he used this incident to advocate a wide-ranging set of legal reforms, including independent and public courts and the extension of the jury system. His substantive political point was that exposure of such abuses should be undertaken systematically by the Social Democrats to elevate political consciousness about the lack of political and civil liberties.

A second strand within his texts advanced political demands for major democratic reforms as he explicitly attempted to raise political consciousness about the lack of liberty. This is best illustrated by his treatment of the penal servitude regulations of 1901 (Lenin, 1901b; 1901c) that governed the conditions under which peasants—then experiencing a serious famine—could be drafted into labor gangs to undertake public works. Lenin underlined how these rules once again enslaved the peasants, forty years after emancipation. He exhorted the Social Democrats to distribute copies of these regulations, along with leaflets explaining their implications, to generate agitation against forced labor. This approach was part of his wider political objective, namely, to extend the struggle against tsarism into the countryside and thus fit with Lenin's insistence, in opposition to the "economistic" trend within the party,[10] that the industrial working class, because of its small size, could not "emancipate itself without emancipating the whole people from despotism" (Lenin, 1901a:418).[11]

Several of Lenin's other articles and pamphlets of this period attempted to disseminate and popularize the democratic demands of the Social Democrats for full political liberties (such as freedom of assembly and freedom of the press), for a Constituent Assembly, and for full equality for the peasantry (Lenin, 1903). For example, in one pamphlet Lenin (1903a) highlighted the demands for securing the political and civil liberties of the peasantry and for discarding all remnants of feudalism; he offered a sustained contrast between Russian autocracy and the democratic advances of Western Europe. He emphasized the general significance of the struggle for democracy: "The entire working class and the entire country are suffering from this absence of rights; it is on this that the Asiatic backwardness in Russian life rests" (Lenin, 1903:351).

A major theme of his writing, particularly prior to 1905, concerned factory legislation. Here again we see the publicist's insistence on the importance of explaining to the workers the detailed implications of successive legislative devices. For example, his early pamphlet "The New Factory Law" (Lenin, 1899) provided a detailed commentary and critique of the 1897 factory legislation. This piece exemplified his repeated analysis that the securing of such legislation was a tribute to the tenacity and struggle of the factory workers themselves, although it had often been facilitated by factory owners who were concerned with minimizing strikes and other forms of disruptions and who, accordingly, pressed the autocracy for these concessions. However, Lenin was keen to demonstrate that in practice the detailed content of the legislation, as well as the methods and procedure provided for its implementation and enforcement, often rescinded its erstwhile benefits.[12]

In an *Iskra* article of 1902, Lenin analyzed a proposal to repeal a new law that made it a criminal offense for workers to leave their employment or to strike. He argued that this provision served to embitter workers and that the commencement of proceedings against large numbers of individual employees was time-consuming and inefficient for both the employers and the authorities. The law embodied "the practical considerations of the manufacturers, which break right through the traditional juridical arguments" (Lenin, 1902:219). The contradiction between legal requirements and practical economic considerations enabled the working class to act upon the contradiction "between the developing bourgeoisie and moribund absolutism" (Lenin, ibid., 223). In the next year Lenin (1903b) argued that the increased level of struggle had won a number of reforms. For example, he detailed the legislative provisions on injury compensation allowing employees to appoint factory stewards. After criticizing the inherent limitations of this reform, he exhorted the Social Democrats to encourage participation and thereby increase the propaganda for political liberty.

In addition to providing detailed analyses of contemporary legislation, Lenin advanced democratic demands of immediate relevance to the industrial workers. Along with such general demands as the legalization of trade unions, Lenin promoted several particular reforms. For example, over a number of years he urged the establishment of special courts to resolve conflicts within the factories; his major demand was for elected workers to sit next to the employers as judges. In this case he was less concerned with promoting a particular model of industrial relations than he was with linking the demand for industrial democracy to that for political democracy in general, to make the political demands relevant in the trade union context and vice versa.

The 1905 revolution achieved considerable gains for the democratic and liberal forces (Carr, 1966, 1:57–69). However, a period of fierce repression ensued that destroyed many short-run advances. In the aftermath Lenin scrutinized the use of reactionary constitutional forms by the Social Democrats. He regarded the issue of whether they should participate in elections and take up seats as a tactical question whose sole consideration was how best to promote the party's political objectives. The years between 1905 and 1917 were marked by the need to combine, in varying ways, legal and illegal activities. For example, there were long periods when RSDLP members sat in the Duma, whilst the party itself was illegal and some or all of its leaders were in exile abroad. Lenin thus insisted that "it was obligatory to combine legal and illegal forms of struggle" (1902a:454–467).

In pursuing a flexible strategy toward participation in the largely unreformed constitutional structure of tsarism, the Social Democrats employed a propagandist approach to the use of the Duma. Their representatives used the Duma as a tribune to attack the system and to demand democratic reforms. They also learned to employ the tactic of introducing draft legislation that they could not in any way enact but that served to provide valuable propaganda in favor of the party's policy and program. The aim was that the whole text, or some part of it, should be published in newspapers, whether friendly or otherwise, and that it could be issued as a leaflet. Among the bills they introduced were ones to secure the eight-hour working day,[13] to abolish disabilities for Jews and non-Russians, and to recognize national rights. Whilst following this flexible strategy toward participation in the Duma, Lenin adopted a flexible attitude toward participation in the courts. At different times and in different contexts, he advocated that party members use the courts to defend the party's action and that they should not surrender themselves to stand trial.

Russian political life after 1905 was full of debate about constitutional reform. Lenin consistently argued that constitutions themselves settled nothing because they reflect the results of class struggle: "Written and unwritten constitutions . . . are merely a record of the *results of struggle obtained through a series of hard-won victories* of the new over the old" (Lenin, 1913:564). He frequently warned against the danger of the illusion that the adoption of an appropriate constitution was the primary objective of political struggle, a position consistent with his jaundiced view of the commitment by the bourgeoisie to parliamentary democracy.[14] Simultaneously, he flexibly deployed this general position within the field of political practice, and in so doing allowed the Social Democrats to use their small but growing forces to the greatest effect. With the crisis over the downfall of tsarism in February 1917, the Bolsheviks were at first surprised by the rapidity of events. But in the short eternity between February and October 1917, they secured the overthrow of the Provisional Government and were themselves in a powerful, if not necessarily commanding, position in the soviets. Accordingly, we can now attend to Lenin's views on the role of law in securing the gains of the October revolution and in socialist construction.

III. Law in the Transition to Socialism

There are at least two difficulties about giving an account of Lenin's view of the role of law in socialist construction. First, there is the risk of imposing, consciously or otherwise, an artificial coherence on his utterances that is not actually present; this is precisely what happened with the canonization that occurred after Lenin's death and which became consecrated as "Marxism-Leninism." Second, when one attempts to remain faithful to the fragmented character of Lenin's views on a topic that was not among his major concerns, the diffuse nature of his observations create some hardship for an order of presentation. Any form of presentation is easily transformed into an order of priority. Our method stems from the threefold conceptual schema that Lenin himself employed in his theoretical discussion of stages of the revolutionary process: (1) the securing of power and the DoP; (2) the socialist transition; and (3) the construction of communism. However, these stages are not chronologies that can be imposed mechanically on the history of the Russian revolution because much of Lenin's discussion about the role of law in the socialist transition occurred before the Civil War. Moreover, during the extreme conditions of the War, especially from spring 1919 until November 1920, the problems associated with the securing of power regained prominence. Similarly, much of Lenin's discussion of communism occurred immediately before and just after the October revolution. We claim no superiority for this method of exposition other than that it is reasonably instructive in assimilating the material at our disposal.

Securing Power and the Proletarian Dictatorship

Lenin's varied texts about state and political power are best exemplified by *The State and Revolution* (Lenin, 1917c). Two emphases in this text must be clarified. First, all major changes in political power would incontrovertibly have to secure that power against both the old order and the factions contending for it. This required calculated coercion against identifiable political forces and institutions. Such coercion could be either reactive or anticipatory; for example, arresting the leaders of a political party demanding armed struggle against the new order would be reactive, while disbanding an army commanded by the prior regime would be anticipatory. However, the measures would have to be calculated precisely. This calculus would be inherently controversial; for example, was it justifiable to exclude the wealthy from the franchise? Such a question was of symbolic importance in the present context in that it had no bearing on the actual course of the revolution because the wealthy classes were excluded from membership in the soviets. The Bolshevik decision to disband the Constituent Assembly—after its first meeting failed to approve the transfer of power to the soviets—made irrelevant the disenfranchisement of the wealthy.[15]

Second, Lenin emphasized that the DoP should be identified with socialism itself. He conceived the DoP as providing the paradigmatic form not only for its governmental structures but also for the whole organization of social, economic, and political life. The interrelationship among these elements—political and socio-economic—can be termed the "constitution of society."[16] Only with the realization of the ultimate goal (communism) would the DoP lose its role. To this second attribute of the DoP we return below.

Lenin was most explicit about the role of the DoP in securing the seizure of power:

> Dictatorship is rule based directly upon force and unrestricted by any laws. The revolutionary dictatorship of the proletariat is rule won and maintained by the use of violence by the public against the bourgeoisie, rule that is unrestricted by any laws. (1918h:236)

Variants of this formulation reoccur regularly: for example, "[t]he scientific term 'dictatorship' means nothing more nor less than authority untrammeled by laws, absolutely unrestricted by any rules whatever, and based directly on force" (Lenin, 1906:246).

There was, then, no equivocation: the immediate objective of the DoP was to suppress the old order and the classes and institutions on which its power was based. However, Lenin provided a number of significant extensions and extrapolations from this position. For example, he directly identified the DoP with the soviets, the institutional embodiment of the Russian revolution: "Soviet power is nothing but an organisational form of the dictatorship of the proletariat" (Lenin, 1918f:265). Again, Lenin offered various parallel characterizations of the soviets as the expression of the DoP, as the embodiment of the direct democracy of the toilers, and as the means of representation of the different sectors of "the masses" and "the working people" (such as workers, soldiers, sailors, peasants, and poor peasants—all of whom had their own soviets at different periods). These different attributes were then conflated so that the soviets were at once legislative institutions and representational expressions of classes (or sections of classes) and the new universal mechanism of socialist democracy and the state form of the revolution. One of the major absences in Lenin's theory is a consideration of the capability of the soviets to fulfill these different and potentially conflicting roles. In seeking to overinvest in this highly distinctive legacy of the revolutionary process, Lenin inadvertently prescribed its demise.

To substantiate this thesis it must be noted that what is referred to as an "absence" in Lenin's thought was not a mere omission but the direct consequence of one of his well-known positions. He often repeated his criticism that the separation of legislative and executive functions reduced parliaments to the status of "talking shops." In contrast, he regarded the endowment of the soviets with legislative, executive, and administrative functions as a distinctive virtue of soviet over parliamentary institutions, without specifying in what this advantage consists. Moreover, Lenin failed to consider whether, in the attempt to fulfill all these functions, the soviets' roles would conflict with one another. Thus, by overendowing the soviets he inserted a potential contradiction in the very core of the institutional apparatus of the new socialist order.

Lenin's view of the coercive function of the DoP was not, he insisted, an endorsement of an unbridled resort to political violence. While he supported the direct use of force in both theory and practice, he also saw law as a normal part of the operation of the DoP, for "[a]s the fundamental task of the government becomes, not military suppression, but administration, the typical manifestation of suppression and compulsion will be, not shooting on the spot, but trial by court" (Lenin, 1918f:266). Similarly, Lenin insisted that the soviets, even in their role as the agency of the DoP, were "a higher form of democracy" and the "beginning of a *socialist* form of democracy" (ibid., 268). From early on, the Bolsheviks had resolved the tension between democracy and obedience through the principle of "democratic centralism," which encouraged the most wide and free participation in decision making followed by mandatory adherence to majority verdict. In what was perhaps a partial recognition of the problem of overendowment, namely, the assignment of multiple, potentially incompatible roles to the soviets, Lenin observed "[w]e must learn to combine the 'public meeting' democracy of the working people—turbulent, surging, overflowing its banks like a spring flood—with iron discipline while at work" (ibid., 271). This process of consolidation involved confirming and securing that which had been made law and been decreed. Lenin's elaborations upon the DoP's fundamental task of suppressing the old order led to a model of the institutionalization of the victorious revolution that required law, rules, and regulations and in which trial by court was preferred to the firing squad in confronting counterrevolutionary forces. At the same time, Lenin claimed that the DoP, as the institutional model for socialism, would be replaced only with the advent of communism. This more expansive role of the DoP is less well supported by justificatory argument.

The Function of Law in the Socialist Transition

For Lenin, the DoP had its most important ramifications beyond the initial problem of securing power. It is therefore necessary to examine his view of the role of law in the more extended period of the socialist transition. Lenin offered no neatly encapsulated account of the functions of law in the socialist transition. Rather, we must examine *seriatim* six distinct yet intersecting themes which are both complementary and contradictory: (1) eradication, (2) education, (3) discipline, (4) transition, (5) participation, and (6) routinization, or accounting and control.

Eradication. Beyond the suppressive functions of the DoP, a number of tasks and consequences flowed from them to which Lenin devoted some attention. While some institutions of the old order were swept away during revolutionary action, others were removed by decree.

In the nine months after October 1917 the All-Russian Central Executive Committee (CEC) and the Council of People's Commissars (CPC) issued 950 decrees and other instructions.[17] These abolished, *inter alia*, targets Lenin set forth in "The April Theses" (Lenin, 1917h) and elsewhere: the standing army, the police, and the bureaucracy. These legislative devices had a multiplicity of forms and included laws, decrees, proclamations, and ordinances. Some, such as "On Combating the Famine" and "To the Population," had no legal status; others were issued largely for purposes of education and propaganda. Their source lay not only in the CEC and the CPC but also in bodies like the Council of Workers' and Peasants' Defense, various commissariats, *volost* land committees, local revolutionary committees, Cheka, and the Revolutionary Military Council. In response to critics who charged that the Bolsheviks had issued too many decrees, Lenin explained:

> If we had refrained from indicating in decrees the road that must *must* be followed, we would have been traitors to socialism. These decrees, while in practice they could not be carried into effect fully and immediately, played an important part as propaganda. . . . *Decrees are instructions* which call for practical work on a mass scale. (Lenin, 1919a:209)

After securing political power the revolution faced "the most important and most difficult aspect of the socialist revolution, namely, the task of organization" (Lenin, 1918f:237). It was thus necessary to establish some alternative institutions. According to Lenin, the courts themselves best illustrate this process,[18] for "[i]n place of the old court [the October revolution] began to establish a new . . . Soviet Court, based on the principle of the participation of the working and exploited classes . . . in the administration of the state" (Lenin, 1918e:217). Additionally, he recognized that the eradication of the old social order would lead, in the short run at least, to chaos and to an increase in "crime, hooliganism, corruption and outrages of every kind" (Lenin, 1918f:237), which established the need for revolutionary order and courts. A small illustration of the problems associated with this process was Lenin's comment about the abolition of the "bourgeois legal bar"; he noted the tendency of such institutions to return in new guises, for example, as "Soviet pleaders.'' These ''professional'' advocates emerged in 1918, but were abolished in October 1920 (Lenin, 1920a:115).

Education. Lenin continually stressed the educative function of both the content and implementation of law in the socialist transition: ''We transformed the court from an instrument of exploitation into an instrument of education'' (Lenin, 1918b:464); ''A single decree putting an end to landed proprietorship will win us the confidence of the peasantry'' (Lenin, 1917f:240); ''From the very outset we gave the ordinary workers and peasants an idea of our policy in the form of decrees'' (1922a:303). Even when the content of these decrees could not be implemented, they still played an important propagandistic role (Lenin, 1919a:209). However, Lenin emphasized that this role had limited historical significance. In 1922 he stated forcibly: ''*The phase of propaganda by decrees is over.* The masses will understand and appreciate *only* business-like practical work'' (Lenin, 1922d:574). Lenin's stress on the educative role of law was tied strongly to what we may call his ''revolutionary realism'': ''[W]e want a socialist revolution with people as they are now. . . . [I]t is inconceivable that people will immediately learn to work without any legal norms after the overthrow of capitalism'' (Lenin, 1917c:467).

Discipline. The educative role of law and regulation in Lenin's thought was closely associated with discipline. Describing the role of the soviet courts, he identified their initial task as one of eradication: ''But, in addition the courts . . . have another, still more important task. This task is to ensure the strictest discipline and self-discipline of the working people'' (Lenin, 1918e:217). But his concept of discipline was far from authoritarian, however, as was signaled in his conjunction of ''discipline'' and ''self-discipline.'' This connection of law and discipline is captured in his assertion that it was ''not yet sufficiently recognised . . . that the courts are an instrument for inculcating discipline'' (Lenin, 1918f:266). Moreover, Lenin emphasized that the Russian people had previously experienced rules, regulations, laws, and courts as external impositions that were exclusively coercive and oppressive. This experience inculcated a negative response that was part of the general backwardness of Russian civil society. Hence, for Lenin, discipline and culture were also closely connected. The object must be ''to establish uniformity of law and develop at least the minimum of culture'' (Lenin, 1922b:365). He counterposed this combination of discipline and culture to the ''semi-savage habit of mind'' and the ''ocean of illegality'' within the parochialism of rural life which was ''the greatest obstacle to the establishment of law and culture'' (ibid.).

Transition. Adjacent to the functions of law outlined above—all of which point to Lenin's attribution of an important role to law within the socialist transition—was a quite different thrust of law as transitory. It accordingly provided a useful, even necessary, function, but one that was subservient to politics and to the needs of the revolution: ''[H]e is a poor revolutionary who at a time of acute struggle is halted by the immutability of law. In a period of transition laws have only a temporary validity; and when law hinders the development of a revolution, it must be abolished or amended'' (Lenin, 1918g:519).

The problem posed by formulations of this type is not one of logical contradiction. Rather, Lenin regarded them as operating at different levels of generality. At the highest level he insisted on the marginality of law, but at the more concrete level of each specific stage of socialist construction he saw the role of law as useful and necessary. This does not abolish the difficulty, for it fails to address the problem of by whom and when it is to be decided that the wider exigencies of the revolution require the abolition or amendment of law. If politics are dominant, then an enormous burden is placed on the political process (that is, ultimately, the party) as the historical agency of the revolution.

Participation: Anybody Can Be a Judge. A key point of reference that allowed the Bolsheviks to distinguish between the forms of social regulation that they were creating and the bourgeois law which they replaced was the appeal to democratic participation. Thus, Lenin explained about the soviet courts that ''we did not have to create a new apparatus, because anybody can act as a judge basing himself on the revolutionary sense of justice of the working class'' (Lenin, 1919a:182). At first, appeal to direct popular participation bears the hallmark of the concern to secure political power. Thus,

> it is not yet sufficiently realised that the courts are an organ which enlists precisely the poor, every one of them, in the work of the state administration . . . [and] that the courts are an *organ of the power* of the proletariat and of the poor peasants. (Lenin, 1918f:266)

But this appeal was also intimately linked to one of Lenin's core conceptions of the future communist society. Both of his key programmatic texts (Lenin, 1917c; 1918f) that straddle October 1917 insist that the strategic objective of ''the withering away of the state'' was not an *abolitionist* idea. Instead, its objective was the construction of a radically new form of social administration in which the state would disappear. The state would be increasingly dissipated as a mechanism of social power when more and, eventually, all citizens participated in its activities.

> For the first time a start is made by the *entire* population in learning the art of administration. . . . [O]ur aim is to ensure that every toiler, having finished his eight hour ''task'' in productive labour shall perform state duties *without pay.* (Lenin, 1918f:272–273)

In this Lenin assumed, problematically, that the division of labor could be so transformed as to abolish the need for a special category of administrative functions, because modern capitalism

> has *created* large-scale production, factories, railways, the postal service, telephone, etc., and *on this basis* the great majority of the functions of the old "state power" have become so simplified and can be reduced to such exceedingly simple operations of registration, filing and checking that they can be easily performed by every literate person. (Lenin, 1917c:420–421)[19]

Lenin's position here remained largely exhortatory. His concern with the growth of "red tape" and bureaucracy attested to events actually in conflict with the universal participation to which he was committed. But he never addressed the project of administrative democratization in more concrete terms when discussing the fight against bureaucracy.

Routinization, or Accounting and Control. Almost immediately after October 1917, Lenin stressed the importance of accounting and control. Although he forged no concerted link between these tasks and the role of law in Soviet society, we suggest, first, that this aspect of Lenin's thought has been neglected, and second, that it has profound implications since it thereby commits him to a model of legalistic regulation as a necessary feature of socialism. As a result, despite some of the more radical and democratic functions discussed above, Lenin advanced an overall view of the necessary relationship between law and the socialist transition that was incompatible with much of his commitment to radical, participatory, nonlegal social regulation.

Frequently, Lenin defined accounting and control as the main economic task confronting the revolution and as "the *essence* of socialist transformation" (Lenin, 1918a:410). In one lengthy discussion he identified the problem as one of overcoming popular suspicion of any form of central regulation so as to "instil into the people's minds the idea of *Soviet* state accounting and control" (Lenin, 1918f:254). But Lenin never clarified precisely in what the demand for accounting and control consists. To understand this omission, its connection with some other related aspects of his thought must be seen.

Between February and October 1917 Lenin belabored the inability and the unwillingness of the Provisional Government to control the capitalist economic power on which its political power rested. He demanded measures of control over capital, for example, over the banks through the abolition of commercial secrecy (Lenin, 1917b:339). He stressed that the Western capitalist powers had already taken successful measures to control the banks and major sectors of production and distribution, and that such measures could be implemented in Russia. In September 1917 he demanded the nationalization of the banks and capitalist syndicates (Lenin, ibid., 328–329). At this stage, and then just after October 1917, the main objective of control was the surveillance and the subsequent breaking up of the power of private capital.

After October 1917 the issue of control was most often raised in terms of workers' control. This concept was then employed with a dual focus: as an expression of the syndicalist aspiration to regulate the economy by the associated producers, and as a reference to the role of workers within the enterprises of control over the activities of the owners to ensure that there was no sabotage of the soviet authorities (Lenin, 1917e:105). With the increasing socialization of private capitalist enterprises, an important shift in emphasis occurred as the definition of control changed from surveillance/supervision to the detailed accounting of all forms of economic resources. In "The Immediate Tasks of the Soviet Government," for example, Lenin (1918f) defined both "worker's control" and "soviet accounting and control" as preconditional to the passage to the next stage of socialism. This shift in emphasis emerged in the context of an economic emergency (famine) bordering on complete social collapse. The exigencies of War Communism complicate the distinction between what Lenin and the Bolsheviks saw as desirable, when measured against the yardstick of their conceptions of socialism, and what was the forced requirement of necessity.

Accounting and control stemming from necessity and from principle blur into a distinctive conception of the economics of the socialist transition.[20] Lenin spoke in broad strategic terms of the need for "a prolonged, complex transition through socialist accounting and control from capitalist society" (Lenin, 1921c:62–63). Elsewhere, his concept of accounting and control was marked by more pressing considerations: "Account must be taken of every single article, every pound of grain, because what socialism implies above all is keeping account of everything" (Lenin, 1917i:288). This rather uninspiring conception of the socialist economy Lenin tried to alleviate by calls for its democratic and popular transformation. Thus, he wrote that socialist control and accounting "can be exercised only by the people" (Lenin, 1918a:410) and "socialists demand the *strictest* control by society *and by the state* over the measure of labour . . . exercised not by a state of bureaucrats, but by a state of armed workers" (Lenin, 1917c:470). This call for "democratic control" was predicated on the inevitable *simplification* of administration achieved under capitalism. In discussing the requirement that all citizens should work equally, Lenin argued that "the accounting and control necessary for this have been *simplified* by capitalism to the utmost and reduced to the extraordinarily simple operations—which any literate person can perform—of supervising and recording" (Lenin, 1917c:473).[21] Elsewhere, he offered a rather unexpected "accounting" vision of the future: "control and accounting will become universal, all-powerful, and irresistible" (Lenin, 1917d:38).

The importance of accounting and control was not for Lenin directly linked to the role of law under socialism, but they were inescapably linked: accounting and control must be rule-bound. Even the simplest accounting measure requires a minimum set of rules about what is to be counted and how. Such activities require and generate rules, and are dependent on bureaucratic institutions that collect and analyze the data; these are collected in forms that allow, for example, comparison between localities or institutional forms. Lenin's discussion of the functions of law in the socialist transition contains major elements consistent with a theoretical and political commitment to a form of social organization and regulation that depends little upon the existence and development of law. But the other aspect of this account must dominate if we take seriously what he actually says. This aspect entails a model of law as a necessary and unavoidable mechanism for forms of routinization that are preconditions for the socialist transition. Routinization was both inevitable and necessary *prior* to the longer term objectives of socialist construction. This notwithstanding, discussion of these matters always occurred in the context of the transitional character of the Russian revolution, dependent as it was on the success of the proletarian revolutions in the more economically developed capitalist nations.

If Lenin's argument leads to a conclusion that he himself wanted to avoid, there were, predictably, major questions about the form and content of socialist law that he either did not consider or attended to only scantily. In general, crucial absences occurred when Lenin relied on the good sense, judgment, and "revolutionary conscience" of party and soviet officials. As we shall see, these very officials, because of their power, were the most difficult to control but although Lenin realized that legal regulation had to be achieved, he never relinquished a utopian commitment to the self-regulatory virtue of the party as the primary agency of revolutionary change and construction.

The Development of Socialist Law

Lenin was involved in the growth of law of the new socialist state as he was in so many other features of the forming society. Yet his involvement was episodic and without a theoretical framework. Our concern here, however, is with neither the growth of Soviet law and legal institutions nor the intense debate among Soviet jurists about the possibility and limits of socialist law. Important and interesting though these debates were, Lenin did not participate in them, and the record does not suggest that he paid much attention to them.[22] His abstention from these debates reflects his abstention from the early stages of constitutional deliberation, which we will discuss in the next section. As we have seen in the discussion of his jurisprudence, Lenin had a number of rather general and unexplored positions about the nature of law and socialist law in particular. We will focus here on the issues arising from his direct involvement in the development of Soviet law.

Lenin was an active participant in the enactment of the early decrees of Soviet power in his capacity as chair of the CPC. He himself penned many of the drafts of these decrees. Among those enacted in the early months of the revolution were the "Decree on Land," "Draft Regulations on Workers' Control," "Decree on the Dissolution of the Constituent Assembly," and "Declaration of Rights of the Working and Exploited People." In addition, he actively commented on, criticized, and amended other decrees. Rather than itemize Lenin's part in this varied legislation, we will explore the wider issues that emerge from the details of his activity.

At the level of general theory, Lenin attributed no very significant role to law. At a more immediate level, as has been indicated in regard to his conceptions of the functions of law in the socialist transition, he gave it some practical significance. Because Lenin devoted no sustained attention to questions of law and socialism, obvious contradictions existed in his position, such as between aspects of his centralism and his commitment to adaptation to local circumstances. In a note on the political control of procurators,[23] he urged that "the law must be uniform, and the root evil of our social life, and of our lack of culture is our pandering to the ancient Russian view and semi-savage habit of mind, which wishes to preserve Kaluga law as distinct from Kazan law" (Lenin, 1922b:364). Again, without insisting upon "the uniformity of the law for the whole Federation [of Soviet Republics] it will be impossible to protect the law, or to develop any kind of culture" (ibid., 365). Simultaneously, he argued that Soviet law

> will be applied everywhere by the soviets in accordance with their local conditions. We are not bureaucrats and do not want to insist on the letter of the law everywhere....
>
> The local soviets, depending on time and place, can amend, enlarge and add to the basic provisions worked out by the government. Creative activity at the grass roots is the basic factor of the new public life. (1918:285, 287–288)

These contradictory stances manifest a more general tension in Lenin's thought between centralism and control from below.

Insofar as a general approach can be attributed to him, Lenin recognized the need to develop a body of socialist law as part of the wider task of contributing to socialist political and economic objectives. But this legal development had to be self-consciously distinct from the bourgeois law that it replaced. This argument emerged clearly in his discussion of the preparation of a new civil code, on which he is worth quoting at some length:

> The new civil legislation is being drafted. . . . [T]he task [of the People's Commissariat of Justice] is to create a new civil law, and not to adopt (rather, not to allow itself to be duped by the old and stupid bourgeois lawyers who adopt) the old, bourgeois concept of civil law. . . . We do not recognise anything "private," and regard *everything* in the economic sphere as falling under *public* and not private *law. We allow only* state capitalism, and as has been said, it is we who are the state. Hence, the task is to extend the application of state intervention in "private legal" relations; to extend the right of the state to annul "private" contracts; to apply to "civil legal relations" not the *corpus juris romani* but *our revolutionary concept of law.* (Lenin, 1922d:562–563)

Before we attribute to Lenin enthusiasm for the project of developing a total system of socialist law, it should be noted that the letter quoted above is entitled "On the Tasks of the People's Commissariat of Justice Under the New Economic Policy." The NEP, of course, was a conscious retreat reviving capitalist economic relations (albeit, he insisted, *state* capitalist relations) first, to consolidate the political alliance with the middle peasantry and, second, to achieve a level of economic development for long-term socialist transformation. During this period most, if not all, of Lenin's "pro-law" formulations occured. In this context he demanded an end to excesses against the peasantry, and the trial of officials and rich peasants abusing the NEP's legal framework. He insisted that "greater revolutionary legality" (Lenin, 1921d:176) was needed to develop relations with the peasantry and to promote trade. Similarly, he demanded that Soviet officials adhere to the legal content of the "tax in kind" which substituted, for direct requisitioning, a variable percentage tax on all agricultural production thereby permitting the producers to exchange their surplus (Lenin, 1921a).

Lenin displayed tangible pride in the substantive content of Soviet legislation. For example, he delighted in the introduction of the eight-hour day, and here and elsewhere he commended the rapid advances recorded in Soviet law in contrast to the legislation of the bourgeois democracies (Lenin, 1922c:392). Again, he often returned to the decrees affecting the position of women, stating that "no other state and no other legislation has ever done for women a half of what Soviet power did in the first months of its existence" (Lenin, 1919f:43). Over a wide range of social questions Soviet legislation underlined a fundamental political lesson for the Bolsheviks: the struggle for reforms did not prepare the way for revolution, but the revolution itself created the conditions for the most far-reaching social reforms. Although many of the advances were later to be curtailed or rescinded, the early years of Soviet power produced much exemplary social legislation, of which that relating to women, marriage, and divorce (Berman, 1963:330–334) and environmental conservation (Zile, 1971) was especially developed.[24]

Lenin's conception of socialist law was deeply affected by his appeal to "socialist legal consciousness," which provided the link between the new institutional structure of courts and the commitment to popular participation. He insisted that judges should "enforce the will of the proletariat, apply its decrees, and in the absence of a suitable decree, or if the relevant decree is inadequate, take guidance from your socialist sense of justice" (Lenin, 1919:131). This conception was explicitly incorporated into the "Decree on the Courts" of February 1918.

The concept of revolutionary legal consciousness served a dual function. It made a powerful appeal to the sovereignty of the people which provided important legitimation to the October revolution—as it has done to all other revolutions. At the same time it marked out the separation between revolutionary and bourgeois law, and made a revolutionary virtue of its inherent variability and situational character. Yet again, this strongly libertarian thrust conflicted with the demand for uniformity and centralization; more seriously, their very coexistence created a politically legitimate mechanism for overriding formal legality just as it does for bureaucratic formalism. The juxtaposition of revolutionary exceptionalism and bureaucratic formalism concentrates the determination of the outcome in the hands of that person or body empowered to effect the choice between the antithesis and then, with equal legitimacy, to swing to the opposite moment. Insofar as Lenin created and justified this alternation between revolutionary justice and legal formalism, he bears historical responsibility for the subsequent deployment of this sublime instrument of authoritarianism by the Stalinist regime.

Law and Bureaucracy

A distinctive feature of Lenin's concept of law and the socialist transition was his identification of law's object as largely Soviet officialdom. His emphasis on the importance of securing adherence to socialist legality by soviet and party officials (see, e.g., Lenin, 1917f:241; 1919e:556; 1922d:562) can be connected with his mounting concern about the struggle against bureaucracy. The depth and tenacity of Lenin's concern with this struggle are indisputable. But how did it relate to the wider context of his political and theoretical positions? An important transition occurred in his analysis of bureaucracy, but it is uncertain whether Lenin himself was aware of it. Immediately after October 1917 he understood bureaucracy as a *legacy* or *survival* resulting from the need to retain and rely on tsarist officials whose habits and politics were expressed in bureaucratic practices. Such officials needed to be subject to constant surveillance: "The capitalists are still fighting us. . . . [M]any thousands are still here, waging war against us according to all the rules of the art of bureaucracy" (Lenin, 1921b:427). In addition to his view of the tsarist state as inherently bureaucratic, Lenin also held that capitalism and bureaucracy had a structural connection that originated in the typical separation of citizens from the administration: "every bureaucracy . . . is purely and exclusively a bourgeois institution" (Lenin, 1895:420). Later, he discarded this exclusive association and indicated that the developed capitalist states had more efficient bureaucracies. Comparing the German and Russian bureaucracies, he argued that the German "bureaucratic apparatus passed through an extensive school, which sucks people dry but compels them to work and not just wear out armchairs as happens in our offices" (Lenin, 1919a:182); whereas the tsarist bureaucracy was constructed on feudal patronage and as a result was characteristically corrupt and inefficient. Lenin must have approved of Rykov's reminder to Soviet officials that "labor is the relation of man to nature and not to paper" (quoted in Liebman, 1975:324).

In the second variant of his analysis of bureaucracy he identified as its ubiquitous source the general cultural backwardness inherited by the Russian revolution. The roots of bureaucracy lay in

> the atomised and scattered state of the small producer with his poverty, illiteracy, lack of culture, the absence of roads and exchange between agriculture and industry . . . the absence of connection and interaction between them. (Lenin, 1921a:351)

The destruction and disorganization resulting from the Civil War exacerbated the sources of bureaucracy. "Bureaucratic practices . . . [are] a legacy of the 'siege' and the superstructure built over the isolated and downtrodden state of the small producer'' (Lenin, 1921a:352). For Lenin revolutionary realism dictated that bureaucratic legacies could not be eradicated quickly; rather, their elimination will require patience, persistence, and the development of new nonbureaucratic styles. In this context he approved of flexibility and informality as alternative modes of organization. In this version of the analysis, therefore, Lenin did not view bureaucracy as a result of the Soviet form itself.

In general terms Lenin applauded the nonbureaucratic character of Soviet power (a ''new type of state without bureaucracy'' [Lenin, 1918d:133]) and administration. This programmatic position was revealed clearly in *State and Revolution* (Lenin, 1917c:425): ''to *smash* the old bureaucratic machine at once and to begin immediately to construct a new one will make possible the gradual abolition of all bureaucracy.'' The Soviet state was able to transcend bureaucracy precisely because it could overcome the separation between citizens and administration. Hence Lenin's commitment to mass popular participation as a defining characteristic of Soviet power. This power was desirable in its own right and constituted a bulwark against bureaucracy: ''We can fight bureaucracy to the bitter end, to a complete victory, only when the whole population participates in the work of government'' (Lenin, 1919a:183).

In Lenin's texts and speeches are references to a novel, if unelaborated, type of bureaucracy, deriving partly from deficiencies in existing party and state institutions. Sometimes Lenin treated this Soviet bureaucracy as a means of survival. Insofar as the legacy/survival analysis becomes less frequent and is not replaced by any other explanation, however, we must suppose that he had no specific analysis of the new bureaucratic form. In the early days of the revolution he seemed fairly confident of a quick victory over bureaucracy, but at the VIIIth Party Congress he identified ''a partial revival'' of bureaucracy within the Soviet system, believing that ''the fight against the bureaucratic distortion of the Soviet form of organization is assured by the firmness of the connection between the soviets and the 'people' '' (Lenin, 1918f:274). His solution was the extension of public participation in administration:

> The more varied must be the forms and methods of control from below in order to counteract every shadow of a possibility of distorting the principles of Soviet government, in order repeatedly and tirelessly to weed out bureaucracy. (Ibid., 275)

Later Lenin saw the struggle as being more protracted:

> We shall be fighting the evils of bureaucracy for many years to come. . . . [It] requires hundreds of measures, wholesale literacy, culture and participation in the activity of the Workers' and Peasants' Inspection. (Lenin, 1921a:351)

By 1921 Lenin (1921c:75) was obviously concerned with failures in the fight against bureaucracy and red tape: ''Why then have we achieved no success in this struggle?" But his solution remained much the same: "It can be done if the masses of the people help" (ibid.), while also proposing a major purge of the party's membership. Significantly, Lenin's (1923; 1923a) last two writings both concern the struggle against bureaucracy. But there is no evidence that his attitude to it changed as he began to understand its persistent and deforming effects on Soviet life. Indeed, he continued to deny the possibility of a causal connection between the Soviet form and bureaucracy:

> Our state apparatus is so deplorable, not to say wretched, that we must first think very carefully how to combat its defects, *bearing in mind that these defects are rooted in the past, which although it has been overthrown, has not yet been overcome.* (Lenin, 1918j:487 [emphasis added])

Because Lenin was convinced that the cure lay in control and surveillance *from below*, he attached great importance to the Workers' and Peasants' Inspection (WPI). Established in 1919, the WPI was an institutional expression of his commitment to the mass participation of workers and peasants in the control and supervision of every institution.[25] It was to function by instituting enquiries and by "cleansing" (*chistka*, the same term used to designate the regular review/purging of party membership). These hearings enabled a janitor to complain against his director and expressed, at least in theory, the idea of workers' control. But by 1920 Lenin admitted that the WPI "exists more as a pious wish; it has been impossible to set it in motion because the best workers have been sent to the front" (Lenin, 1920b:423). His ultimate return to the project of making the WPI effective suggests that he remained committed to the project of control from below through parallel institutional mechanisms. The substance of his proposal to the XIIth Party Congress was greatly to reduce the WPI's size (12,000 in its central body, excluding all regional apparatuses). But a decisive shift of emphasis occurred to which insufficient attention has been paid. In its original conception the WPI was to draw upon teams of rank and file workers (as their cultural level was raised, the peasantry was to be included as well) to monitor and control not only the state apparatus but also all soviet institutions.[26] But by 1923, although he still intended to involve rank-and-file workers, Lenin's hopes for the eradication of bureaucracy depended not on "our best party forces" (Lenin, 1923:482); instead, he proposed to merge the Inspectorate with the Central Control Commission (established in 1920 as a parallel institution to the Central Committee). The latter's role was to review complaints against party officials from the membership below. These fused bodies were to have a staff of "three or four hundred persons, specially screened for conscientiousness and knowledge of our state apparatus" (ibid.). In other words, Lenin now relied upon a professionalized but supervirtuous party membership to check and control both the party and state apparatus; hence the slogan "Better Fewer, but Better" (Lenin, 1923a). He seems to have little appreciated that democratic control from below (that is, by the nonparty masses) had disappeared. Indeed, Lenin's myopic strategy sought to remedy the deficiencies of existing institutions by creating new ones. These, in turn, became bureaucratized and the end result was a further ossification of the whole system. His strategy was therefore doomed.

Lenin's approach to bureaucracy assumed a crucial connection among class situation, political experience and education, and "virtue." Immediately after October 1917, he regarded the proletariat itself as the repository of revolutionary virtue. With the decimation of the working class, his confidence was increasingly placed in an amended conception of "the vanguard," which he equated with Bolshevik party members. This is the first and decisive stage along the road of "substitutionism"—the replacement of the masses as both the subject and the object of the revolutionary process, originally by the party, then by its leadership, and ultimately by the leader. This perspective was at best inherently utopian and at worst naive. Lenin had no proper reason to identify a specific social origin as a privileged source of virtue or rectitude. Nor are there any sound reasons for believing that people, whose virtue stems from their lack of contamination with bureaucratic apparatuses, have the means or capacity to control those very bureaucracies whose strength rests upon their monopolization of organizational experience and technical knowledge.

It must be conceded that Lenin identified bureaucracy as a major problem for the young Soviet state. Not only did it nullify the form of socialist accounting and control that he regarded as a precondition of socialist economic development, but it also had pervasive and debilitating effects upon political and social life. Moving testimony to Lenin's concern appears in his account of the inefficiency, incompetence, and waste on the railway system that he encountered on his first journey when traveling "not as a 'dignitary' " (1922e:432). Yet it must be concluded that the regulatory and institution-building strategy that he advanced was a failure, and that in turn it exacerbated bureaucratization and engineered the peculiar union of authoritarianism and bureaucracy that became the hallmark of Soviet society.

Law and the Transition to Communism

What role, if any, did Lenin conceive for law in the transition to the higher stage of communism? We can give an unqualified answer: none. He was committed to a theoretical perspective in which the withering away of the state and of formal political democracy necessarily implied the withering away of law, although it should be noted that he does not explicitly use this formulation. Lenin's notion of communism, like Marx's, was very limited. Despite well-known passages about the withering away of the state in *The State and Revolution* (Lenin, 1917c), he had little else to say on this matter. In his final reflections on the future of the revolution, Lenin was so preoccupied with the immediate problems of socialist construction that he was unable even to consider the transition to communism.[27]

The forceful argument in *The State and Revolution* is nevertheless controversial.

In Lenin's view, the people would become increasingly cultured in the course of socialist construction, all would participate in public affairs, and the division between mental and manual labor would progressively be overcome. Most important would be the abolition of all classes and thereby the prevalence of social, economic, and political conflict. In this process "people will *become accustomed* to observing the elementary conditions of social life *without violence* and *without subordination*" (ibid., 456). Democracy will by its universalization itself become superfluous:

> Only [when the state ceases to exist] then will a truly complete democracy become possible and be realised, a democracy without any exceptions whatever. And only then will democracy begin to *wither away*, owing to the simple fact that . . . people will gradually *become accustomed* to observing the elementary rules of social intercourse. (Ibid.)

Lenin therefore envisaged a society with rules but without law and with shared consensus about "the elementary rules of social life." Insofar as society may require detailed and technical rules, we may presume that he conceived of such rules as being without authoritative or coercive mechanisms. Lenin's general thesis (derived directly from Marx and Engels), that social life under communism will be fundamentally simplified because of the absence of class conflict and technological advance, supports a conception that does not foresee the need for a framework of rules extending beyond the general requirements of the consensually developed rules of social intercourse: "We give the name communism to the system under which people form the habit of performing their social duties without any special apparatus of coercion" (Lenin, 1919h:284).

This presentation of the withering away of law has serious omissions. Even if we accept for expository purposes that the abolition of classes massively reduces the possibility of social conflict, Lenin's "optimism" was dangerously crude. Even if interpersonal conflict either disappears or is handled by nonlegal mechanisms of conflict resolution, his account entirely omits institutional relations and the continuing necessity of mechanisms for allocating resources. It is possible to imagine a society in which there is an abundance of the immediate needs of life, but no abundance could ever be envisaged that would either abolish the need to make choices about resource allocation or eliminate conflicts about the priority between alternative projects and aspirations.

IV. The Constitution of Soviet Society

In the introduction we indicated that the problem of constitution traversed an important paradox: The political and theoretical objections to constitutionalism, which motivated Lenin and the Bolsheviks, contributed greatly to the ultimate failure to constitute Soviet society in a form by which the radical democratic motives of the revolutionary process could be realized. Indeed, this failure was a dangerous vacuum that within a decade of Lenin's death was filled with the paradoxical coexistence of law and terror (Sharlet and Beirne, *infra*, chapter 6). Our argument extends beyond the standard liberal critiques of the Soviet Union that point to the absence of a separation of powers between party and state as the origin of the authoritarian potentiality exemplified under Stalinism. This failure, we contend, was only a symptom. The problem of Soviet society is the failure to develop a civil society able to provide and sustain processes for handling social conflicts and choices, compatible with some sustainable conception of democracy and an expanding public participation as needed in any attempt to construct a viable socialist society.

Lenin's critique of constitutionalism began with his rigorous adherence to the orthodox Marxist view of the state as an instrument of rule by a single class. Each historically dominant class has a characteristic form of state power, with parliamentary democracy being "the best possible political shell for capitalism" (Lenin, 1917c:393). In this schema the separation of powers is a temporary, unstable phenomenon when two classes (for example, the feudal aristocracy and the bourgeoisie) vie for power; thereafter, it is nothing more than a constitutional illusion, because, when a single class holds power, the different organs are expressions of the same class interest:

> Bourgeois states are most varied in form, but their essence is the same: all these states, whatever their form, in the final analysis are inevitably the *dictatorship of the bourgeoisie*. The transition from capitalism to communism is certainly bound to yield a tremendous abundance and variety of political forms, but the essence will inevitably be the same: *the dictatorship of the proletariat*. (Ibid., 413)

Lenin's analysis of the state form of a successful proletarian revolution is predicated on an interweaving of two distinct strands. The first, syndicalist strand emphasizes the possibility of the direct exercise of popular power. In this, the unitary conception of class power conflates political and economic power; hence, in much of Lenin's discussion "all power to the soviets!" and "workers' control!" are synonymous. It is here that Lenin elaborated the idea of the withering away of the state. The second strand appears in the argument advancing the need for the DoP. Decisively, this state power is devoid of any specific form, for "*the people* can suppress the exploiters even with a very simple 'machine,' almost without a 'machine,' without a special apparatus, by the simple *organization of the armed people*" (ibid., 463). He then added in parentheses: "(such as the Soviets of Workers' and Soldiers' Deputies, we would remark, running ahead)" (ibid.).

Remarkably, and without contradiction, this formulation contains two different arguments. On the one hand, there is a syndicalist conception of popular power; on the other, there is an insistence upon an instrument, the DoP with a very specific state function, namely, an essential but fundamentally transitional role in eradicating the class power of the old ruling class. In Lenin's analysis the fusion and interpenetration of these two strands most clearly appeared in his discussion of the Russian form of the dictatorship, namely, the Soviets. These are simultaneoulsy mass organizations of a class and the state form of the dictatorship.

Lenin's unique contribution to Marxist political theory before 1917 was his analysis of the party, and it was to be the primary instrument of the revolution. Yet the party was not present in *The State and Revolution* (1917c), the key text linking the creation of the revolutionary instrument and its political triumph. Moreover, this text contained no theory or account of representation, which tends to explain both the specific omission of the party and also Lenin's apparent lack of concern with the political/constitutional form of the revolution.[28] These silences were manifest in the failure to explore a question that he touched on time and time again: the way in which classes can be said to be agents, or, in what sense, if any, do classes act? Much socialist discourse typically speaks of actions such as the working class "struggling" or the capitalist class "retreating." Such formulations operate as a serviceable shorthand, but they wrongly tend to be taken literally. Classes *as such* never act; rather, historical agents always "act" as some specific social force, such as trade unions or political parties. But the corollary of this truism is that the form of the agency has a distinctive effect upon the content and style of the action taken. For example, trade unions act differently than political parties. A central question for any form of political theory, therefore, is the consideration and selection of forms of political representation that are appropriate to its objectives.

At one level Lenin's whole project from the mid-1890s onward was to develop the concept of the revolutionary party as the form of working-class representation. Yet at another level he constantly conflated the interests of this class with the form of its representation. In the prerevolutionary period this imagery did not do great violence; much politics involved competition between rival parties and factions for the allegiance of the small urban proletariat. The tsarist system allowed few arenas for political competition; in comparison, bourgeois democratic systems with complex civil societies generate many different locations for and forms of political representation. However, after February 1917 major transformations increasingly occurred that posed the question of representation over a wide range of social and economic activities and in connection with a series of new institutions. In this context Lenin's analysis was problematic. It is true that the intense nature of the political struggle legitimates analysis presented in terms of assertions about a direct relationship between classes and parties. But this analysis conceals the complex forms of representation developing within the new concatenation of social, economic, and political forces created by the revolution.

Among the Bolsheviks this issue came to center stage in the controversy over the role of the trade unions. In 1920 the substantive issue was the militarization of labor:[29] would the trade unions retain any capacity to represent the interests of their members and workers in particular enterprises or in a specific industry vis-à-vis management, planning bodies, or the state? Lenin at first supported Trotsky's proposals[30] for militarization, but increasingly retracted this position as he recognized the need for a specific mechanism to represent the immediate interests of labor even within a proletarian state. Frequently, the role of the trade unions was debated in relation to the legitimacy of strikes. Lenin was prepared to accept that workers needed to retain some means of struggle against management, but he marginalized the problem by treating it as a *survival* of capitalism:

> [T]he strike struggle in a state where the proletariat holds political power can be explained and justified only by the bureaucratic distortions of the proletarian state and by all sorts of survivals of the old capitalist system in the government offices on the one hand, and by the political immaturity and cultural backwardness of the mass of the working people on the other. (Lenin, 1922:186–187)

In recognizing the independent, representational role of the trade unions in the short term, Lenin in effect agreed to the abolition of the problem of representation because the interests of workers, managers, party, and state would be unanimous. We must now draw out the implications of Lenin's persistent tendency to insist upon the fusion of different interests and constituencies. Before focusing on this issue, however, it is important to establish how it relates to questions about law and legality.

Representation and Fusion

Lenin paid scant attention to the debates preceding the promulgation of the first constitution of the Russian Soviet Federative Socialist Republic (RSFSR) of July 1918.[31] But he held what we term a "fusion model" of the constitution of a socialist society, believing that it should overcome the separation of state and people through the progressive fusion of popular and mass organizations with the decision making and administrative work of the state. Although Lenin never espoused this position in its general form, we contend that it underlay all his declared views about the constitution of socialist society in its broadest and most important sense, namely, the relations between state and civil society.

One facet of the fusion theory had a fairly high profile in Lenin's thought because of its usage in *The State and Revolution.*

Here he claimed that the superiority of soviet to parliamentary democracy consisted in its *overcoming* the separation of legislative and administrative functions within the state. He found little need to support this view because he derived it from the authority of Marx's commentary on the lessons of the Paris Commune: "The Commune was to be a working, not a parliamentary body, executive and legislative at the same time" (Marx, 1871 [1969]:220).[32] Lenin elaborated Marx's idea into "the conversion of the representative institutions from talking shops into 'working' bodies" (Lenin, 1917c:423). The substance of this claim for the inherent superiority of soviets is not clear. One of the advantages of soviet government was that

> it makes it possible to combine the advantages of the parliamentary system with those of immediate and direct democracy, i.e., to vest in the people's elected representatives both legislative and *executive* functions. . . . this is an advance in democracy's development which is of world-wide, historic significance. (Lenin, 1917e:103–104)

We may presume here that Lenin claimed that the fusion of legislative and administrative functions would render the legislature more effective, that is, it would not experience bureaucratic obstruction by the administration typically castigated by left and radical governments in parliamentary democracies. There is perhaps also a claim that fusion promotes the virtue of realism, ensuring that the legislature has its feet on the ground and in contact with the people, in that it has not only to decide policy but must also be responsible for its implementation. Fusion would "bring the state apparatus closer to the working people" (Lenin, 1919:108). But it is unclear why Lenin thought this was true. Other claims that we may presume Lenin would have made for fusion, and thus implicitly against the separation of powers, rest on a rather naive view of the role and function of administration, which, as we have seen, he presumed would be profoundly simplified. We have indicated our serious reservation about this, but should add that Lenin's view leads to his failure to address the more difficult issues surrounding the capacity to achieve effective legislative surveillance of the implementation of law.

A second, more important version of the fusion theory in Lenin's writing has attracted almost no attention, yet it contains the grounds for the most significant criticism of Lenin's failure to address the conditions for the development and preservation of socialist democracy. Lenin was committed to the fusion of mass organizations (such as the soviets) with the state. But the fusion of legislature and administration occurs only *within the state*. To propose a merger between the primary mechanisms of popular representation and the institutions of the state is tantamount to uniting state and civil society. The roots of such a project are part of the theoretical trajectory proposing the withering away of state and law (the higher stage of communism). In this the abolition of classes results in nonantagonistic social, economic, and political relations whereby the state—as an apparatus of class oppression—will be superfluous. Insofar as the withering away of the state is a process rather than an act of abolition, an important step in overcoming the separation of state and people is its removal by fusing or merging mass organizations with state organs. It is thus part of the thesis so influential in Lenin's thought, and already often encountered here, that the distinguishing feature of socialist democracy must be popular participation in governmental and administrative activity. If popular organs are fused with state organs then one stage on the road to communism and the withering away of the state is realized. His consequential espousal of the "withering away of democracy" is an assertion that mechanisms of representation are unnecessary in a society with no class divisions and no separation between state and people.

Fusion and the Soviets

The soviets, as the primary instrument of popular power, provided the core legitimation of the October revolution. The slogan "All power to the soviets" was the vehicle through which political power was seized and on whose behalf the old state machine was smashed. It was to the soviets that political power was given: "Comrades, workers, soldiers, peasants and all working people! Take *all* into the hands of *your* soviets" (Lenin, 1917g:297). In the early months of the revolution the local soviets operated with great autonomy and usually guarded it jealously. But the direct popular power found in the local soviets was gradually absorbed by the central state agencies. Although this story has already been recorded and we will not add to it,[33] the relative importance of the particular and general causes of the decline of the soviets must be mentioned here.

The exigencies of the Civil War destroyed many local soviets, and inevitable pressures tended toward centralization and militarization and toward the absorption of the soviets by the state. The most salient pressure was the basic claim of soviet power that the soviets were the source of sovereignty and that they provided the central tenet of the 1918 Constitution. Thus, the soviets were invested with two major roles: they were the basic representative organ for the expression and articulation of popular politics, and at the same time they were to become the new state apparatus rather than merely the basis of its sovereignty. In the absence of the separation between legislative and executive functions, the soviets were transformed into departments of state. Did this involve an overinvestment of power? As the soviets increasingly became administrative state agencies, their capacity to fulfill their role as the organ of popular representation suffered. The "de-sovietization" of political life ensued. Political and administrative power was rapidly transferred to the state apparatus; at all levels the congresses of soviets met less and less often and began to serve the function of legitimation and ex post facto ratification.

The tragic paradox was that the process that served to debilitate soviet power involved those very features that Lenin praised as the great merit of the new system:

> The Soviets are a new state apparatus . . . [that] provides a bond with the people . . . far more democratic than any previous apparatus . . . and so constitutes an apparatus by means of which the vanguard of the oppressed classes can elevate, train and lead the *entire vast mass.* (Lenin, 1917e:103; see also 1918k:100; 1919:106–107)

Lenin (1918f:273) himself applauded the fusion of representation and administration in terms of the relations between the soviets and the commissariats. Moreover, he proposed that experimentation be followed by legislative incorporation: "[A]ll steps that are taken in this direction—the more varied they are the better—should be carefully recorded, studied, systematised, tested by wider experience and embodied in law" (Lenin, 1918h:273). Given the party's assigned roles—as universal political agent and as a mechanism of systematization, coherence, and leadership—then the soviets' capacity to articulate popular opinion would either disappear or be so hedged about by the party and administration that it would become superfluous. Indeed, Lenin was usually diffident about the relationship between the party and the state. Most of his utterances on this were constructed on the belief that the party's role was *leadership*, always suggesting a separation between the leaders and the led. When he returned briefly to the question of the relations among the party, state, and soviet institutions, he asked if it was "improper" to amalgamate or fuse party and soviet institutions. His pragmatic answer clearly regarded such arrangements as atypical. He referred to "this particular amalgamation" (Lenin, 1923a:496), but found it acceptable if it worked in a given case. In his polemic with Kautsky, Lenin pondered whether transforming the soviets from "combat organizations of a class" into state organizations would destroy their democratic character (Lenin, 1918h:259–262). His reaction to Kautsky was so intense that he simply did not reply to the point of substance. Instead, he construed his opponent as arguing that the working class should not seek to capture state power, whereas the real problem posed by Kautsky was whether the mechanism through which the working class organized itself and then won political power could become the workers' and peasants' primary mass organization and thus the institutional basis of the new state. But this issue remained dormant.

While Lenin consistently advocated the fusion of soviet and state roles he was, as noted above, more ambivalent about whether the trade unions should be fused with the economic administration. On occasion he decided in favor of fusion, but more often he recognized the important capacity of unions to represent the interests of workers with reference to enterprise management and in the planning institutions. His preferred role for the trade unions used an analogy with schools. The trade union, he argued, "is not a state organization.... It is an organization designed to draw in and train; it is, in fact, a school; a school of administration, a school of economic management, a school of communism" (Lenin, 1921:20).

The model of fusion underlying Lenin's attitude to constitutional issues could fulfill the diverse functions that the theory assigned to it only if one major condition was met: that the end of Russian capitalism would actually vitiate serious social, political, and economic conflict. In turn, this condition depended on the contention that class struggles were the only sources of antagonistic conflict.[34] From this assumption it followed that all the mechanisms of representation, decision making, and administration are capable of functioning harmoniously. Although class antagonism is a major, or even the most important, single source of conflict, if conflict has other sources (for example, the sexual division of labor) that persist under socialism, then the mechanisms of conflict resolution are important and necessary features of the constitution of a socialist society. More broadly, does recognition of the necessarily conflictual and thus pluralistic features of a viable socialism require a particular role for law as a specific mechanism? An alternative case could be made (see, for example, Abel, 1982; Cain, 1985) that informalism and delegalization are the most apt mechanisms of conflict resolution under socialism.

Contrary to Lenin's fusion thesis, a strong case exists for a socialist theory of the separation of powers. Within capitalist societies the potency of this doctrine stems from the existence of strong private associations, both economic (including the organizations of labor and capital) and political. The separation of powers, and with it the role of law, are sustained by the tension between state and civil society. In a socialist society the very attempt to overcome the negative consequences of the separation of public and private spheres generates the role and location of law. The very process of reducing the conflict of private interests necessitates the presence of an effective public law. We therefore agree with Lenin's contention that a peculiarity of socialist law is the transformation of private law into public law. But against him we insist that public law must guarantee the democratic conditions of decision making. This requires a constitutional arrangement explicitly directed to the prevention of the overinvestment of power within any one institutional apparatus. The need for this form of public law is the major lesson in the history of the first socialist experiment and the contribution to it—with its strengths, its weaknesses, and its silences—of Lenin.

Notes

1. The main protagonists in this literature are by now well known, and their specific contributions to it need no rehearsal here. The varied writings include: Thompson (1975, 1980); Cohen (1977); Hirst (1979:96–176, 1986); Fryer, Hunt, McBarnet, and Moorhouse (1981); Beirne and Quinney (1982); Buchanan (1982); Collins (1982); Campbell (1983); Fine (1984); Lea and Young (1984); Geras (1985); and Hirst (1986).

2. For present purposes socialism is a transitional stage—of a more or less protracted period—that spans the conquest of political power and the emergence of communism as a classless society in which capitalist social and economic relations have been wholly expunged. No existing society satisfies these conditions.

3. See Stuchka (1925), Pashukanis (1925), Krylenko (1934), and Bratous (1970).

4. Examples of these "if only" histories are provided by Cohen (1973), Makepiece (1980), and Medvedev (1981).

5. However, Lenin occasionally argued that the Bolsheviks should use the old bourgeois state against the bourgeoisie. For example, in his famous lecture on the state, at Sverdlov University, he argued that "so far we have deprived the capitalists of this machine [the State] and have taken it over. We shall use this machine, or bludgeon, to destroy all exploitation" (Lenin, 1919d:488).

6. While bourgeois revolutions had varying degrees of continuity with the feudal orders they replaced, the transition from capitalism to socialism was conceived as a more fundamental rupture or break necessitating a total transformation in all arenas of economic and political life.

7. Narodnism was a late-nineteenth-century populist doctrine based on the political advancement of the Russian peasantry. Its decline was coextensive with the rise of the Russian Social-Democratic Labor Party (RSDLP).

8. Similar formulations can be found in Lenin (1919b:353–354; 1919c:380; 1919d:482; 1919f:42; 1919g:121).

9. In the specific historical context of the 1914–1918 War this thesis had some justification. Subsequently, the course of European politics in the inter-war period, in particular the rise of fascism, led this thesis to play a central part in the politics of the Comintern and it was a central tenet of the ultrasectarian politics of the "third period," which refused to recognize any difference between bourgeois democracy and fascism. It is much easier, from the vantage point of the defeat of fascism and the continuing vitality of bourgeois democracy, to see the underlying error in Lenin's original position.

10. "What is To Be Done?" (Lenin, 1902a) was the culmination of Lenin's struggle against the economistic trend in the RSDLP. For a brief account of this controversy see Carr (1966, 2:105–108).

11. Lenin contrasted the harsh regulations against the peasantry with a law passed in the same year providing for the leasing of unoccupied lands in Siberia to the "poor" landowning nobility who, in turn, he contrasted with the landless poor in the United States who were encouraged to settle on vacant land (Lenin, 1901d:99–100).

12. This demystification closely paralleled Marx's (1867 [1967]: vol. 1, chap. 10, pp. 231–302) analysis of the early Factory Acts in England, although Lenin himself did not refer to Marx's writings.

13. Lenin demanded that this bill expressly provide for the "gradual" introduction of the shorter working day to demonstrate the "technical, cultural and economic practicality of the Social-Democratic programme" (1909:115).

14. Accordingly, he stressed that the revolt of major sections of the Tory Party and of the officer core of the British Army over the Irish Home Rule crisis in 1914 showed that the ruling classes would dispense with legality, the rule of law, and the constitution when their class interests were threatened (Lenin, 1914). There was even less reason to trust the Russian ruling classes than the British, he argued.

15. The history of the Bolsheviks' relationship with the Constituent Assembly need not be retold here. Our concern is to focus on its implications for Lenin's thought on the place of constitutions. It is well known that the Bolsheviks disagreed about whether to allow the Constituent Assembly to function. Lenin had indicated as far back as April 1917 that the Bolsheviks would not be satisfied with a "bourgeois parliamentary democratic republic" but should press on to achieve a "democratic workers' and peasants' republic" (1917:471). His major justification for closing the Assembly involved two related arguments. Firstly, because the news had not reached most rural areas by the time the votes were cast for the Constituent Assembly, the election results (in which the SRs gained a handsome majority) belied the fact that the soviets had taken power in St. Petersburg and Moscow. Second, the votes were unreliable because when the Assembly was to convened, the "victors" had already divided into the Left-SRs (who supported the Bolsheviks and who participated in the soviets and their executive bodies) and the Right-SRs. In general these arguments applied practically the thesis outlined above—that constitutions do not create but merely reflect, confirm, and legitimize political power. The rapidity of the revolutionary process had eluded the Constituent Assembly. Power was now firmly in the hands of the soviets, and to revert to the Constituent Assembly would be to retreat in the face of historical reality. To argue otherwise was to fall under the spell of "constitutional illusions."

16. The term "constitution" implies both the formal process of constitution-making, or constitutionalism, and a broader set of processes by and through which societies are constituted. We employ this concept like Giddens (1984) when he refers to the whole complex of relations—economic, political, and cultural—through which each society is constituted and in which great importance is attached to the relationship that exists between the state and civil society.

17. *Sobranie Uzakonenii* (Collection of Laws) lists 1,033 entries for 1917–1918 and

596 for 1919. The *Sobranie Uzakonenii* (hereinafter *S.U.*) was first published as a systematized collection in 1921 as *Sobranie uzakonenii i resporiazhenii rabochego i krest'ianskogo pravitel'stva, sistematicheskii sbornik vazhneishkikh decretov 1917–1920*. On the difficulties of distinguishing the statuses of the various legislative devices, see further Feldbrugge (1964:28–29) and Makepiece (1980:75–59).

18. Prior to the passage of the first decrees on the courts there was considerable discussion among the Bolsheviks about the proper relation between the revolution and the old legal system. One faction argued that the prerevolutionary courts should be retained as a necessary apparatus for the period of socialist transition; indeed, a judge of the new Moscow court reminisced that it was hoped somehow to have been possible to postpone the task of creating a new judiciary until the Moscow city government could solve some more pressing problems (Hazard, 1960:1). Another faction insisted that all law and all legal institutions should be abolished at once because they were incompatible with socialism. Following the lead of those such as Lunacharsky (1917), Lenin himself effected a compromise between these two factions in "Decree No. 1 on the Court," (*S.U.*, 1917–1918, no. 4, item 50) which he himself initiated and which was issued through CPC Indeed, according to Stuchka (1925), Lenin was an enthusiastic supporter of this decree and in order to faciltiate its passage he agreed to release it solely through CPC rather than the Central Executive Committee where, although it probably would have been adopted, it would have met with opposition from the coalition parties.

19. For discussion and criticism of this "simplification" thesis see Hunt (1985).

20. The key Bolshevik texts in the great debate about the economics of the socialist transition were Bukharin and Preobrazensky (1919) and Bukharin (1920). For commentary on this debate see Cohen (1974:83–106) and Nove (1976:119–135).

21. In turn, Lenin linked this simplification with Engels's superficially attractive claim that under communism "the government of persons is replaced by the administration of things" (1880:147). Lenin's formulation was that when "the more important functions of the state are reduced to such [simplified] accounting and control . . . it will cease to be a 'political state' and public functions will lose their political character and become mere administrative functions" (1917c:473). This formulation is decidedly "un-Marxist" in that it is difficult to conceive of any way in which changes in the administration of things do not have necessary implications for some sets of social relations. Its anarchic implications were carried to their logical extreme by the radical wing of the commodity exchange school of law—see especially Pashukanis (1924:40–131).

22. Among Marxist jurists the leading texts of this period were Stuchka (1921) and Pashukanis (1924). For commentary on the respective juristic positions embodied in these texts, and on the development of Soviet legal theory until the rise of Stalinism, see Beirne and Sharlet (1980:1–36).

23. Discussions of Lenin's views of the political relations between central authorities and local legal officials can be found in Hazard (1960: chs. 5–7) and Solomon (1985).

24. Arguably, a major exception to these advances was the continuation of capital punishment. For Lenin's own presentation of his complicated position on capital punishment and the regularization of "red terror," see, e.g., Lenin (1917b:341; 1917g:294; 1918c:33; 1918i:336; 1920c:167) and Carr (1966, 1:162).

25. For example, he urged that even illiterate workers were to be involved in the work of the WPI, assisting and learning from their literate comrades, and that "*women*, literally *every woman* must be drawn into this work" (Lenin, 1920:301).

26. As Deutscher comments: "With his characteristic belief in the inherent virtues of the working classes, Lenin appealed to the workers against his own bureaucracy" (1961:231).

27. Lenin's so-called Last Testament is usually taken to include the brief papers

dictated between January and March 1923. For a full discussion of this period see Lewin (1969).

28. Representation concerns the forms in which social groups, forces, and classes manifest and advance their interests vis-à-vis other classes, groups, etc. One of us (Hunt, 1983) has argued elsewhere that there is a similar absence in Marx when he fails to address the implications of the changed forms of representation that were the consequence of the extension of the franchise toward the end of the nineteenth century.

29. For accounts of the debate over the trade unions see Dewar (1956) and Carr (1966, 1:372–376).

30. For Trotsky's account of the case for the militarization of the unions as an extension of War Communism, see Trotsky (1975:482–485).

31. The best introductory discussion of the debates around the Soviet constitution is Carr (1966, 1:pt. 2, 115–237).

32. Incidentally, Marx provided no supporting argument in favor of the fusion of legislative and administrative functions.

33. For a general introduction see Liebman (1975) and Rigby (1979).

34. "Antagonistic conflict" refers to those conflicts regarded as being fundamental in the sense that the conflicting interests are incapable of resolution. Other than through the victory of one side, Marxist theory traditionally regards the conflict between labor and capital as such a fundamental or antagonistic conflict, while conflicts within classes or other social groups are regarded as nonfundamental and thus nonantagonistic.

References

Authors' note: All works by Lenin are from *Lenin: Collected Works* [*LCW*], 45 vols. (Moscow: Progress Publishers, 1960–1970).

Works by Lenin

(1895) "The Economic Content of Narodnism and the Criticism of It in Mr. Struve's Book," *LCW* 1:133–507.
(1899) "The New Factory Law," *LCW* 2:267–315.
(1901) "Beat—But Not to Death," *LCW* 4:383–402.
(1901a) "The Drafting of 183 Students Into the Army," *LCW* 4:414–419.
(1901b) "Penal Servitude Regulations and Penal Servitude Sentences," *LCW* 5:243–249.
(1901c) "Review of Home Affairs," *LCW* 5:251–301.
(1901d) "The Serf-Owners at Work," *LCW* 5:95–100.
(1902) "The Draft of a New Law on Strikes," *LCW* 6:217–226.
(1902a) "What Is to Be Done?" *LCW* 5:349–529.
(1903) "The Autocracy Is Wavering . . . " *LCW* 6:348–353.
(1903a) "To the Rural Poor," *LCW* 6:361–432.
(1903b) "An Era of Reforms," *LCW* 6:510–517.
(1906) "The Victory of the Cadets and the Tasks of the Workers' Party," *LCW* 10:199–276.
(1908) "The Handicraft Census of 1894–95 in Perm Gubernia and General Problems of 'Handicraft' Industry," *LCW* 2:355–458.
(1908a) *The Development of Capitalism in Russia. LCW* 3:21–607.
(1908b) "The Agrarian Programme of Social-Democracy in The First Russian Revolution 1905–1907," *LCW* 13:217–431.

(1909) "Explanatory Note on the Draft of the Main Grounds of the Bill on the Eight-Hour Working Day," *LCW* 16:110–116.
(1910) "Two Worlds," *LCW* 16:305–313.
(1913) "An Increasing Discrepancy," *LCW* 18:562–579.
(1914) "Constitutional Crisis in Britain," *LCW* 20:226–229.
(1916) "The Socialist Revolution and the Right of Nations to Self-Determination," *LCW* 22:143–156.
(1916a) "A Caricature of Marxism and Imperialist Economism," *LCW* 23:28–76.
(1917) "Materials Relating to the Revision of the Party Programme," *LCW* 24:455–479.
(1917a) "A Contradictory Stand," *LCW* 25:88–90.
(1917b) "The Impending Catastrophe and How to Combat It," *LCW* 25:319–365.
(1917c) *The State and Revolution. LCW* 25:381–492.
(1917d) "The Russian Revolution and Civil War," *LCW* 26:28–42.
(1917e) "Can the Bolsheviks Retain State Power?" *LCW* 26:87–136.
(1917f) "Meeting of the Petrograd Soviet of Workers' and Soldiers' Deputies," *LCW* 26:239–241.
(1917g) "Speech at a Joint Meeting of the Petrograd Soviet of Workers' and Soldiers' Deputies and Delegates from the Front, November 4 (17), 1917," *LCW* 26:293–295.
(1917h) "The Tasks of the Proletariat in the Present Revolution" [The April Theses], *LCW* 24:19–26.
(1917i) "Meeting of the All-Russia Central Executive Committee, November 4, 1917," *LCW* 26:284–292.
(1918a) "How to Organise Competition?" *LCW* 26:404–415.
(1918b) "Third All-Russia Congress of Soviets of Workers', Soldiers' and Peasants' Deputies," *LCW* 26:453–482.
(1918c) "The Socialist Fatherland Is in Danger!" *LCW* 27:30–33.
(1918d) "Extraordinary Seventh Congress of the R.C.P.(B.)," *LCW* 27:85–158.
(1918e) "Original Version of the Article 'The Immediate Tasks of the Soviet Government,' " *LCW* 27:203–218
(1918f) "The Immediate Tasks of the Soviet Government," *LCW* 27:235–277.
(1918g) "Fifth All-Russia Congress of Soviets of Workers', Peasants', Soldiers' and Red Army Deputies," *LCW* 27:505–532.
(1918h) *The Proletarian Revolution and the Renegade Kautsky. LCW* 28:227–325.
(1918i) "To G. Y. Zinoviev," *LCW* 35:336.
(1918j) "To G. Y. Zinoviev," *LCW* 35:487.
(1918k) "The Democratism and Socialist Nature of Soviet Power," *LCW* 42:100–101.
(1919) "Draft Programme of the R.C.P.(B.)," *LCW* 29:97–140.
(1919a) *Eighth Congress of the R.C.P.(B.), LCW* 29:141–225.
(1919b) "First All-Russia Congress on Adult Education," *LCW* 29:333–376.
(1919c) "Foreword to the Published Speech 'Deception of the People With Slogans of Freedom and Equality,' " *LCW* 29:377–381.
(1919d) *The State. LCW* 29:470–488.
(1919e) "Letter to the Workers and Peasants Apropos of the Victory Over Kolchak," *LCW* 29:552–560.
(1919f) "The Tasks of the Working Women's Movement in the Soviet Republic," *LCW* 30:40–46.
(1919g) "Soviet Power and the Status of Women," *LCW* 30:120–123.
(1919h) "Report on Subbotniks Delivered to a Moscow City Conference of the R.C.P.(B.)," *LCW* 30:283–288.
(1920) "Remarks on and Addenda to Drafts for 'Rules for the Workers' and Peasants' Inspection,' " *LCW* 30:300–301.

(1920a) *"Left-Wing" Communism—An Infantile Disorder*. *LCW* 31:17–118.
(1920b) "Our Foreign and Domestic Position and the Tasks of the Party," *LCW* 31:408–426.
(1920c) "Speech at the Fourth Conference of Gubernia Extraordinary Commissions, February 6, 1920," *LCW* 42:166–174.
(1921) "The Trade Unions, The Present Situation and Trotsky's Mistakes," *LCW* 32:19–42.
(1921a) "The Tax in Kind," *LCW* 32:329–365.
(1921b) "Tenth All-Russia Conference of the R.C.P.(B.)," *LCW* 32:399–437.
(1921c) "The New Economic Policy and the Tasks of the Political Education Departments," *LCW* 33:60–79.
(1921d) "Ninth All-Russia Congress of Soviets," *LCW* 33:141–181.
(1922) "The Role and Functions of the Trade Unions under the New Economic Policy," *LCW* 33:184–196.
(1922a) "Eleventh Congress of the R.C.P.(B.)," *LCW* 33:259–326.
(1922b) " 'Dual' Subordination and Legality," *LCW* 33:363–367.
(1922c) "Speech at the Fourth Session of the All-Russia Central Executive Committee, Ninth Convocation, October 31, 1922," *LCW* 33:390–395.
(1922d) "On the Tasks of the People's Commissariat for Justice Under the New Economic Policy," *LCW* 36:560–565.
(1922e) "To I. S. Unschlicht and V. V. Fomin," *LCW* 45:432–433.
(1922f) "Notes for a Speech on March 27, 1922," *LCW* 36:571–575.
(1923) "How We Should Reorganise the Workers' and Peasants' Inspection," *LCW* 33:481–486.
(1923a) "Better Fewer, but Better," *LCW* 33:487–502.
(1923b) "Pages from a Diary," *LCW* 33:462–466.
(1923c) "On Co-operation," *LCW*:467–475.
(1923d) "Our Revolution," *LCW*:476–486.

Other Works

Abel, Richard L. (ed.) (1982): *The Politics of Informal Justice*. 2 vols. New York: Academic Press.
Beirne, Piers, and Robert Sharlet (eds.) (1980). *Pashukanis: Selected Writings on Marxism and Law*. Tr. Peter B. Maggs. London: Academic Press.
Beirne, Piers, and Richard Quinney (eds.) (1982). *Marxism and Law*. New York: John Wiley.
Berman, Harold J. (1963). *Justice in the U.S.S.R.* Cambridge: Harvard University Press.
Bratous, S. N. (1970). "Lenin's Ideas on Soviet Law and Socialist Legality," *Review of Contemporary Law* 1:21.
Buchanan, Allen (1982). *Marx and Justice*. London: Methuen.
Bukharin, N. I. (1920). *Ekonomika perekhodnogo perioda* [The Economics of the Transition Period]. Moscow.
Bukharin, N. I., and E. Preobrazhensky (1919) (1969). *The ABC of Communism*. London: Pelican Books.
Cain, Maureen (1985). "Beyond Informal Justice," *Contemporary Crises* 9:335.
Campbell, Tom (1983). *The Left and Rights*. London: Routledge & Kegan Paul.
Carr, E. H. (1966). *The Bolshevik Revolution*. 3 vols. London: Pelican.
Cohen, G. A. (1978). *Karl Marx's Theory of History: A Defense*. Princeton, N.J.: Princeton University Press.
Cohen, Stephen F. (1974). *Bukharin and the Bolshevik Revolution: A Political Biography, 1888–1938*. New York: Alfred A. Knopf.
Collins, Hugh (1982). *Marxism and Law*. Oxford: Clarendon Press.

Deutscher, Isaac (1961). *Stalin: A Political Biography*. London: Oxford University Press.
Dewar, M. (1956). *Labour Policy in the U.S.S.R. 1917–1928*. London: Royal Institute of International Affairs.
Engels, Friedrich (1880) (1969). "Socialism: Utopian and Scientific," 3:95–151 in *Karl Marx and Frederick Engels: Selected Works*. 3 vols. Moscow: Progress Publishers.
Feldbrugge, F. J. (1964). "Law in Eastern Europe," in *Soviet Criminal Law: General Part*. No. 9. Leyden: A. W. Sijthoff.
Fine, Bob (1984). *Democracy and the Rule of Law*. London: Pluto.
Fryer, Bob, Alan Hunt, Doreen McBarnett, and Bert Moorhouse (1981). *Law, State and Society*. London: Croom Helm.
Geras, Norman (1985). "The Controversy About Marx and Justice," *New Left Review* 150:47.
Giddens, Anthony (1984). *The Constitution of Society*. Cambridge: Polity Press.
Hazard, John N. (1960). *Settling Disputes in Soviet Society: The Formative Years of Legal Institutions*. New York: Columbia University Press.
Hirst, Paul (1979). *On Law and Ideology*. London: Macmillan.
——— (1986). *Law, Socialism and Democracy*. London: Allen and Unwin.
Hunt, Alan (1983). "Marx—the Missing Dimension: The Rise of Representative Democracy," in B. Matthews (ed.), *Marx: A Hundred Years On*. London: Lawrence & Wishart.
——— (1985). "The Future of Rights and Justice," *Contemporary Crises* 9:309.
Krylenko, N. V. (1934). *Lenin o Sude* [Lenin on the Courts]. Moscow.
Lea, John, and Jock Young (1984). *What Is To Be Done about Law and Order?* London: Penguin.
Lewin, Moshe (1969). *Lenin's Last Struggle*. London: Faber & Faber.
Liebman, Marcel (1975). *Leninism Under Lenin*. Tr. Brian Pearce. London: Merlin.
Lunacharsky, A. (1917). "Revoliutsiia i Sud" [Revolution and the Court], *Pravda*, no. 193.
Makepiece, R. W. (1980). *Marxist Ideology and Soviet Criminal Law*. London: Croom Helm.
Marx, Karl (1867) (1975). *Capital*. 3 vols. New York: International Publishers.
——— (1871) (1969). "The Civil War in France," 2:178–244 in *Karl Marx and Frederick Engels: Selected Works*. 3 vols. Moscow: Progress Publishers.
Medvedev, Roy (1981). *Leninism and Western Socialism*. London: Verso and New Left Books.
Nove, Alec (1976). *An Economic History of the USSR*. London: Penguin.
Pashukanis, E. B. (1924) (1980). *The General Theory of Law and Marxism*, in Beirne and Sharlet (eds.), *Pashukanis: Selected Writings on Marxism and Law*. Tr. Peter B. Maggs. London: Academic Press.
——— (1925) (1980). "Lenin and Problems of Law," in Beirne and Sharlet (eds.).
Rigby, T. H. (1979). *Lenin's Government: Sovnarkom 1917–1922*. Cambridge, Mass.: Cambridge University Press.
Sharlet, Robert, and Piers Beirne (1984). "In Search of Vyshinsky: The Paradox of Law and Terror," *International Journal of the Sociology of Law* 12:153.
Sharlet, Robert, Peter Maggs, and Piers Beirne (1988) (eds. and tr.). "Editors' Introduction" in *Stuchka: Selected Writings on Soviet Law and Marxism*. Armonk, N.Y.: M. E. Sharpe.
Solomon, Peter H. (1985). "Local Political Power and Soviet Criminal Justice, 1922–41," *Soviet Studies* 37:305.
Stuchka, P. I. (1921) (1951). *The Revolutionary Part Played by Law and the State—A General Doctrine of Law*. In John N. Hazard (ed.), *Soviet Legal Philosophy*. Tr. Hugh W. Babb. Cambridge: Harvard University Press.
——— (1925). "Lenin i revoliutsionny dekret" [Lenin and the Revolutionary Decree], *Revoliutsiia prava: Sbornik I*, pp. 33–39.

Thompson, E. P. (1975). *Whigs and Hunters*. London: Penguin.
——— (1980). *Writings by Candlelight*. London: Merlin.
Trotsky, Leon (1975). *My Life*. Harmondsworth: Penguin.
Zile, Zigurds L. (1971). "Lenin's Contribution to Law: The Case of Protection and Preservation of the Natural Environment," in B. W. Eissenstat (ed.), *Lenin and Leninism*. Lexington, Mass.: D. C. Heath.

Chapter 5

Lenin, Crime, and Penal Politics, 1917-1924

Piers Beirne and Alan Hunt

> In the fight against crime the reform of social and political institutions is much more important than the imposition of punishment.
>
> —Lenin (1901a:394)

I. Introduction

In this chapter we examine Lenin's pronouncements on crime and penal politics ("penality") during the critical period of early Bolshevik power between October 1917 and his death in early 1924.

Our intent is twofold. First, it is to extend to Lenin's perspective on crime and penal politics our critical analysis of his view of law and the constitution of Soviet society in the previous chapter (Beirne and Hunt, *supra*, chapter 4). In our analysis there we tried to identify Lenin's diverse views about the nature of legal relations in the period of socialist transition between capitalism and communism. The implications of Lenin's various pronouncements about such relations we placed within a broad conception of the constitution of Soviet society. In that conception, we argued, Lenin failed to secure, or even to specify, a coherent space either for an institutional separation of powers or for a juridical (or other) means of sustaining the boundaries between them. This failure, we concluded, greatly contributed to the intensification of authoritarian centralism during the late 1920s which was, afterwards, a defining characteristic of the Stalinist period. However, as will shortly become clear, we largely disagree with the widely held Whig interpretation (see Gouldner, 1977:7–11; Cohen, 1985:38–70) that, within Russian Bolshevism, the link between Leninism and Stalinism was an ineluctable straight line.

What follows here is an exploration of Lenin's view of a specific aspect of

We wish to thank Peter Solomon for his helpful comments on an earlier version of this chapter.

the constitution of Soviet society, namely, the field of crime and penal politics.[1] As we outline, this field was the object of a mass of pronouncements by Lenin in the early years of Bolshevik power. Given his close and apparently domineering relationship with key Bolshevik personnel in the Commissariat of Justice, such as P. I. Stuchka and D. I. Kursky, it is reasonable to suppose that Lenin must have been aware of and have implicitly condoned all of the major shifts in Bolshevik penal strategies (see, for example, Stuchka, 1925; Pashukanis, 1925). With few exceptions, no decree of importance was enacted in this period without Lenin's direct or indirect approval. He himself wrote and revised hundreds of decrees and other legislative instruments, several of which he actually dictated at CPC meetings. Whenever he presided over these meetings, regardless of who subsequently signed the minutes, it was Lenin who personally worded all the decisions (Bratous, 1970).[2] However, as in his discourse on law and the constitution of Soviet society, Lenin rarely analyzed crime and penality as explicit theoretical objects. For this reason, and also for others that lie within the intellectual history of modern criminology (but which cannot concern us here), there has to date been no sustained treatment of Lenin's conception of the field of crime and penal politics either in the literature of criminology and social control or in that of political theory.

Our second, more expository intention here is therefore to describe Lenin's discourse on crime and penal politics. In this discourse we identify three key elements:

(1) a neoclassical view of criminality in socialist and communist societies;

(2) adherence to various progressive features in Bolshevik penal strategies;

(3) a simultaneously coherent and contradictory fusion, within the penal complex, of strategies of law and terror.

Lenin's discourse on crime and penal politics must be situated in the general context of his political theory, important aspects of which include: the relationship between authoritarian and libertarian tendencies, specifically as this was reproduced in his concept of the dictatorship of the proletariat (hereinafter DoP); whether there was a revolution in Bolshevik penal strategies between 1917 and 1923 and, if so, then of what sort and to what extent; and the paradoxical relation between law and terror, especially as it was manifest in specific fields of the penal complex such as "red terror," show trials, and capital punishment. Our underlying thesis is that the origins of authoritarianism in general, and of authoritarian penal practices in particular, were intrinsic neither to the early Bolshevik project nor to Lenin's discourse as its major exponent. Rather, authoritarianism was the unintended consequence of the silences, omissions, and absences in Lenin's political theory and practice, including its libertarian tendencies. Specifically, it derived from the absence of any sustained theory of what we have designated as the constitution of Soviet society. Finally, by way of tentative conclusion, we summarize the lessons provided by Lenin's contribution to the first socialist experiment in the field of crime and penality.

II. Politics, Law, and Penality

Two key tendencies can be identified in Lenin's diverse theoretical views concerning the constitution of Soviet society: an authoritarian tendency and a libertarian one. It is in the terms of the rhetoric supplied by this couplet of authoritarianism and libertarianism that many of the prevailing questions about Lenin's contribution to Marxist political theory have been couched.[3] For example, was Lenin's claim about the emancipatory *aim* of the revolution—"[w]e do not all differ with the anarchists on the question of the abolition of the state" (1917:436)—a clever strategy to gain the much-needed allegiance, prior to their planned annihilation by the Bolsheviks, of ultraleftists such as anarchists and syndicalists? Which aspect of the couplet of authoritarianism and libertarianism was typically dominant, and why? Did Lenin actually subscribe to both tendencies simultaneously? If he did, was this position one of simple contradiction or, rather, a "realist" one that depended on his pragmatic assessment of the configuration of class forces at any given moment?

Such questions can readily be compressed into yet another: What was the relation between authority and liberty in Lenin's extension of theory to the realm of the concrete? An underlying premise of our argument about Lenin's view of crime and penality is that, although for heuristic purposes they can easily be disengaged, for Lenin himself the tendencies of authoritarianism and libertarianism were not concretely separated in practice by some yawning political chasm. On the contrary, they often overlapped and, ultimately, were indissolubly interwoven. Both libertarianism and authoritarianism lay at the heart of Lenin's crucial concept of the DoP, for example, and nowhere did the convoluted interplay of these tendencies penetrate more deeply than in his classic text on the DoP, the much debated *State and Revolution* (Lenin, 1917).

In *State and Revolution*, Lenin urged that an all-encompassing commitment to the DoP was a defining characteristic of Marxism itself (1917:412; and see 1918:231–242). The practical implications of the role that Lenin envisaged for the DoP during the socialist transition therefore comprised a crucial point of reference next to which his pronouncements about crime and penality should be situated. Lenin was adamant that a Marxist commitment to the DoP had to be practiced at three levels. First, he insisted that the DoP must entail a rigorous and rapid conquest of political power by the revolutionary forces so as to prevent the restoration of the old order. At this level, in its conquest of political power, the DoP was to be an exceptional, quasi-military, and temporary phase needed for securing the complete defeat of the old regime, but not in itself constitutive of socialism. Second, Lenin contended that during the DoP the revolutionary forces should not utilize the institutions of the overthrown capitalist state because these were inappropriate for achieving the objectives of the socialist revolution. This contention, in turn, derived from Lenin's broader thesis that there must be a complete rupture between the periods of capitalism and socialism. To effect this rupture the institutions of the old capitalist state needed to be ruthlessly suppressed and then supplanted by proletarian organizations such as soviets.[4] Third, Lenin urged that the DoP should be a constructive period that actively promotes the institutions and social relations for the transition from socialism to communism. Socialism differed from all earlier revolutions not only because it was the first revolution made on behalf of the majority of the population but also because of the principled importance that it attached to a second (i.e., communist) revolutionary transformation. At this level, then, the DoP was to be less negative and coercive than active and educative in its quest for communism.

In Lenin's view, practical commitment to the DoP involved both an uncompromising insistence on the necessity to smash (*razbit'*) the old order and also a determination to unleash the creative energy of the people. It therefore entailed both authoritarian and libertarian practices. Its authoritarianism was largely predicated on Lenin's insistence that the old order must be utterly smashed—because otherwise, like a weed whose roots are left in the soil, it would reassert itself and eventually suffocate the red flower of the revolution. Its libertarianism cultivated both the unleashing of the creative energies of mass popular initiative unfettered by bureaucratic and legalistic restraints, and also the valorization of spontaneous popular participation in democratic processes associated with the concept of "socialist legality."[5]

Only iron-willed discipline, Lenin reasoned, could transform social relations as thoroughly as this. For Lenin, in other words, authoritarianism and libertarianism were integral parts of the same revolutionary struggle. Only the practice of iron-willed authority could ensure the success of the libertarian project.

Let us reiterate our claim that the libertarian and authoritarian tendencies in Lenin's writings and practice were coterminous in such basic concepts as the DoP. In *State and Revolution*, Lenin (1917; and see 1919e:420) viewed the DoP as a transitional period whose political structure was circumscribed in extent and duration. As Medvedev (1981:47–49) has documented, Lenin subscribed to the classical notion of dictatorship rather than to its post-Machiavellian, modern meaning. He conceived the DoP as a transitional period directed to *both* the completion and consolidation of political power *and* the development of alternative participatory democracy within Soviet power. He saw both strategies as being employed simultaneously and coextensively. Whichever tendency became dominant, this interpretation implies, would depend upon the specific and largely unpredictable configuration of historical forces. For example, had no Western military intervention occurred in 1918 and had the Civil War not been so protracted, then the emergent Soviet society would have developed, or at least could have developed, in a far more libertarian direction. Two such directions did in fact have a brief and prefigurative existence. One direction was the radical libertarian trajectory heralded by the 1921 Kronstadt revolt (Avrich, 1970). The other was the coexistence of different modes of production, and the likelihood of a corresponding political pluralism, that emerged between 1921 and 1923 during the early years of the New Economic Policy (NEP). Although we recognize that the absence in Lenin's texts of a politico-constitutional theory could have resulted in very sharp problems for either of these two trajectories, we disagree with the assumption that the path to authoritarianism was inevitable.

Before we examine Lenin's view of crime and penality, our claim about the theoretico-practical fusion of authoritarianism and libertarianism must be contrasted with the otherwise similar thesis of Polan's (1984) book *Lenin and the End of Politics*. We agree with Polan that authoritarianism was deeply imbricated in *both* the authoritarian *and* libertarian traditions. However, our disagreement is not with Polan's conclusion about the dichotomy of authoritarianism and libertarianism within Leninism.[6] It is with his definition of the two tendencies in Lenin's work as existing in *a priori* contradiction with each other rather than, as we argue, as coterminous. Such an *a priori* characterization largely ignores the fact that Lenin rarely employed these tendencies on the same theoretical or temporal plane. Neither Lenin's intentions nor their cultural effects on the project of socialist emancipation, for example, were necessarily contradictory when he asserted both: (a) "[d]ictatorship . . . is rule based directly upon force and unrestricted by any laws" (1918:236), and (b) "legality must be raised (or rigorously observed), since the basis of laws in the RSFSR has been established" (1918a:110). Couplets such as this pervade Lenin's texts.[7] But only if they are extracted from their specific conditions of production can they be adduced as sufficient evidence for a contradictory political project. In short, their theoretical context, their political objects, and their intended effects resided at quite different levels of analysis, and must therefore be understood as such.[8]

Did Lenin's pronouncements encourage in the domain of penality the institutionalization of a systematic authoritarianism during the period of Stalinism? If so, how, and to what extent? It must be recognized, in addressing these questions, that the same fusion of authoritarianism and libertarianism that resided in Lenin's concept of the DoP also inhabited many of his pronouncements on penality. In the domain of penality an important source of this fusion arose in the political linkages that Lenin encouraged between the socialist law of the DoP and the complex of Bolshevik penal strategies. Although similar in form to its bourgeois counterpart, in that each was commonly seen as a set of injunctions with the whole population as its disciplinary object, the socialist law of the DoP was applauded by Lenin (e.g., 1922c:364; see Beirne and Hunt, *supra*, chapter 4) for its explicit subservience to socialist politics (as in class societies, he insisted, it always was) and to the needs of the revolution.

The principled subservience of socialist law to politics during the DoP was manifest in three major ways.[9] First, the dictates of socialist law were envisaged as providing only a temporary basis for the consolidation of Bolshevik policy. As Lenin himself argued, "In a period of transition, laws have only a temporary validity; and when law hinders the development of a revolution, it must be abolished or amended" (1918o:519). A second linkage forged between socialist law and Bolshevik penal strategies was doctrinal and institutional antiformalism. A key point of reference that allowed the Bolsheviks to distinguish between the forms of social regulation which they were creating and the bourgeois law which they replaced was the "principle of the participation of the working and exploited classes . . . in the administration of the state" (Lenin, 1918n:217). The new institutions of socialist justice were therefore to be liberated from the shackles of bourgeois ideology and composed of a popular rather than a professional staff. The temporary and antiformalist nature of Bolshevik law has been widely recognized in the scholarly literature. But in the early years of Bolshevik power the relation of law to penal strategies had a third, largely unrecognized feature—namely, a differential emphasis upon the legal regulation, control, and discipline of the representatives of Soviet power. Indeed, a distinctive feature of Lenin's approach to crime and penality during the DoP was his insistence that a chief object of socialist law should be the soviet official. However, his views on the use of law to regulate the conduct of party and soviet functionaries should be considered in the context of Lenin's overriding political end, namely, the achievement of the future communist society. To his sparse views on this we now turn.

Among many of the Bolsheviks, including Lenin, there was every expectation that because formal law was essentially a bourgeois phenomenon, nonlegal and socialist forms of regulation would emerge with the weakening of capitalist relations of production. Although he occasionally remarked about these new forms of regulation, it must at once be noted that Lenin (e.g., 1917:457), like Marx and Engels before him, opposed detailed descriptions of the future communist society as fanciful utopianism. One reason for this stance was that he was so involved with the immediate problems of socialist construction that he was simply unable to concern himself with the future communist society, the date of whose introduction he was continually forced to postpone. Another reason is the implicit idealism that he believed to inhere in laboratory-like projections of the good society. Thus,

> what distinguishes Marxism from the old, utopian socialism is that the latter wanted to build the new society not from the mass human material produced by bloodstained, sordid, rapacious, shopkeeping capitalism, but from very virtuous men and women reared in special hothouses and cucumber frames. (1918k:388)

Lenin's brief but significant arguments about the nature of communist social relations were the condensed outcome of his prior analyses of politics, bureaucracy, and culture under conditions of the DoP. Lenin (1917:459–474) envisaged the DoP, or the period of socialist construction, as the first phase of communism. During this first phase he saw the period of the DoP as one in which a "new socialist person" was to be created. This was to be accomplished in a variety of ways, but chiefly in the process of work.

> We must learn to combine the "public meeting" democracy of the working people—turbulent, surging, overflowing its banks like a spring flood—with *iron* discipline while at work. (1918i:271)

Social classes would gradually disappear during socialist construction and so, correspondingly, would the structural sources of social, economic, and political conflict. People would become increasingly accustomed to collective life. All would learn to participate in public life. In turn, and linked with Engels's attractive claim that under communism "the government of persons is replaced by the administration of things" (1880:147), Lenin argued that when

> the more important functions of the state are reduced to such [simplified] accounting and control . . . it will cease to be a "political state" and public functions will lose their political character and become mere administrative functions. (Lenin, 1917:473; see also ibid., 420–421)[10]

> We give the name of communism to the system under which people form the habit of performing their social duties without any special apparatus of coercion, and when unpaid work for the public good becomes a general phenomenon. (1919f:284–285)

Under communism one section of society would no longer dominate others because "people will *become accustomed* to observing the elementary conditions of social life *without violence* and *without subordination*" (Lenin, 1917:424).

Lenin's (1917:464) most extended pronouncement about crime in communist society occurred in *State and Revolution*:

> only communism makes the state absolutely unnecessary, for there is *nobody* to be suppressed—"nobody" in the sense of a *class*, of a systematic struggle against a definite section of the population. We are not utopians, and do not in the least deny the possibility and inevitability of excesses on the part of *individual persons*, or the need to stop *such* excesses. In the first place, however, no special machine, no special apparatus of suppression, is needed for this; this will be done by the armed people themselves, as simply and as readily as any crowd of civilised people, even in modern society, interferes to put a stop to a scuffle or to prevent a woman from being assaulted. And, secondly, we know that the fundamental social cause of excesses, which consist in the violation of the rules of social intercourse, is the exploitation of the people, their want and their poverty. With the removal of this chief cause, excesses will inevitably begin to "*wither away.*" We do not know how quickly and in what succession, but we do know they will wither away. With their withering away the state will also *wither away*. [emphases in original]

Elsewhere Lenin urged that during socialist construction the DoP should be a dictatorship of the people "without any police" (1920b:352), because

> the people, the mass of the population, unorganised, "casually" assembled at the given spot, itself appears on the scene, exercises justice and metes out punishment, exercises power and creates a new, revolutionary law. (ibid., 353)

However, it must be stressed that Lenin's concept of communism was far from being an abolitionist one. In two texts which straddle the October revolution, Lenin (1917:395–401; 1918i) recommended that the strategic objective of the withering away of law should not be nihilist or abolitionist in nature. Instead, its objective was to be the construction of a radically new form of social administration in which the state would disappear. The state would increasingly be dissipated as a mechanism of social power when more and, eventually, all citizens participated, without remuneration, in its activities (Lenin, 1918i:272–273). Only under communism, when social classes and the state have disappeared,

> will democracy begin to *wither away*, owing to the simple fact that, freed from capitalist slavery, from the untold horrors, savagery, absurdities and infamies of capitalist exploitation, people will *become accustomed* to observing the elementary rules of social intercourse . . . without force, without coercion, without subordination. . . . (Lenin, 1917:462)

III. Penal Strategies in the "Normal" State

The entire range of pre-Stalinist Bolshevik penal strategies has tended to be characterized in the rhetoric of the "straight line" theory referred to earlier in this chapter. In this characterization, prominently employed in the analysis of the carceral archipelago by the otherwise instructive writings of Solzhenitsyn (e.g., 1973:26–39), the origins of the Stalinist labor camps, for example, are firmly identified as the expanded focus of the penal strategies of early Soviet power. But this portrayal mistakenly vilifies much in early Bolshevik history that was genuinely enlightened. Indeed, to look backwards from the depths of the gulags, as Solomon (1980:195) has rightly complained,

> is to take a selective or partial view of early Soviet penal history, for the civil war period contained the embryo of another penal policy, a progressive policy, which differed radically from that practiced by the Cheka and OGPU. And it was this progressive policy, not the Cheka's approach, which gained the predominant position during the NEP years.[11]

Although Lenin's own—on balance, unintentional—contribution to the rise of the *gulags* will soon be acknowledged here, it is instructive to indicate, prior to beginning that task, just how enlightened some of the often forgotten "normal" strategies of Bolshevik penality actually were.

In the Neoclassical Vanguard

The Bolshevik theorization of socialist penality embodied, at a very abstract level, various aspects of the terrain of neoclassical criminology emerging elsewhere in Europe (Gsovski and Grzybowski, 1959, 2:926–927; Garland, 1985; Beirne, 1987). The key element in neoclassicism was the compromise established between the overdetermined object of positivist criminology and the volitional legal subject of classical jurisprudence. In Lenin's own implicit theorization, the proper articulation of penal strategies was to be based on a compromise between a positivist concept of crime, on the one hand, and a voluntaristic concept of rehabilitation on the other. While conceptual compromise was the essence of neoclassicism, the many features that clustered around it naturally varied from one country to another.

In the early years of Soviet power, the terms of neoclassicism were erected, first, on the positivist (and largely economistic) assumption that the "causes" of crime lie in exploitative, and especially capitalist, social relations (private property, the capitalist state, ideology, etc.) and second, on the voluntaristic assumption that (except for incorrigible class enemies) the criminal character could be reformed through moral rehabilitation. As we will see, because of his acceptance of the first assumption, Lenin insisted that a chief object of socialist law should be remnants of the old capitalist system and corrupt soviet and party officials. Because of the second assumption, Lenin determined that, with the use of voluntaristic penal strategies associated with socialist construction, it would be possible drastically to reduce the extent of exploitation, violence, and other injustices in the future communist society.

For at least two years after the October 1917 revolution, and despite the publication of numerous decrees in the field of crime and penality, the Bolsheviks were extremely reluctant to articulate in juridical terms the basic concepts underlying their penal strategies. The flexible category of "violation," for example, was often preferred to the legalistic concept of "crime."[12] Juridical concepts such as "guilt" and "responsibility" were condemned as medieval errors, deleted from the vocabulary of criminalization, and replaced by nonlegal concepts such as "social danger" and "social harm." The concept of "punishment," oscillating between repression and education, was retermed "measures of social defense"; "imprisonment" became "deprivation of freedom." The coercive principle of "retribution" was abandoned for the humananistic language of conversion, correction, and reeducation. This doctrinal antiformalism was matched by a desire to deprofessionalize the composition of socialist legal institutions.

Even when compared with other systems of criminal justice elsewhere in Europe, it is fair to say that Russian Bolshevism was in the vanguard of the neoclassical movement. Many of the key strategies of early Bolshevik penality conformed with the neoclassical principles of "rehabilitation" and "individualization." These strategies can be summarized as follows (Dallin and Nicolaevsky, 1947:149–163; Carr, 1960:421–454; Juviler, 1976:35–36; Solomon, 1980:196–199):

• the decriminalization of certain common crimes;

• the use of noncustodial sanctions including fines, suspended sentences, and compulsory work for a great variety of offenses;

• the use of neoclassical principles of sentencing policy that allowed judges to consider a convict's motive, mental capacity, age, social circumstances, and degree of recidivism;

• minimum prison sentences that reflected the aim of rehabilitation rather than retribution, and which led to a reduction in the average length of prison terms actually served;

• a sweeping institutional reform of the prison system, including the introduction of the progressive stage system, semiopen agricultural colonies and educational programs, and socially useful labor (sometimes as a substitute for incarceration) paid at trade union rates;

• a reliance on unsupervised parole; and,

• a great reduction in the use of capital punishment.

Under Lenin's guidance between 1917 and 1923, these innovative policies were inaugurated by the Commissariat of Justice, rapidly and successfully in some spheres but slowly and without visible effect in others.[13] Lenin himself was highly selective in the attention that he gave, or could afford to give, to the various aspects of Bolshevik penality. He rarely concerned himself, for example, with the precise calculus of pain required by neoclassical philosophies of sentencing and incarceration. However, during debates on the 1919 Bolshevik Party Program, Lenin himself urged a reduction in the use of incarceration and he encouraged (1) extensive use of conditional convictions; (2) increased use of public censure; (3) replacement of imprisonment by compulsory labor at home; (4) replacement of prison with educational institutions; and (5) introduction of comrades' courts to handle certain categories of crime (Carr, 1960, 2:421; Bassiouni and Savitski, 1979:189–190).

Lenin recognized that the eradication of the old social order would lead, in the short run, to chaos and to an increase "of crime, hooliganism, corruption, profiteering and outrages of every kind" (1918i:264) during the socialist transition.[14] "To put these down," he continued, "requires time and . . . *an iron hand*" (ibid.). This requirement necessitated "[d]ictatorship . . . government that is revolutionarily bold, swift and ruthless in suppressing both exploiters and hooligans" (ibid., 265).[15]

From the very beginning of the October revolution, the Bolsheviks distinguished between "ordinary" crimes typically committed by the powerless, and "counter-revolutionary crimes" typically committed by those with military, economic, or political power. Lenin himself was not equally concerned with "every kind" of crime; the traditional crimes of the powerless, for example, commanded very little of his attention. Indeed, during the Civil War years (1918–1920) the Bolsheviks altogether abolished certain of these categories, including abortion, some sexual offenses, and most crimes by juveniles.[16]

In 1923, certainly with Lenin's knowledge and probably with his active consent, a special commission (led by the old Bolshevik Aron Solts and the Moscow prosecutor Shmuel Fainblit) granted general amnesty to large numbers of poor peasants convicted of the crime of home brewing (Solomon, 1981:16; Weissman, 1986). Between mid-1924 and early 1925, just after Lenin's death but presumably with his prior knowledge and tacit approval, there was a massive decriminalization of an even wider set of offenses. These included home brewing for personal use, poaching small amounts of timber for personal use, hooliganism committed for the first time, and petty thefts in factories (Solomon, ibid., 16–17).

In many of Lenin's pronouncements, and in much early Bolshevik practice, the crimes of soviet economic and political cadres were as much an object of criminal law as were the typical crimes of the powerless. An important reason why Lenin condemned "red-collar crimes" (Lós, 1988:147) is that he envisaged a simplified bureaucracy as a crucial feature of postrevolutionary society. Thus, he argued that in addition to the chiefly oppressive apparatus (the standing army, the police, and the bureaucracy), the modern state possesses an accounting and bookkeeping apparatus (banks, syndicates, postal service, consumers' societies, and office employees' unions) which will be "the *skeleton* of socialist society" (Lenin, 1917d:106). Lenin himself was especially concerned with two sorts of crime: (i) economic crimes by war-profiteers and remnants of the old bourgeoisie, and (ii) offenses by state officials, whether bureaucrats or party members, that stemmed from or included the abuse of their political power. For the first sort of crime Lenin reserved his most vehement condemnation. Thus, he suggested that war-profiteers "are the worst that [have] remained of the old capitalist system and are the vehicles of all the old evils; these we must kick out . . ." (1918l:468–469). Indeed, one of the very first CEC decrees ("On Workers' Control" of November 1917) ordered that "[t]hose guilty of concealment of materials, products and orders, improper keeping of accounts and other such malpractices are held criminally responsible."[17] In mid-1918, immediately prior to the passage of a new law on embezzlement, Lenin requested that the Commissariat of Justice ensure "speedier and more ruthless court action against the bourgeoisie, embezzlers of state property, etc." (1918m:77). At the same time he demanded the expulsion from the party of judges who had given lenient sentences to four members of the Moscow Commission of Investigation charged with bribery and blackmail (Lenin, 1918h:331, n.317). Again, Lenin insisted that in order to proceed with the nationalization of the banks, "real success must be had" in "catching and *shooting* bribe-takers" (1918i:252; see also 1921g:78). He ordered that "everything must be done" to identify and capture bandits, capitalists, and landowners because they were "saboteurs, who stop at no crime to injure Soviet power" (Lenin, 1919i:556). In June 1921, capital punishment was fixed as the maximum penalty for state officials who aided theft from state warehouses (Hazard, 1951:302).[18] Moreover, it should be stressed that the provisions of the code indicate that the Bolsheviks were more concerned with embezzlement by state officials than by private citizens—the latter could only be punished by incarceration for a period no longer than six months.[19]

Our claim that red-collar criminals (i.e., soviet and party officials) were an important object of Bolshevik criminal law was only implicit in Lenin's writings. Although this claim was never developed theoretically by Lenin himself in the explicit form in which we express it here, it can nevertheless be derived from numerous pronouncements in his writings and speeches. From these it is evident that for Lenin a major object of Soviet law and socialist legality was the disciplining of the agents or representatives of Soviet power. Their somewhat unenviable position derived from Lenin's conception of socialist law as a mechanism for achieving the standards of conduct and responsibility expected of public officials if they were to fulfill their "leading role" as representatives of the most advanced section of the proletariat. Indeed, for all practical purposes, Lenin regarded the encumbents of this role as synonymous with the party membership itself. As occurred so often in Lenin's thought, we find here a mixture of practical exigency and political principle. The practical considerations arising from the immediate requirements of Soviet power entailed reliance upon cadres who were inexperienced, undereducated, and impatient. In this context, it was only to be expected that the agents of Soviet power would commit "errors" and "excesses." Yet these actions provided dangerous ammunition for counterrevolutionary forces, weakened the loyalty of allies, and undermined popular commitment to the socialist project. Accordingly, Lenin reminded the representatives of Soviet power that "the strictest revolutionary order is essential for the victory of socialism" (1917c:241). The violation of legality could have serious political consequences.

> The slightest lawlessness, the slightest infraction of Soviet law and order is a *loophole* the foes of the working people take immediate advantage of, it is a *starting-point* for Kolchak and Denikin victories. (Lenin, 1919i:556)

Similarly, albeit in another context, Lenin stressed the need for the strictest adherence to legality in economic relations with the peasantry so as to preserve and promote the fragile political alliance on which the revolution depended:

> those who contrary to the laws of Soviet power, treat the peasants unjustly must be ruthlessly fought, immediately removed and most severely prosecuted. (Lenin, 1923:502; see also Lenin, 1918j:252; 1919i:556; 1919b; and 1922c)

He argued that the lessons of such mistakes must be recognized and that soviet authorities must investigate, bring to trial, and punish all such "violations" and "excesses." On another occasion (the attempt to develop commodity exchange at the beginning of NEP), Lenin (1921f:387) demanded detailed reports about whether such activities had been investigated and, if so, whether the perpetrators had been punished. In a letter of 1918 to Kursky, he urged that it was essential for a bill to be drawn up prescribing that the penalties for bribery, extortion, and graft should be no less than ten years' imprisonment in addition to ten years of compulsory labor (Lenin, 1918h:331). Significantly, he demanded that differential or exemplary punishments be imposed on party members: "triple penalties should be inflicted on Communists, as compared with non-Party people" (Lenin, 1922:562). Elsewhere, he challenged functionaries in the People's Commissariat of Justice:

> every worker in this Commissariat should be assessed according to his record, on the strength of the following figures: how many Communists have you jailed with triple sentences? . . . How many bureaucrats have you jailed? (Lenin, 1922:562)

Lenin's emphasis on the importance of securing adherence to socialist legality by soviet and party officials was closely associated with his concern about the struggle against bureaucracy. In the period prior to his death he became more strident in his demand for action against the bureaucrats. He ordered that bureaucracy and red tape should be exposed and punished: "We must not be afraid of the courts . . . but must drag bureaucratic delays out into daylight for the people's judgment" (Lenin, 1921:556). He demanded exemplary trials of "the more 'vivid' cases" (Lenin, 1921a:522), and sent numerous missives to the People's Commissariat of Justice for action against red tape and for the reorganization of state control (Lenin, 1918j; 1919c; 1919d:486; 1921b:180; 1921c; and 1922d).

Penality and the Courts

However, the center of Bolshevik penal strategies is not to be found in the differential emphasis on class enemies and red-collar offenders, even though this strategy was arguably Bolshevism's most original feature. Nor, we believe (*pace* Solzhenitsyn), did it lie in the spheres of incarceration and sentencing. Indeed, the precise articulation of these two spheres was conceived by the Bolsheviks as lying at the end point rather than at the center of their policies. At the center of Bolshevik penal strategies were undoubtedly the courts (Hazard, 1960:1–63), the tsarist forms of which Lenin had earlier referred to as "instrument[s] of exploitation" (1918l:464) and "organs of bourgeois rule" (1919j:131; and see Krylenko, 1934:44). Moreover, it was precisely toward the innovative contribution of courts to the revolutionary process that many of Lenin's pronouncements about penality were directed.

One of Lenin's (1901a) earliest commentaries on courts had been sparked by a case of police brutality. Lenin's subsequent attack on the tsarist police was set within the general context of an 1887 law which had removed crimes by and against officials from the jurisdiction of courts sitting with a jury, and which had then transferred them to courts of crown judges and representatives of the estates. In his polemic, he distinguished between the respective merits of "state trials" and "street trials":

> Trial by the street is valuable because it breathes a living spirit into the bureaucratic formalism which pervades our government institutions. The street is interested, not only, and not so much, in the definition of the given offence (insulting behavior, assault, torture), or in the category of punishment to be imposed; it is interested in exposing thoroughly and bringing to public light the significance and all the social and political threads of the crime, in order to draw lessons in public morals and practical politics from the trial. The street does not want to see in the court "an official institution," in which functionaries apply to given cases the corresponding articles of the Penal Code, but a public institution which exposes the ulcers of the present system, which provides material for criticising it and, consequently, for improving it. Impelled by its practical knowledge of public affairs and by the growth of political consciousness, the street is discovering the truth for which our official, professorial jurisprudence, weighed down by its scholastic shackles, is groping with such difficulty and timidity—namely, that in the fight against crime the reform of social and political institutions is much more important than the imposition of punishment. (Ibid., 393–394)

Lenin concluded that street justice was the better form of justice, especially if the citizenry was sufficiently educated to understand and press for its "rights."[20] While Lenin never advocated street justice as a form of proletarian regulation, his polemic here disclosed his abiding preference for a system that was "closer to the people" than formalistic adjudication. Indeed, after the ravages of the Civil War, Lenin stressed that the Russian people had previously experienced courts as external impositions, as exclusively coercive and oppressive. This experience inculcated a negative response, itself part of the general backwardness of Russian civil society that was akin to a "semi-savage habit of mind" and an "ocean of illegality" that was "the greatest obstacle to the establishment of law and culture" (Lenin, 1922c:365).

So important to Lenin was the role of the courts during the DoP that the first legislation on courts (Decree No. 1 on the Court) was enacted only a few weeks after the October revolution, in November 1917. The Decree (as modified several times in the next seven months) dictated the basic elements of the new court system and abolished existing legal institutions such as the Procuracy, the Bar, and all but the most basic of laws.[21] It transpires, in numerous of Lenin's pronouncements, that from the beginning of the revolution the new Bolshevik system of courts was burdened with a heavy political agenda. While the local and people's courts had ordinary crimes as their chief targets, the revolutionary tribunals were created to combat counterrevolutionary forces. By order of Trotsky, in 1917, military discipline was to be adjudicated through a system of comrades' courts. Apart from eradicating the old social order, the courts were to be a leading agency for the inculcation and propagation of socialist virtues. As Lenin put it: "the courts . . . have another, still more important task . . . [namely] to ensure the strictest discipline and self-discipline of the working people'' (Lenin, 1918n:217; and see 1918c). Thus, Lenin wrote:

> Soviet power . . . immediately threw the old court on the scrap-heap. By that we paved the way for a real people's court, and not so much by the force of repressive measures as by massive example, the authority of the working people, without formalities; we transformed the court from an instrument of exploitation into an instrument of education on the firm foundations of socialist society. There is no doubt that we cannot attain such a society at once. (1918l:464; see also 1921d:351)

Lenin played an important part in forming the structure of the revolutionary tribunals, and he insisted that they be set up to deal with ''counter-revolutionaries, bribe-takers, disorganisers and violators of discipline'' (1918q:220). He intended that, taken together, these courts would spearhead the elimination of the old social order and also propagate discipline and culture. In the context of addressing the question of how to restore the ''discipline and self-discipline'' of the masses, Lenin offered some comments about the dual roles of the new courts:

> [S]pecial mention should be made of the important role now devolving on the courts of law. In capitalist society, the court was mainly an instrument of oppression, an instrument of bourgeois exploitation. Hence the bounden duty of the proletarian revolution lay not in reforming the judicial institutions . . . but in completely destroying and razing to its foundations the whole of the old judicial apparatus. . . . The new court has been needed first and foremost for the struggle against the exploiters. . . . But, in addition, the courts—if they are really organised on the principle of Soviet institutions—have another, still more important task. This task is to ensure the strictest discipline and self-discipline of the working people. (1918n:217)

Like socialist legal institutions as a whole, the new courts were intended to be temporary, popular in composition, and selective in their handling of different categories of crime and criminality.[22] The new courts were quite explicitly located at a lower level, and included local (later, people's) courts and revolutionary tribunals. The local courts were devised for civil cases involving suits not exceeding 3,000 roubles and for criminal cases punishable with not more than two years imprisonment. They were to be staffed by a permanent local judge and two alternate assessors who were instructed to abide by the old laws insofar as they had not been abolished by the revolution and contradicted neither revolutionary conscience nor revolutionary legal consciousness.

We can discern several new features about the new courts. First, there was an attempt to politicize their principles of adjudication. For example, in trying cases, the courts were instructed to be guided by extant laws if they had not been annulled by the CEC or CPC and if they did not contradict socialist legal conscience.[23] Again, for both civil and criminal cases the existing courts' rules of procedure were held to be operative only if they did not "run counter to the legal consciousness of the working classes."[24] People's courts were to be free from formal considerations when deciding what evidence to accept as relevant in a given case.[25] In all cases, courts were not to be bound by formal law at the expense of substantive justice.[26] According to Decree No. 3 on the Court (July 1918), which increased the jurisdiction of the local courts, judges were henceforth never to permit formalities to hinder a just decision.[27]

Second, the staff of the new courts was popularized. As Lenin explained about the soviet courts, "we did not have to create a new apparatus, because anybody can act as a judge basing himself on the revolutionary sense of justice of the working class" (1919g:182). Moreover, a note added to Decree No. 2 on the Court declared that the size of the daily fees of assessors was to be determined by the soviets, "bearing in mind the gradual obligatory transition to gratuitous performance by citizens of the state duty of administering justice."

Third, some concern was shown with respect to due process and procedural safeguards. For example, according to Decree No. 2 on the Court, there was to be a limited system of appeals from the new people's courts of 1918 overseen by a Supreme Supervisory Authority in Petrograd.[28] The types of cases that could be appealed were expanded in 1918.[29] In July 1918 the Commissariat of Justice issued an Instruction, signed by Stuchka, about procedure in the people's courts.[30] Procedural rules were largely confined to the pretrial stage and related to jurisdiction, the calling of witnesses, and sufficiency of evidence. These instructions were expanded by the Decree on the People's Court of November 30, 1918, and here we meet the first mention of appeal for procedural errors and violations: decisions could be overturned if court procedure was violated.

However, in certain key respects it is evident that all was not well with the new court structure. Lenin's position about the simplification of state functions produced by popular participation in the courts, for example, probably remained largely exhortatory. According to the Bolshevik Vinokurov (cited in Hazard, 1960:389), by 1924 the courts were largely proletarian in composition: 87 percent of the people's judges and 72 percent of the judges in the provincial courts were of worker or peasant background; 75 percent of the former and 80 percent of the latter were Bolsheviks. But, from the NEP onwards, Lenin's mounting concern with bureaucracy attested to events actually in conflict with the universal participation to which he was committed. Moreover, he never addressed the project of administrative democracy in concrete terms. In 1918 it was provided that old legal officials could still be elected to both judicial and investigation institutions.[31] Thus, exactly how influential Decree No. 1 was in practice is unclear. Stuchka, the second Commissar of Justice, wrote in August 1918 that some jurisdictions had already replaced the old courts before the Decree's enactment, while others had been unable to replace them after it; the central authorities had to content themselves with the issuance of general directives (see further Hazard, 1960:8 and n.16). Lenin himself complained that

> our revolutionary and people's courts are extremely, incredibly weak. One feels that we have not yet done away with the people's attitude toward the courts as something official and alien. . . . It is not yet sufficiently realised that the courts are an organ which enlists precisely the poor, every one of them, in the work of state administration. (1918c:266)

Problems of the composition of the new court structure were exacerbated, moreover, by a certain confusion which Lenin, unintentionally and carelessly, created in the respective jurisdictions of the different courts. For example, he demanded that the People's Commissariat of Justice should push the people's courts to conduct "noisy model trials" (Lenin, 1922:561–562) of those who abused NEP; yet, at the same time, he urged that such trials (specifically, of bureaucratic negligence) should be held in the revolutionary tribunals (Lenin, 1922a). Therefore, there was also an increasing blur between political crimes and ordinary crimes. This was itself intensified by the lack of clear guidelines between the types of crime respectively dealt with by the people's courts and the revolutionary tribunals.

Thus far, we have suggested no more than that in the differential objects of its criminal law lay the seeds of a revolution in the "normal" strategies of Bolshevik penality. In that Bolshevik penality had as its chief objects the illegalities of soviet and party officials, rather than those of the powerless Russian masses, its intentions were arguably quite revolutionary. The neoclassical principles of Bolshevik penality were undoubtedly far more enlightened than either the antiquated policies of the tsarist system or the classical schemes of the Socialist Revolutionaries (SRs), their main rivals for power.

IV. Penal Strategies in the "Exceptional" State

Our concern now is to explore the extent to which Lenin encouraged the use of *exceptional* forms of penal strategies. Was this encouragement linked to, or did it even cause, the low priority accorded to individual civil liberties and lack of legal constraints on party and state power in the subsequent history of Soviet society? E. H. Carr has identified the paradox of the Bolshevik conception of crime as the product of a disordered society and punishment as an act of reclamation and education, on the one hand, and the Bolshevik use of revolutionary terror to combat counterrevolution on the other (1960, 2:421–422).

> The paradox of the tension between ultimate humanitarian ideals and the immediate necessities of a revolutionary situation was . . . particularly acute. The tension could be resolved only on the heroic assumption that the harshest

> penalties applied to class enemies were temporary measures necessitated by the revolutionary struggle for power, and had nothing in common with the permanent methods and policies of the régime. (Ibid., 421)

By way of responding to this paradox, we should begin by noting that Lenin's libertarianism was significantly *weaker*, in a specific sense, than his authoritarianism. However, it was not "weaker" because he was less strongly committed to his libertarianism, but because he failed either to specify or to create the organizational and institutional forms for its realization. In contrast, Lenin's authoritarianism can properly be seen as the *dominant* element within Bolshevism precisely because its manifestations secured early institutional expression. Only in this specific sense, we suggest, is it correct to identify a strong continuity between Leninism and Stalinism. Indeed, Lenin's view of the authoritarian dimension of the DoP never amounted to an endorsement of unbridled violence or to an abstract preference for centralism. So, Lenin insisted that

> as the fundamental task of the government becomes, not military suppression, but administration, the typical manifestation of suppression and compulsion will be, not shooting on the spot, but trial by court. (Lenin, 1918i:266)

How, then, can we account for Lenin's encouragement of *specific* facets of the arsenal of authoritarianism, namely, the various strategies that we have thus far referred to as those of the "exceptional" state? We will explore this thorny question by briefly considering his views on three items in the authoritarian inventory: model (or "show") trials, capital punishment, and "red terror."

Model Trials

Lenin undoubtedly bears some historical responsibility for the Soviet institution of the model or "show" trial. Consistent with our rejection of the thesis of simple linearity between Leninist and Stalinist authoritarianism, our view is that Lenin's use of show trials unwittingly provided the institutional framework later deployed with such devastating effect in the Stalinist 1930s. However, whereas Lenin typically conceived of show trials as vehicles of public education, their very publicity was transformed in the 1930s into a purely repressive mechanism that served to inhibit and eventually to destroy all possibility of legalized political opposition.

Model trials do not seem to have been conceived of by Lenin in the same sense of stagedness as used later in Stalin's show trials. In 1922 Lenin sent instructions to the People's Commissariat of Justice insisting that "several model trials" be held in Moscow, Petrograd, and other key centers (1922:561; 1922a). The chief purpose of these trials was to ensure that counterrevolutionaries knew that their crimes would be detected, tried, and punished according to law. At the same time, these trials were to be held in conjunction with educative political meetings and with the widest possible press coverage. Lenin's espousal of these public displays was premised on a belief in their potential educative value in underlining and publicizing the policy and the ethics of socialism. For example, he wrote to the Moscow Revolutionary Tribunal about a case of bureaucratic procrastination that

> it is of exceptional importance—both from the Party and the political standpoint—to have the proceedings in the red tape case arranged with the greatest solemnity, making the trial *educational*, and the trial sufficiently impressive. (Lenin, 1921e:348)

The most important, and the most well known model trial with which Lenin was associated was that of the leadership of the Right Socialist Revolutionaries (SRs) in mid-1922.[32] While allowing that the Bolsheviks acted abominably during the SR trial (see e.g., Burbank, 1986:108–110), it is nevertheless difficult to determine Lenin's conduct in it. According to the very partisan account of Jansen (1982:27), for example, Lenin orchestrated the entire affair, despite his grave illness. Yet others have suggested, implicitly (Carr, 1961, 1:189) or explicitly (Medvedev, 1971:382), that Lenin, who was seriously ill during the whole trial, played no role in it at all, and that it had been instigated by the Chekist leader (Dzerzhinsky), and organized by the General Secretary (Stalin).

The trial of the SRs resulted in considerable opposition from all branches of the international socialist movement, and a delegate from the Comintern—meeting with representatives from the other two Socialist Internationals—agreed that the Soviet government would allow international observers at the trial and that it would not apply the death penalty against any of the defendants. Lenin disagreed with these concessions. But having argued his case, he concluded that, an agreement having been made, the Bolsheviks should adhere to it (Lenin, 1922b:330).[33]

It is perhaps strange that Lenin should have been opposed to the participation of foreign observers since, if nothing else, publicity for the Bolshevik contention about the duplicity of the SRs would have been maximized by the presence of foreign observers. Because such trials were consciously transformed into political events, they necessarily generated demands for observer status from other interested groups. It is perhaps fair to say that Lenin's opposition articulated a persistent Soviet preoccupation with the right to national self-determination—which implied a sharp separation between internal and external affairs. The logic of the show trial, which Stalin understood better than Lenin, was that the greatest impact could be achieved with the maximum internationalization of the proceedings. It seems clear that Lenin had not thought through the logic of the maximum use of show trials as a political strategy, nor did they play anything more than an occasional role in early Soviet political life. Their elaboration and full deployment was, of course, to come later; however, while Lenin's authoritarianism coexisted with his libertarianism in an uneasy and often contradictory tension, no such ambiguity existed in the social order of Stalinism.

Capital Punishment

Any discussion of Lenin's position on capital punishment must acknowledge a cardinal distinction between those who were executed according to the due processes of Bolshevik law, on the one hand, and those who died through extralegal (although often officially approved) means in the course of purges, for example, or during the Red Terror, on the other. In what follows we begin with a discussion of the former.

Although Lenin clearly shared the traditional hostility of Russian progressive thought to state executions, he nevertheless maintained an ambivalent position toward capital punishment.[34] In February 1917 Kerensky's Provisional Government had abolished the death penalty. The abolition was met with unanimous approval, although there was a deafening silence about it in the Bolshevik press (*Pravda* and *Izvestiia*)—a silence that probably indicated a refusal to pay any tribute to the government, rather than any hostility to the measure itself. One month later, with the impending collapse of the Russian army, the Provisional Government restored the death penalty for "traitorous" soldiers at the front. The Bolsheviks, in alliance with the SRs, now campaigned actively for its abolition. However, there is some evidence to suggest that, even at this time, Lenin himself would have supported the retention of the death penalty for class enemies. For example, in a brief discussion of the Petrograd Soviet's resolution to abolish capital punishment, which he supported, Lenin remarked that "the situation would be different if it were a weapon against the landowners and capitalists" (1917f:263).[35]

In one of its first decrees, in November 1917, the Second Congress of Soviets abolished capital punishment. Lenin was not apparently present, although Trotsky reported that at the time Lenin had reservations about the abolition. Moreover, Trotsky attributed to Lenin the observation that "[t]his is madness. . . . How can we accomplish a revolution without shooting?" (1925:133).[36] Trotsky's report of Lenin's attitude is confirmed in one of Lenin's own pamphlets written in mid-1917:

> It is right to argue against the death penalty only when it is applied by the exploiters against the *mass* of the working people. . . . It is hardly likely that any revolutionary government whatever could do without applying the death penalty to the *exploiters*. (Lenin, 1917a:341)

In the early days of the revolution the Bolsheviks tended to be noticeably lenient with their opponents, often being content to disarm them and then to set them free (Carr, 1950, 1:150–162). By Lenin's own account, "[w]hen we arrested anyone we told him we would let him go if he gave us a written promise not to engage in sabotage" (Lenin, 1917b:294). However, the death penalty reemerged as the Civil War intensified, although not through any formal decision. The evidence suggests that the Cheka began to carry out executions in February 1918; the first summary executions were of bandits, speculators, and blackmailers rather than political enemies (van den Berg, 1983:155). In June 1918, the revolutionary tribunals began imposing the death penalty without regard to the absence of any jurisdictional authority to do so. With Wrangel's military activity in the Crimea and with the Poles advancing in the Ukraine, the use of the death penalty became more regular. Now Lenin openly defended capital punishment and advocated its extension to ever wider categories of opponents. During War Communism and the Civil War these new categories included the avoidance of labor service (1918c:33); unlicensed possession of arms (1918d:35); indiscipline in the supply services (1918e:406); prostitution (1918f:349); those assisting the "predatory campaign of the Anglo-French imperialists," if resisting arrest (1918p:114–115), "formal and bureaucratic attitudes to work" in the food-purchasing board (1919:499); and informers giving false information (1918g:115).[37] At the beginning of NEP Lenin also showed a willingness to broaden the categories of those liable for capital punishment; these new categories included "abuse of NEP" (1922:561); assistance to the international bourgeoisie and striving to overthrow the communist system of property by violence, blockade, espionage, financing the press (1922e).

However, in early 1920, after Denikin's defeat, Lenin again placed the abolition of the death penalty on the agenda. The use of terror had only been imposed, he argued, in response to counterrevolutionary terrorism. With victory, he insisted, "we shall renounce all extraordinary measures" (Lenin, 1920:328). In the same month, he referred more cautiously to the same decision to end Cheka's use of the death sentence: "[A] reservation was made at the very beginning that we do not by any means close our eyes to the possibility of restoring capital punishment" (Lenin, 1920a:167). Capital punishment was restored in early May 1920.

Finally, reference should be made to the statutory provisions for capital punishment enacted while Lenin was in power, especially those contained in the RSFSR Criminal Code of 1922. It should be noted that, during the debates prior to enactment of the Code, considerable protest (led by Riazanov) had occurred among the Bolsheviks about the restoration of capital punishment (Adams, 1972:82). While the CEC was preparing the draft, Lenin wrote to Kursky, then Commissar of Justice, urging that the death penalty be used against those assisting the international bourgeoisie (1922e:358; and see van den Berg, 1983:156). The 1922 Code contained a large number (forty-seven) of capital offenses—and to these should be added nine more offenses that violated a decree or an administrative order. Significantly, the language of the Code revealed a serious intent by the Bolsheviks to punish by death an almost unique concatenation of crimes: crimes by and against public officials, counterrevolutionary crimes, military crimes, economic crimes, and crimes against socialist property. Indeed, for only three "ordinary" crimes (robbery, aggravated rape, and aggravated murder) was the death penalty in effect. According to Adams's content analysis of Soviet decrees and statutes relating to capital punishment, these three had a far lower likelihood of being carried out than most other capital offenses (Adams, 1972:89–90).[38]

It is important to draw attention to the consequences of the particular way in which these capital offenses were drafted. Some offenses were defined in such a way as to require no proof either of specific conduct or of determinable intent. Rather, they explictly required ex post facto judgement as to the political ramifications of the conduct complained of. Thus, for example, "sabotage" (*diversiia*) and "wrecking," "participation in a counterrevolutionary organization," "undermining state institutions," and "aiding the international bourgeoisie" were all extremely broad catch-all offenses.[39] Indeed, Lenin's dislike of legal formalism predisposed him to favor broad statutory provisions, of which the avoidance of repressive interpretation could be entrusted to the good sense of the proletarianized courts. There is an obvious naivety in this cavalier rejection of legal formalism, to which we will soon return.

About Lenin's several views on capital punishment, then, it can be said that they entailed a tension unresolved by the explanation that he only accepted its use in the extreme conditions of Civil War. As van den Berg writes, "already under Lenin, the direct relationship between the necessity of terror in a revolution and the death penalty no longer governed actual policy" (1983:156). Once introduced on grounds of expedience, then legitimized, and finally expanded in scope, capital punishment later became so familiar a feature of the political landscape that there was only minimal resistance to its reintroduction as a normal strategy for responding to political disputes.

Red Terror

Both model trials and capital punishment were important parts of the exceptional penal strategies directed to the establishment of Bolshevik hegemony. They were exceptional not only because, unlike the neoclassical strategies of Bolshevism discussed earlier in this chapter, they were understood to embody authoritarian rather than libertarian practices, but also because their use was expected to be of short duration.

The third and most insidious weapon in the arsenal of exceptional penal strategies was undoubtedly terrorism, officially referred to by the Bolsheviks themselves as "red terror." The several organs of red terror were a crucial aspect of Bolshevik penal strategies during and after the Civil War. Institutionally, they included an extensive secret police network (the infamous Cheka), the revolutionary tribunals, and a special system of camps that originally existed in parallel with the prisons of the neoclassical regime. Local units of the Cheka soon comprised a grid covering the entire Soviet Republic—all major cities, county seats, provincial capitals, railroads, ports, and the army (Heller and Nekrich, 1986:65).

As we have seen, Lenin's principled opposition to terrorism before 1917 stands in stark contrast to the emergence, and his own explicit endorsement of, red terror during and after the period of the Civil War.[40] What was involved in Lenin's apparent change of position toward terror?

Prior to 1917, Lenin had emphasized that the struggle for democracy was a necessary stage of development within the prebourgeois political formation of tsarist Russia. In this he differed profoundly from the many Russian political movements which advocated almost unqualified terrorism (Woodcock, 1963:376–400). His clear and unambiguous message was that Russian revolutionaries should campaign without violence for the realization of bourgeois democracy and legality because it offered the most advantageous conditions for the development of the struggle against both tsarism and the bourgeoisie, of whom the latter Lenin (1905:300) insisted were the long-term enemy.[41] Indeed, immediately after the seizure of power, Lenin denied that Bolsheviks had engaged in terrorism. In November 1917, for example, he wrote, "we are accused of resorting to terrorism, but we have not resorted, and I hope will not resort, to the terrorism of the French revolutionaries who guillotined unarmed men" (Lenin, 1917b:294).

Lenin consistently criticized political tendencies that resorted to terroristic forms of struggle. He employed two main arguments against terrorism. Firstly, he argued that it was an essentially petty-bourgeois activity (e.g., Lenin, 1902:471). This was so because it expressed the opportunism of those intellectuals who, lacking systematic contact with either the working class or the peasantry, were inclined to favor spontaneity and sensationalism. As a political strategy, terrorism was opposed to mass political action. Second, he insisted that it was futile to engage in abstract discussions of terrorism "in principle" (e.g., Lenin 1901:19). Against such abstractions, Lenin countered that the issue should be posed in terms of whether or not terrorism was appropriate or harmful "under the present conditions." There is no trace in his extensive discussion of the concept of the DoP of any *general* or principled endorsement of revolutionary terror.

We therefore reject the popular view (e.g. Leggett, 1975) that all along Lenin was a covert authoritarian and that, having secured political power, he at once displayed his "true colors." Rather, we suggest that his endorsement of terror was largely a response to the brutal reality of the "white terror" unleashed by the forces of the counterrevolution.[42] The establishment of repressive organs such as the Cheka and the revolutionary tribunals was an urgent response to the military fact that, barely six weeks after the revolution, southeastern Russia was overrun by Cossack armies and other white forces, western Russia was threatened by the Germans, and the Ukraine was heavily infiltrated by French and British influence. "At the critical moment of a hard-fought struggle," reflects E. H. Carr, "the establishment of these organs can hardly be regarded as unusual" (1950, 1:167–168). Moreover, Chekist energies were at first only directed to (i) the sabotage of Bolshevik administration by the bourgeoisie, (ii) destruction and rioting by drunken mobs and, (iii) banditry "under the flag of anarchism" (see Carr, ibid.).[43] The particular combination of external military intervention and internal civil war added a real desperation to the maintenance of power, and Lenin's urgent telegrams to the "fronts" in 1918 and 1919 reveal the perilous circumstances of Bolshevik power. In these circumstances the resort to terror, for Lenin, was an unavoidable necessity. Characteristically, Lenin made a virtue out of necessity. He thus explicitly argued for the political necessity of resorting to revolutionary terror—red terror, in contrast to the white terror of the counterrevolution.

At the same time, however, Lenin increasingly began to argue for the regularization and even the "legalization" of red terror. He wrote to Zinoviev, for example, only four days before an assassination attempt on his own life, criticizing him for restraining Petrograd workers who wanted to respond with mass terror to the murder of a leading Bolshevik. Instead of restraint, urged Lenin, "[w]e must encourage the energy and mass character of the terror against the counterrevolutionaries" (1918b:336). As an objective, moreover, the regularization of red terror outlasted the most perilous period of the Civil War. Soon thereafter, according to Trotsky's recollection, "at every passing opportunity" Lenin now began to equate the DoP with the absolute necessity of the terror (1925:137–138).[44] About a new article for inclusion in the Criminal Code that would justify and legalize the institutionalization of terror, Lenin wrote to Commissar of Justice Kursky that

> the courts must not ban terror—to promise that would be deception or self-deception—[we] must formulate the motives underlying it, legalise it as a principle, plainly, without any make-believe or embellishment. (1922e:358)

His very next sentence has considerable import:

> It must be formulated in the broadest possible manner, for only revolutionary law and revolutionary conscience can more or less widely determine the limits within which it should be applied. (1922e:358)

From a temporary and exceptional penal strategy, then, red terror had by 1922 been more or less consciously perverted by Lenin and transformed into a normal one. It is not possible here to address either the dimensions or the putative justifications of Lenin's contribution to this double perversion, a tragic transformation the concrete unfolding of which has been presented in great detail elsewhere (e.g., Shub, 1948; Carr, 1960, 2:421–454; Andics, 1969; Bettelheim, 1976). However, we would be remiss if we failed to point out that, when normal and exceptional penal strategies are so conflated, red terror is nothing less than official lawlessness. The very problem of official lawlessness, of which Lenin was so well aware, and which returns us to our original argument about Lenin's inadequate theorization of the constitution of Soviet society, demanded mechanisms of regulation involving a certain degree of separation of powers. The absence of such mechanisms, whilst not in itself authoritarian, created the conditions in which official lawlessness was able to flourish, as it did under Stalinism.

Nowhere were the consequences of the absence of mechanisms for "policing the police" more dire than in the intersection of Chekist practices with the attempted development of neoclassical forms of incarceration. Indeed, the gradual transformation of the enlightened, neoclassical prisons into the infamous system of gulags originated in the indistinct boundaries between the jurisdiction of the courts and the legal (and extralegal) activities of the Cheka—a deadly muddle to which Lenin, with his disdain for legal formalism, decidedly contributed but which, at the same time, he clearly did not intend (Feldbrugge, 1986).[45] During his last attendance at a Party Congress, Lenin (1922g) somewhat obliquely bemoaned the overinvestment of carceral power in the security apparatuses. Far too late, in other words, Lenin himself seems pathetically to have realized that when in the same political project libertarianism and unchecked authoritarianism intersect, libertarianism is inevitably the bloody loser.

V. Conclusion

> Freedom only for the supporters of the government, only for the members of one party—however numerous they may be—is no freedom at all. Freedom is always and exclusively freedom for the one who thinks differently. Not because of any fanatical concept of "justice" but because all that is instructive, wholesome and purifying in political freedom depends on this essential characteristic, and its effectiveness vanishes when "freedom" becomes a special privilege.
>
> —Rosa Luxemburg (1918:69)

In this chapter we have offered what we believe is a necessary palliative to the widely held view that the chief source of the degeneration of Soviet society was the dominance of the authoritarian over the libertarian tendencies within Bolshevism. The authoritarian roots of Leninist penality, we have suggested, lay in *both* the authoritarian and libertarian tendencies within his political thought, and in the specific combination of the two that was manifest in his chosen penal strategies. Within both these traditions there was a failure to advance, either theoretically or concretely, a model of political and constitutional relations that could provide and secure the minimum conditions of democratic life under socialism. These provisions would have needed to include a secure public space for political discussion and political competition. Additionally, they would have needed to specify and to mandate the policing of the boundaries between the different levels of institutional powers and competencies.

An inescapable tension existed between the regularization or legalization of suppression against "counterrevolutionary crimes" and the reliance upon mass initiative and revolutionary conscience to govern the circumstances and the degree of its operation. Ultimately, Lenin's position amounted to an act of political faith in the moral rectitude either of the proletariat as a whole, or of party members and state officials, that legal powers would be applied with circumspection and good judgment. With his disdain for legal formalism, and his tendency to castigate all legally empowered rights as intrinsically bourgeois, Lenin failed to provide any institutional guarantees against the abuse or violation of rules by individual agents of revolutionary power. Such provision, characteristically, is a distinguishing feature of the doctrine of "the rule of law."

But we should not be understood as advancing the naive position that all would have been well if Lenin had insisted on the institutionalization of the rule of law. Commitment to "the rule of law," of course, does not in itself guarantee that official lawlessness is effectively banished. Rather, we hold the view that Lenin can, and indeed must, be criticized for relying on the naive and moralistic view that political commitment can in itself be a guarantee against authoritarian practices by party and state officials. Lenin's position was epitomized in his letter to Kursky in the alternative drafts of the definition of "counterrevolution":

> *Variant 1:* Propaganda or agitation, or membership of, or assistance given to organisations the object of which . . . is to assist that section of the international bourgeoisie which refuses to recognise the rights of the communist system of ownership. . . . (1922ea:358)

> *Variant 2:* Propaganda or agitation that objectively serves . . . the interests of that section of the international bourgeoisie which (as above). . . . (1922ea:359)

Lenin indicated his preference for *Variant* 2. The contrast is clearly posed. The former required both some identifiable conduct and an intention, such as to assist an external political agent. The latter had no requirement either of specified conduct or of intention; it sufficed that there was some conjuncture which could be construed as "serving the interests of the international bourgeoisie." The application of such a rule required great and, we suggest, unreasonable faith in "revolutionary conscience," quite apart from its inherent capacity to spill over into a license for generalized repression.

Lenin clearly attached great significance to a combination of socialist legality, nonlegalistic rules (such as exhortation to revolutionary conscience) and, beginning with the Civil War and War Communism, the several organs of red terror. This combination vividly emerged in a set of draft theses on "strict observance of the laws." Here Lenin urged that "emergency measures of warfare against counterrevolution should not be restricted by the laws." Such measures were subject to what is in essence both a declaratory and reporting condition that

> an exact and formal statement be made by the appropriate Soviet body or official to the effect that the special conditions of civil war and the fight against counterrevolution require that the limits of the law be exceeded. (Lenin, 1918a:110)

This provision was self-evidently dependent upon officials' revolutionary conscience, and Lenin clearly had such a generalized confidence. It may be significant that he was himself prepared to intervene, to demand explanation, or to institute investigation where some irregularity or persecution had been reported to him. However, personal intervention depends on the disposition and prestige of the leader, of the flow of information and access to the leader. Such a system cannot itself be a solution to the supervision and control of exceptional powers.

What emerges from and extends beyond Lenin's practical and exhortatory concern to punish violations by soviet officials is a broad conception of socialist legality as an appeal to an exemplary moral order. How far is it correct to push the analogy between the conception of the party and that of an elect moral agency? Lenin himself would have clearly rejected such an analogy as confusing the role of example and leadership with that of an idealist conception of moral agency. However, it remains true that there was a serious tension in Lenin's thought between a materialism, which rejected concepts like moral agency, and a voluntarism, which emphasized the role of will and determination as final arbiters of the historical process. This dualism is not unique to Marxism but it lies at its core. It is epitomized in Marx's own celebrated dictum that "[m]en make their own history, but they do not make it just as they please" (Marx, 1852, 1:398). Indeed, in *State and Revolution* Lenin was virtually silent about the question of the relation between the party and the masses. His sole mention of this question is pregnant with dangerous possibilities:

> By educating the workers' party, Marxism educates the vanguard of the proletariat, capable of assuming power and *leading the whole people* to socialism, of directing and organising the new system, of being the teacher, the guide, the leader of all the working and exploited people in organising their social life. . . . (Lenin, 1917:404)

The key feature of this formulation is its overinvestment in the voluntarist burden allocated to party personnel. Our contention is not simply a version of a skepticism which denies the very possibility of an organic relation between party and masses. Rather, we have been anxious to focus attention on Lenin's disregard of the need for the institutional protection of legal and political processes from bureaucratic or authoritarian tendencies. These absences are consistent with, but not necessarily justified by, Lenin's sincerely held view that the exceptional measures he advocated were only to be short-lived, a necessary but temporary consequence of the need to secure power and to defeat the counterrevolution in the Civil War.

The libertarian strain in Lenin's thought was undoubtedly conceived as the dynamic element initiating the long road to the communist future. The self-activating participatory democracy of Lenin's conception of communism was accorded no resources apart from its own revolutionary consciousness. Without proper resources it was unable to resist the institutionalization of the dual process of exceptionalism and bureaucratism; it simply had no supports or guarantees outside the voluntaristic inspiration of the revolutionary élan once that institution had itself become an agency of the very exceptionalism and bureaucratism which undercut its revolutionary vocation. Thus, the conjunctural history of the revolution and its institutionalization became the bearer of precisely those processes which first postponed, and then abandoned, the experimental and humanitarian impulse of Bolshevik penal strategies.

Notes

1. According to one secondary source, although we have been unable to confirm this in any original texts, Lenin "gave his approval to the study of crime and penal practices, in the apparent hope that progress would result from such study" (Connor, 1969:28). In our analysis we ignore the many occasions when Lenin used only polemically the vocabulary of crime and penality and with no serious theoretical intent. In *Lenin's Collected Works* we have therefore ignored such meaningless entries as, for example, Lenin's utterance about a conference to found a Third International in August 1917, that "[i]t would be simply criminal to postpone now the calling of a conference of the Left" (1917e:321).

2. These diverse activities still seem to provide theoretical grist for the understanding of crime and penality. Indeed, several recent texts (e.g., Bucholz, Hartman, Lekschas, and Stiller, 1974; Bassiouni and Savitski, 1979:101–129; Avanesov, 1981; Korobeinikov, 1985; and Vigh, 1985) profess to have discovered the relevance of Lenin's pronouncements for a modern-day socialist criminology. According to Bucholz et al., for example, "socialist criminology sees the Marxist-*Leninist* concept of the causes of crime as its principal scientific foundation" (1974:8) [our emphasis]. However, this "Marxist-Leninist" criminology has very little to do with socialism or, indeed, with the respective projects of Marx, Engels, and Lenin. Far from it, it most closely resembles a crude amalgam of biologism and late-1940s structural functionalism, whose combined objects are well-worn and bankrupt concepts like "criminology as science," "causes of crime," "criminal personality," "criminological prediction," and "organization of social prevention."

3. We firmly reject the view that Lenin covertly subscribed to only one aspect of this couplet and that his pronouncements about the other aspect were mere facade. Anticipatory versions of our account of the relation between the authoritarian and libertarian tendencies can be found in the dichotomy of popular initiative/elite direction (Evans, 1987) and the view that Lenin's tracts on the proletarian dictatorship, especially *State and Revolution*, were *genuinely* based "on the audacious project of directly proceeding with and actually encouraging the dissolution of the state" (Harding, 1983, 2:187).

4. However, see Lenin's somewhat different formulation in his lecture "The State" (1919h:488).

5. Lenin's concept of the democratic process referred not only to the democratization of institutions but also, and perhaps more importantly, to the dictatorship of the masses over the exploiters. Every democracy (a term of bourgeois legal ideology), for Lenin, is a class dictatorship; see Balibar, 1977:66–77. Lenin tended to see the concept of socialist legality as a peculiarly socialist form that mediated between democracy and dictatorship and transcended their individual bourgeois components; see Carr (1960, 2:468–471).

6. The conclusions we draw are very much the same as those arrived at by Polan: "The central absence in Lenin's politics is that of a theory of political institutions . . . Lenin's state form is one-dimensional. It allows no distances, no spaces, no appeals, no checks, no balances, no processes, no delays, no interrogations and, above all, no distribution of power" (1984:129).

7. The quotations in the couplet above, for example, which occurred in *The Proletarian Revolution and the Renegade Kautsky* (Lenin, 1918) and the "Rough Thesis of a Decision on the Strict Observance of the Laws" (Lenin, 1918a), respectively, were produced in wholly different circumstances and had altogether different objects. The former was in part directed to factions within German Social Democracy that articulated socialist demands in legalistic terms; the latter was concerned to secure obedience to a socialist legality that avoided the inflexibility of formal law.

8. Polan himself approaches this position with an argument appealing to Weber rather than Lenin: "There are certain situations where the rule of law cannot exist. Clearly, the rule of law cannot be assumed to exist in a society undergoing revolutionary reconstruction. . . . This reconstruction is at very least a time-consuming and complex process. A multitude of contradictory interpretations of the newly dominant ideology will for some time obtain" (1984:113).

9. In almost their first legislative act (Decree No. 1 on the Court), the Bolsheviks (1) abolished the "existing general judicial institutions," including the old hierarchy of tsarist courts, the system of justices of the peace, and the procuracy; (2) invalidated, in a note inserted by Lenin, all existing laws if they contravened CEC decrees or the Bolshevik/SR minimum programs; and (3) established a new court system (see *infra*). The legislative measures of the young Soviet Republic were of various sorts, including largely symbolic decrees such as "To the Population" and "To Workers, Peasants and Soldiers!" About the new decrees Lenin proclaimed, "we shall not regard them as absolute injunctions which must be put into effect instantly and at all costs" (1919g:209). On the difficulties of distinguishing the various forms of Bolshevik law, see Makepeace (1980:75–76).

10. Soon thereafter, Pashukanis (1924) and the commodity exchange school of law elevated this sort of argument to a theoretical foundation for the distinction between "legal" and "technical" rules. By the early 1930s, with the virtual disappearance of public provision for private rights and liberties, the anarchic attractions of this distinction, however brilliant its proponents, turned out to be tragically superficial (Beirne and Sharlet, 1980; Sharlet and Beirne, 1984).

11. The Cheka ("Extraordinary Commission for the Struggle against Counterrevolution, Sabotage and Official Crimes") was formerly established under the leadership of Felix Dzerzhinskii in November/December 1917. See further Levytsky (1972) and Gerson (1976).

12. For example, the foreword to the 1919 *Basic Principles of Criminal Law* (written by the People's Commissariat of Justice) defined criminal law as "rules of law and other measures by which the system of social relations of a particular class society is protected against violations (crimes) through the use of means of repression (punishment)"; see *Sobranie Uzakonenii* (Collection of Laws, hereinafter *S.U.*), RSFSR, 1919, no. 66, art. 590. Not until legislation of 1922 were Bolshevik penal strategies (definition of crime, stated objectives, etc.) given precise definition (*S.U.*, RSFSR, 1922, no. 15, art. 153).

13. In the "temporary instruction" "On Deprivation of Liberty as a Measure of Punishment and on the Method of Undergoing It," enacted on July 23, 1918, the Commissariat of Justice (*Narkomiust*) attempted to systematize many of the early decrees; see *S.U.*, RSFSR, 1917–1918, no. 53, art. 598. This decree focused on the worthiness of corrective labor as a means of reforming criminals. It also introduced a special category of isolated prison for incorrigibles. See further Carr, 1960, 2:421–424.

14. Despite the decriminalization of certain offenses by 1923, the soviet courts were tremendously congested with new criminal cases. Limitations of space preclude proper discussion here of the interesting but probably unresolvable problem of whether the crime rate actually did increase during the early period of Bolshevik power. However, in an important essay that discusses aspects of this question, Solomon (1981; and see Juviler,

1976:30–31) has argued that there was no increase in "actual" criminal behavior after October 1917. Rather, the new criminal cases in the people's courts resulted from the criminalization of certain common misdemeanors previously adjudicated outside the tsarist criminal courts. Van den Berg (1985:9–16) discusses the difficulties involved in estimating both the volume of crime in the 1920s and also the level of judicial repression.

15. Lenin appropriated the term "hooliganism" (*khuliganstvo*) from the tsarist legal and criminological discourse at the beginning of the century; see further Weissman (1978) and Pearson (1983:106–107; 255–256). For both tsarist and Bolshevik purposes the term referred to such diverse activities as public obscenity, the breaking of windows, the stealing of carriage wheels, rape, arson, and murder. In modern Soviet society, "hooliganism" has occupied a dual role in the vocabulary of penality: on the one hand, as a sociomedical description of alcoholism and, on the other, as a rhetorical device to marginalize political dissent.

16. For Bolshevik support of progressive legislation for women, see Goldman (1984:364–366). In January 1918, Lenin supported a decree, despite strong opposition, that raised the age of criminal responsibility from ten to seventeen (Juviler, 1976:25–26; and on his advocacy of the use of "educational" and "medical" institutions for juvenile delinquents, see e.g., Lenin, 1920c:182–183).

17. *S.U.*, RSFSR, no. 3, art. 35, sec. 10, 1917.

18. The crime of embezzlement was specifically introduced by several sections of the first Criminal Code of the RSFSR in 1922. Article 113 of the code referred to "[e]mbezzlement by an official of money or other valuables, which are under his control by virtue of his official position . . ." (quoted in Hazard, 1951:302); this was punishable by deprivation of liberty for between one and ten years. Another paragraph described the exacerbating circumstances (e.g., officials entrusted with special powers, or embezzlement of very valuable state property) that could lead, on conviction, to the maximum sentence of death.

19. Hazard (1951:304), relying on Utevsky (1948:265), argues that "[t]he giving of precise definition to the crime of embezzlement and the campaign conducted against those who committed it seems to have had little effect . . . following the adoption of the 1922 Code."

20. Although Lenin often advocated enforcement of the legal rights available under tsarism, when and where he selectively deemed it politically appropriate, he altogether lacked a coherent view of rights, justice, and civil liberties (see e.g., 1917d:129). After the 1917 October revolution he occasionally referred to "rights," but because he tended to regard them as mere expressions of bourgeois individualism, they played no positive part in his thinking about the means of securing the interests of the Soviet citizenry. See further Lukes (1985:61–70), Hirst (1986), and Beirne and Hunt (1988:579–581).

21. Because he was disturbed by the political arbitrariness of local authorities, Lenin (1922c; see also Timasheff, 1958:9) personally took the initiative in having the procuracy restored in 1922 (*Sobranie Zakonov*, RSFSR, 1922, no. 36, art. 424). The political question of whether or not procurators should be appointed both by the central authority (People's Commissariat) and by local authorities (Gubernia Executive Committee) was not a simple one. Lenin (1922c:363–364) recognized that dual subordination was a mechanism for ensuring the independence of local authorities from bureaucratic centralism. However, he argued (ibid., 365–367) that local procurators should be subordinate only to the central authority on the grounds that a higher principle was at stake, namely, a uniform law for the RSFSR. Lenin seemed genuinely concerned about the "high-handed" conduct of central authorities and, accordingly, he successfully proposed that if procurators challenged the legality of a local authority's decision, then that decision was not (as before) suspended, but subject to judgment in the courts. In reality, however, the result was a

dangerous expansion in the potential abuse of the democratic wishes of local authorities by the central state organs. See further Hazard (1960:230–232).

22. On February 15, 1918, some of the provisions of Decree No. 1 were amended by Decree No. 2 on the Court (*S.U.*, RSFSR, 1917–1918, no. 26, item 420).

23. Decree No. 2 on the Court, *S.U.*, RSFSR, 1917–1918, no. 26, item 420, s. 36. It should be pointed out that, according to Commissar of Justice Stuchka (1925:90), Lenin himself was not particularly attracted to concepts such as "revolutionary legal conscience" and "revolutionary legal consciousness" because they allegedly had no concrete content.

24. Decree No. 2 on the Court, *S.U.*, RSFSR, 1917–1918, no. 26, item 420, s. 8.

25. Decree No. 2 on the Court, *S.U.*, RSFSR, 1917–1918, no. 26, item 420, s. 14.

26. Decree No. 2 on the Court, *S.U.*, RSFSR, 1917–1918, no. 26, item 420, s. 36.

27. *S.U.*, 1918, no. 52, item 589.

28. *S.U.*, RSFSR, 1917–1918, no. 26, item 420.

29. Decree No. 3 on the Court, *S.U.*, 1918, no. 52, item 589.

30. *S.U.*, 1917–1918, no. 53, item 597. See further Hazard (1960:26).

31. Decree No. 2 on the Court, *S.U.*, RSFSR, 1917–1918, no. 26, item 420, s. 39.

32. After the Civil War, the Bolsheviks had declared an amnesty with the Right SRs, legalizing their party in 1919, and allowing publication of their newspaper *Delo naroda*. However, the crimes committed by the SRs against the Soviet government were not trumped up by the Bolsheviks: they included assassination attempts on the lives of Lenin and other Bolshevik leaders in 1918, and in 1920 they organized and led kulak uprisings in many regions (Medvedev, 1973:382; and see Carr, 1966, 1:190). The indictments therefore reflected serious offenses. As Carr writes, "[i]f it was true that the Bolshevik regime was not prepared after the first few months to tolerate an organized opposition, it was equally true that no opposition party was prepared to remain within legal limits. The premise of dictatorship was common to both sides of the argument" (ibid., 190).

33. Lenin may have agreed not to support the death penalty in this particular SR case, but it did not reflect his general view of the appropriate way of dealing with SR counter-revolutionary activities. For example, in a note to Commissar of Justice Kursky, written just before the start of the SR trial and intended as an addendum to the draft preamble of the new RSFSR criminal code, Lenin urged that "I think the application of the death sentence should be extended (commutable to deportation) . . . to all forms of activity by the Mensheviks, SRs *and so on*" (1922f:419). However, in his vague statements to the Eleventh Party Congress it was not at all clear (*pace* Jansen, 1982:34) that Lenin (1922g:282–283; 313) demanded the death penalty for the SRs.

34. E. H. Carr has observed that a "curious essay might be written on the attitude of the Russian revolution to capital punishment" (1950, 1:162). Were such an essay to be written it might begin by showing that Lenin's ambivalence reflected Marx's. On the one hand, Marx (1853:194) complained that "it would be very difficult, if not altogether impossible, to establish any principle upon which the justice or expediency of capital punishment could be founded in a society glorifying in its civilisation"; on the other, he (Marx, 1849:213) described as "heroic" the actions of those who, in the 1848 Hungarian revolution, dared "to oppose white terror with red terror" (Marx, 1849:213).

35. However, it is difficult to know precisely how to interpret Lenin's remark in his polemical speech "Paper Resolutions." Some (e.g., Adams, 1972: n. 30) have argued that Lenin's comment should straightforwardly be understood as support of capital punishment for landowners and capitalists, nothing more and nothing less. But Lenin's argument here, we suggest, was directed not only to the abolition of capital punishment. It was also cognizant of the fact that its restoration would inevitably result in executions not of "landowners and capitalists" but of "the masses" (or "the masses of soldiers" as

suggested in the Petrograd resolution: see *Collected Works of V. I. Lenin*, New York, 1932, vol. 21, no. 1, pp. 292–293).

36. According to Trotsky, Lenin "proposed changing the decree at once. We told him this would make an extraordinarily unfavorable impression. Finally someone said: 'the best thing is to resort to shooting only when there is no other way.' And it was left at that." (1925:134).

37. Van den Berg (1983:157) notes, while refraining from an assessment, that the official number of death sentences was 16,000 during June 1918 to October 1919, and that the military tribunals alone passed 6,543 such sentences between June 1 and October 31, 1920. Estimates of the number of death sentences and of actual executions during War Communism and the Civil War are legion, and it is impossible to assess which of them, if any, are correct.

38. Adams's analysis was not based on actual executions, but on a rating scale derived from the wording of penalty clauses about capital punishment (ibid., 84–85). The rating scale included a spectrum ranging from a mandatory death sentence to a noncapital penalty. Adams's scale clearly shows that military and counterrevolutionary crimes were most likely to result in executions; the three common crimes of aggravated murder, aggravated rape, and robbery were moderately unlikely to result in execution.

39. It should be noted that pressure to abolish the death penalty did not diminish after the 1922 code. Article 33 of the 1922 code was amended five times in the first thirteen months of operation, thereby restricting executions of pregnant women and minors, and introducing a statute of limitations; see Adams (1970:117, n. 45) and Hazard (1960:343).

40. Accounts of the Cheka's punitive measures are nearly always fragmentary and unreliable (Carr, 1950, 1:174); in the spring and summer of 1918 their victims included "insurgents . . . the bourgeoisie . . . officers and gendarmes . . . white-guard[s] . . . kulaks . . . priests" (ibid.).

41. Lenin saw no contradiction between this demand and the recognition that bourgeois democracy provides "the best possible political shell for capitalism" (1917:393). Political forms had to provide a clear but not inevitable series of stages. The achievement of political democracy would secure both a major victory over the autocracy and also an important new stage in the struggle for socialism. "Marxists know that democracy does not abolish class oppression. It only makes the class struggle more direct, wider, more open and pronounced, and that is what we want" (Lenin, 1916:73).

42. By this claim we do not mean to imply that the Bolsheviks were entirely "innocent" in their introduction of red terror. Quite the contrary, as both Lenin and Trotsky often asserted between 1918 and 1921, red terror was a class-based strategy the need for which—in exceptional circumstances—had been amply demonstrated both by the Jacobin terror of the 1790s in France (see, e.g., Carr, 1950, 1:160–165) and the Russian political theory of Peter Tkachev (Weeks, 1968).

43. Inclinations toward shock or revulsion at the measures taken by the Red Army, or by the Cheka, pale in comparison with the repression meted out by the counterrevolution. Within the party, opposition to the Cheka came from both idealists who disapproved of the terror and from functionaries who objected to the Cheka's usurpation of their domains (Carr, 1950, 1:187). The Cheka was abolished in spring 1922, and its functions conveyed to the GPU (State Political Administration). In October 1922 the GPU acquired the right to apply extrajudicial measures of repression, including execution, to "bandits" (Heller and Nekrich, 1986:220). From the Cheka, the GPU inherited its own armed forces, bureaucrats, and camps (including the infamous *Solovki*). However, at the Eleventh Party Congress, the last that he was able to attend, Lenin (1922g; and see Bettelheim, 1976:288) denounced the irregular extension of the scope of GPU.

44. It is a matter of historical judgment, beyond our present concerns, whether the

objective conditions justified the retention of terror.

45. By the summer of 1918 the people's courts, the revolutionary tribunals, and the Cheka all imposed penalties for various sorts of crime; the first was generally concerned with common crimes, the second and third with crimes that threatened state security. Although the people's courts and the revolutionary tribunals were subject to rules of legal procedure, the Cheka was an administrative organ whose scope was quite unrestricted (Carr, 1960, 2:422–423). After a brief period at the end of the Civil War, when there was a movement to unite the jurisdictional bodies for penitentaries, the NKVD was finally given leading authority in July 1922 (Feldbrugge, 1986:6–7).

In September 1918, the *Decree on the Red Terror* dictated that class enemies should be isolated in detention camps (*S.U.*, 1917–1918, no. 67, art. 710). Lenin first mentioned these camps in a telegram instructing how to suppress an uprising in Penza during August 1918. In it he urged that a reliable force should be organized "to carry out a campaign of ruthless mass terror against the kulaks, priests and white guards; suspects to be shut up in a detention camp outside the city" (1918r:489). The camps originally acted as preventive rather than punitive institutions, and were from the outset controlled by the Cheka, and then administered by Narkomvnudel (RSFSR Commissariat of Internal Affairs, or NKVD). Originally, the Cheka had virtually unlimited powers to detain political offenders, solely, in these camps. But by 1919 their populations began to resemble those of the Narkomiust prison populations subject to forced labor. The original designation of the People's Commissariat of Justice as the body responsible for penitentiaries was changed in May 1919 by two decrees that placed their responsibility under the NKVD or the Cheka. See further Carr, (1960, 2:421–454) and Solomon (1980). The tremendous expansion in the concentration camps under Stalinism occurred, not because of the real difficulties of executing the progressive (Narkomiust) policy "in an unfavorable environment, but because of factors external to penal policy, in particular, the labor demands generated by the decision to pursue forced-draft industrialization" (Solomon, 1980:195).

References

Authors' notes: (i) Unless otherwise indicated, all works by Lenin are from *Lenin: Collected Works* [*LCW*], 1960–1970, Moscow: Progress Publishers. (ii) In the case of entries with two publication dates, the first refers to the original date of publication and the second to the edition that we have used here.

Works by Lenin

(1901) "Where To Begin," *LCW*, 5:13–24.

(1901a) "Beat—But Not to Death (Casual Notes)," *LCW* 4:387–402.

(1902) "What Is To Be Done?" *LCW*, 5:349–529.

(1905) "The Revolutionary-Democratic Dictatorship of the Proletariat and the Peasantry," *LCW*, 8:293–303.

(1916) "A Caricature of Marxism and Imperialist Economism," *LCW*, 23:28–76.

(1917) *The State and Revolution. LCW*, 25:381–492.

(1917a) "The Impending Catastrophe and How To Combat It," *LCW*, 25:319–365.

(1917b) "Speech at a Joint Meeting of the Petrograd Soviet of Workers' and Soldiers' Deputies and Delegates from the Front, November 4 (17), 1917," *LCW*, 26:293–295.

(1917c) "Meeting of the Petrograd Soviet of Workers' and Soldiers' Deputies," *LCW*, 26:239–241.

(1917d) "Can the Bolsheviks Retain State Power?" *LCW*, 26:87–136.
(1917e) "To the Bureau of the Central Committee Abroad," *LCW*, 35:318–324.
(1917f) "Paper Resolutions," *LCW*, 25:261–264.
(1918) *The Proletarian Revolution and the Renegade Kautsky*. *LCW*, 28:227–325.
(1918a) "Rough Thesis of a Decision on the Strict Observance of the Laws," *LCW*, 42:110–111.
(1918b) "To G. Y. Zinoviev," *LCW*, 35:336.
(1918c) "The Socialist Fatherland Is in Danger!" *LCW*, 27:30–33.
(1918d) "Supplement to the Decree of the Council of People's Commissars: 'The Socialist Fatherland Is in Danger!' " *LCW*, 27:34–35.
(1918e) "Theses on the Current Situation," *LCW*, 27:406–407.
(1918f) "To G. F. Fyodorov," *LCW*, 35:349.
(1918g) "Proposals Concerning the Work of the Vecheka," *LCW*, 42:115.
(1918h) "Letter to D. I. Kursky," *LCW*, 35:331.
(1918i) "The Immediate Tasks of the Soviet Government," *LCW*, 27:235–277.
(1918j) "Telegram to V. V. Kurayev," *LCW*, 35:351.
(1918k) "A Little Picture in Illustration of Big Problems," *LCW*, 28:386–389.
(1918l) "Third All-Russia Congress of Soviets of Workers', Soldiers' and Peasants' Deputies," *LCW*, 26:453–482.
(1918m) "To the Commissariat for Justice," *LCW*, 44:76–77.
(1918n) "Original Version of the Article 'The Immediate Tasks of the Soviet Government,' " *LCW*, 27:203–218.
(1918o) "Fifth All-Russia Congress of Soviets of Workers', Peasants', Soldiers' and Red Army Deputies," *LCW*, 27:505–532.
(1918p) "Telegram to S. P. Natsarenus," *LCW*, 44:114–115.
(1918q) "Concerning the Decree on Revolutionary Tribunals," *LCW*, 27:219–220.
(1918r) "Telegram to Yevgenia Bosch," *LCW*, 36:489.
(1919) "Telegram to the Kursk Extraordinary Commission," *LCW*, 36:499.
(1919a) "Extraordinary Seventh Congress of the R.C.P.(B).," *LCW*, 27:85–158.
(1919b) "To All Members of the Boards and People's Commissars of All the Commissariats," *LCW*, 44:282.
(1919c) "Note to D. I. Kursky," *LCW*, 36:517.
(1919d) "Note to Stalin on Reorganisation of State Control," *LCW*, 28:486.
(1919e) "A Great Beginning," *LCW*, 29:409–434.
(1919f) "Report on Subbotniks Delivered to a Moscow City Conference of the R.C.P.(B.)," *LCW*, 30:283–288.
(1919g) "Eighth Congress of the R.C.P.(B.)," *LCW*, 29:141–225.
(1919h) *The State*. *LCW*, 29:470–488.
(1919i) "Letter to the Workers and Peasants Apropos of the Victory over Kolchak," *LCW*, 29:552–560.
(1919j) "Draft Programme of the R.C.P.(B.)," *LCW*, 29:97–140.
(1920) "Report on the Work of the All-Russia Central Executive Committee and the Council of People's Commissars," *LCW*, 30:315–316.
(1920a) "Speech at the Fourth Conference of Gubernia Extraordinary Commissions, February 6, 1920," *LCW*, 42:166–174.
(1920b) "A Contribution to the History of the Question of the Dictatorship," *LCW* 31:340–361.
(1920c) "The Prosecution of Minors," *LCW*, 42:182–183.
(1921) "To P. A. Bogdanov," *LCW*, 36:556–558.
(1921a) "Letter to D. I. Kursky and Instruction to a Secretary," *LCW*, 35:521–522.
(1921b) "Ninth All-Russia Congress of Soviets," *LCW*, 33:141–181.

(1921c) "To D. I. Kursky," *LCW*, 45:368–369.
(1921d) "The Tax in Kind," *LCW*, 32:329–365.
(1921e) "To the Moscow Revolutionary Tribunal," *LCW*, 45:348.
(1921f) "Instructions of the Council of Labour and Defence to Local Soviet Bodies," *LCW*, 32:375–398.
(1921g) "The New Economic Policy and the Tasks of the Political Education Departments," *LCW*, 33:60–79.
(1922) "On the Tasks of the People's Commissariat for Justice under the New Economic Policy," *LCW*, 36:560–565.
(1922a) "To D. I. Kursky," *LCW*, 36:576–577.
(1922b) "We Have Paid Too Much," *LCW*, 33:330–334.
(1922c) " 'Dual' Subordination and Legality," *LCW*, 33:363–367.
(1922d) "To D. I. Kursky," *LCW*, 35:533–534.
(1922e) "To D. I. Kursky," *LCW*, 33:358–359.
(1922f) "Addendum to the Draft Preamble to the Criminal Code of the RSFSR and a Letter to D. I. Kursky," *LCW*, 42:419.
(1922g) "Eleventh Congress of the R.C.P.(B.)," *LCW*, 33:259–326.

Other works

Adams, Will (1972). "Capital Punishment in Soviet Criminal Legislation, 1922–1965: A Code Content Analysis and Graphic Representation." Pp. 78–121 in Roger Kanet and Ivan Völgyes (eds.), *On the Road to Communism: Essays on Soviet Domestic and Foreign Politics*. Lawrence: University of Kansas Press.
Andics, Hellmut (1969). *Rule of Terror: Russia under Lenin and Stalin.* New York: Holt, Rinehart, and Winston.
Avanesov, G. (1981). *The Principles of Criminology*. Moscow: Progress Publishers.
Avrich, Paul (1970). *Kronstadt 1921*. Princeton: Princeton University Press.
Balibar, Etienne (1977). *On the Dictatorship of the Proletariat.* Trans. Grahame Lock. London: New Left Books.
Bassiouni, M. Cherif, and V. M. Savitski (eds.) (1979). *The Criminal Justice System of the USSR*. Trans. L. A. Nejinskaya. Springfield, Ill.: Charles C. Thomas.
Beirne, Piers (1987). "Between Classicism and Positivism: Crime and Penality in the Writings of Gabriel Tarde." *Criminology* 25(4):785–819.
Beirne, Piers and Alan Hunt (1988). "Law and the Constitution of Soviet Society: The Case of Comrade Lenin." *Law & Society Review* 22(3):575–614.
Beirne, Piers and Robert Sharlet (1980). "Editors' Introduction." Pp. 1–36 in P. Beirne and R. Sharlet (eds.), Peter B. Maggs (trans.), *Pashukanis: Selected Writings on Marxism and Law*. London: Academic Press.
Berman, Harold J. (1972). *Soviet Criminal Law and Procedure: The RSFSR Codes.* 2nd edition. Trans. Harold J. Berman and James W. Spindler. Cambridge, Mass.: Harvard University Press.
Bettelheim, Charles (1976). *Class Struggles in the USSR. First Period: 1917–1923*. London: Monthly Review Press.
Bratous, S. N. (1970). "Lenin's Ideas on Soviet Law and Socialist Legality." *Review of Contemporary Law* 1:21–46.
Buchholz, Erich, Richard Hartman, John Lekschas, and Gerhard Stiller (1974). *Socialist Criminology: Theoretical and Methodological Foundations.* Trans. Ewald Osers. Lexington, Mass.: D. C. Heath.
Burbank, Jane (1986). *Intelligentsia and Revolution: Russian Views of Bolshevism, 1917–*

1922. New York: Oxford University Press.
Carr, E. H. (1950) (1966). *The Bolshevik Revolution 1917–1923*. 3 vols. London: Pelican.
——— (1960). *Socialism in One Country*. 2 vols. New York: Macmillan.
Cohen, Stephen F. (1985). *Rethinking the Soviet Experience: Politics and History Since 1917*. New York: Oxford University Press.
Dallin, David J., and Boris I. Nicolaevsky (1947). *Forced Labor in Soviet Russia*. New Haven: Yale University Press.
Evans, Alfred B. (1987). "Rereading Lenin's *State and Revolution*." *Slavic Review* 46(1):1–19.
Feldbrugge, F. J. M. (1986). "The Soviet Penitentiary System and the Rules of Internal Order of Corrective Labor Institutions in Historical Perspective." *Review of Socialist Law* 12:5–29.
Garland, David (1985). *Punishment and Welfare. A History of Penal Strategies*. Brookfield, Vt.: Gower.
Gerson, Lennard D. (1976). *The Secret Police in Lenin's Russia*. Philadelphia: Temple University Press.
Goldman, Wendy (1984). "Freedom and Its Consequences: The Debate on the Soviet Family Code of 1926." *Russian History/Histoire Russe* 11(4):362–388.
Gouldner, Alvin W. (1977). "Stalinism: A Study of Internal Colonialism." *Telos* 34:5–48.
Gsovski, Vladimir, and Kazimierz Grzybowski (1959). *Government, Law and Courts in the Soviet Union and Eastern Europe*. 2 vols. New York: Atlantic Books.
Hazard, John N. (1951). "Soviet Socialism and Embezzlement," *Washington Law Review* 26:301–320.
——— (1960). *Settling Disputes in Soviet Society*. New York: Columbia University Press.
Heller, Mikhail, and Aleksandr M. Nekrich (1986). *Utopia in Power*. Trans. Phyllis B. Carlos. New York: Summit Books.
Hirst, Paul (1986). *Law, Socialism and Democracy*. London: Allen & Unwin.
Jankovic, Ivan (1984). "Socialism and the Death Penalty." *Research in Law, Deviance and Social Control* 6:109–137.
Jansen, Marc (1982). *A Show Trial Under Lenin*. The Hague: Martinus Nijhoff.
Juviler, Peter (1976). *Revolutionary Law and Order: Politics and Social Change in the USSR*. New York: Free Press.
Korobeinikov, B. V. (1985). "Sociopolitical and Legal Principles of Crime Prevention in the U.S.S.R." *Crime and Social Justice* 23:29–50.
Krylenko, N. V. (1934). *Lenin o sude i ugolovnoi politike, k desiatiletiiu so dnia smerti, 1924–1934*. Moscow.
Leggett, G. H. (1975). "Lenin, Terror, and the Political Police." *Survey* 21(4):157–187.
Levytsky, Boris (1972). *The Uses of Terror: The Soviet Secret Police 1917–1970*. Trans. H. A. Piehler. New York: Coward, McCann & Geoghegan.
Lós, Maria (1988). *Communist Ideology, Law and Crime*. New York: St. Martin's Press.
Lukes, Steven (1985). *Marxism and Morality*. Oxford: Clarendon Press.
Luxemburg, Rosa (1918) (1976). *The Russian Revolution and Leninism or Marxism*. Ann Arbor: University of Michigan Press.
Makepeace, R. W. (1980). *Marxist Ideology and Soviet Criminal Law*. London: Croom Helm.
Marx, Karl (1849) (1973). "The Magyar Struggle." Pp. 213–226 in David Fernbach (ed.), *Karl Marx: The Revolutions of 1848*. New York: Random House.
——— (1853) (1979). "Capital Punishment." Pp. 193–196 in Alan Hunt and Maureen Cain (eds.), *Marx and Engels on Law*. London: Academic Press.
Medvedev, Roy A. (1971). *Let History Judge*. Trans. Colleen Taylor. New York: Vintage Books.

Pashukanis, E. B. (1924). *The General Theory of Law and Marxism*. Pp. 37–131 in P. Beirne and R. Sharlet (eds.), Peter B. Maggs (trans.), *Pashukanis: Selected Writings on Marxism and Law*. London: Academic Press.

——— (1925) (1980). "Lenin and Questions of Law." Pp.133–164 in P. Beirne and R. Sharlet (eds.), Peter B. Maggs (trans.), *Pashukanis: Selected Writings on Marxism and Law*. London: Academic Press.

Pearson, Geoffrey (1983). *Hooligan: A History of Respectable Fears*. London: Macmillan.

Polan, A. J. (1984). *Lenin and the End of Politics*. London: Methuen.

Sharlet, Robert, and Piers Beirne (1984). "In Search of Vyshinsky: the Paradox of Law and Terror." *International Journal of the Sociology of Law* 12(2):153–177.

Shub, David (1948). *Lenin*. New York: Doubleday & Co.

Shvekov, G. V. (1970). *Pervii Sovetskii ugolovnii kodeks*. Moscow: Vysshaia shkola.

Solomon, Peter H. (1978). *Soviet Criminologists and Criminal Policy*. New York: Columbia University Press.

——— (1980). "Soviet Penal Policy, 1917–1934: A Reinterpretation." *Slavic Review* 39:195–217.

——— (1981). "Criminalization and Decriminalization in Soviet Criminal Policy, 1917–1941," *Law & Society Review* 16(1):9–43.

Solzhenitsyn, Aleksandr I. (1973). *The Gulag Archipelago 1918–1956: An Experiment in Literary Investigation*. New York: Harper & Row.

Stuchka, P. I. (1925) (1988). "Lenin and the Revolutionary Decree." Pp. 89–96 in Robert Sharlet, Peter B. Maggs, and Piers Beirne (eds. and trans.), *P. I. Stuchka: Selected Writings on Soviet Law and Marxism*. Armonk, N.Y., and London: M. E. Sharpe.

Timasheff, N. S. (1958). "The Procurators' Office in the USSR." *Law in Eastern Europe* 1:8–15.

Trotsky, Leon (1925) (1962). *Lenin*. "Authorized translation." New York: Capricorn Books.

Utevsky, B. S. (1948). *Obshchee uchenie o dolzhnostuki prestupleniaki*. [A General Study of Crimes Committed by Officials]. Moscow.

van den Berg, Ger P. (1983). "The Soviet Union and the Death Penalty" *Soviet Studies* 35(2):154–174.

——— (1985). *The Soviet System of Justice: Figures and Policy*. Dordrecht, Netherlands: Martinus Nijhoff.

Vigh, Józse (1985). "Thoughts About the Essence of Socialist Criminology." *Crime and Social Justice* 24:154–186.

Weeks, Albert L. (1968). *The First Bolshevik: A Political Biography of Peter Tkachev*. New York: New York University Press.

Weissman, Neil B. (1978). "Rural Crime in Tsarist Russia: The Question of Hooliganism 1905–1914." *Slavic Review* 37(2):228–240.

——— (1986). "Prohibition and Alcohol Control in the USSR: The 1920s Campaign against Illegal Spirits." *Soviet Studies* 38(3):349–368.

Woodcock, George (1963). *Anarchism*. London: Penguin.

Chapter 6

In Search of Vyshinsky: The Paradox of Law and Terror

Robert Sharlet and Piers Beirne

The dictatorship of the proletariat is authority unlimited by any statutes whatever. But the dictatorship of the proletariat, creating its own laws, makes use of them, demands that they be observed, and punishes breaches of them.

—Vyshinsky in *The Law of the Soviet State* (1938:48)

Introduction

Solzhenitsyn calls him "evil and quick of mind," a cameo appearance in Arthur Koestler's *Darkness at Noon* has him shouting his infamous line "Shoot them like mad dogs!" and his name becomes an expletive in the Chicago Seven trial as a synonym for blatant judicial persecution in the cause of political justice. Typical assessments of his *Law of the Soviet State*—an authoritative constitutional text published in the USSR in 1938, and first published in English in 1948 under the auspices of the American Council of Learned Societies—include devastating reviews by Lon Fuller (1949) and Harold Berman (1949). Fuller (1949:1157) angrily remarked that it "dodges every real problem its thesis might seem to suggest and substitutes for reasoned analysis the scurrilous and abusive recriminations for which its author-editor has become famous in international conferences"; Berman (1949:595) more soberly concluded that distaste for his invective and distortion should not obscure the very real issues reflected in the book. Not all assessments of him have been so harsh. Harold Laski, for example, said of his early trial work in the 1930s, "[he] . . . was doing what an ideal Minister of Justice would do if we had such a person in Great Britain—forcing colleagues to consider what is meant by actual experience of the law in action" (1935:21). An American Marxist has even recently stated that his jurisprudence "outlines in summary form the Marxist theory of law" (Terrar, 1981:55).

This chapter originally appeared in *International Journal of the Sociology of Law*, 1984, 12:153–177. Reprinted and amended by permission.

These are the prevailing images of Andrei Ianuarevich Vyshinsky, a jurist who exerted considerable influence in the USSR of the Stalinist 1930s, yet who remains an elusive figure in the history of Soviet jurisprudence. Vyshinsky is rarely mentioned in the political histories of the USSR apart from his major role as State Prosecutor in the show trials of Bukharin, Kamenev, Pyatakov, and Radek (e.g., Schapiro, 1971; Gouldner, 1977). In the literature on Soviet education and jurisprudence, Vyshinsky appears but briefly and peripherally as an unwelcome intruder on the historical stage (e.g., Sharlet, 1974:121; Fitzpatrick, 1978:15). Similarly, only fragments of Vyshinsky's several careers have been documented and these are scattered piecemeal throughout the memoir literature of East and West. In these memoirs, we catch glimpses of Vyshinsky with fellow prosecutors in the early phase of the New Economic Policy (Orlov, 1953:331), traveling south by train with the poet Mandelstam and his wife in the late 1920s (Mandelstam, 1974:190), addressing a Chemistry Faculty on curricular changes during the cultural revolution of the 1930s (Ostrovitianov, 1967:219), at lunch with the American ambassador to Moscow in the late 1930s (Davies, 1941:55), and seeing off the British Foreign Minister at the Belorussian train station in Moscow in the mid-1940s.

Official Soviet literature has hardly been more revealing about a man who was awarded six Orders of Lenin for his public service, the Order of the Red Banner of Labor for his work in the Kirov affair, and a Stalin Prize for his legal scholarship; who rose (along with Brezhnev) to candidate membership in the Presidium in the twilight of the Stalin era; and who became procurator general of the USSR, Minister for Foreign Affairs of the USSR (1949–1953), and then chief Soviet delegate to the United Nations. Upon his death in 1954, in the year following Stalin's, Vyshinsky was officially eulogized as "a true son of the Communist Party" whose dedicated service to the party would not be forgotten (*SGiP*, 1954, 8:10–12). His ashes were immured in the wall of the Kremlin and his name emblazoned on the Academy of Science's Law Institute *imeni Vyshinskogo*.

Vyshinsky had been an active force in legal policy and legal scholarship to the very eve of his death. However, his voluminous and heretofore authoritative writings were soon ignored, except for an occasional citation of his work on international law and a passing reference to him as "one of the leading Soviet jurists" (*SGiP*, 1955, 2:17 and 6:104). Even two years after his death, at the Twentieth Congress of the CPSU in 1956, what criticism there was of Vyshinsky was cautious and moderate, sometimes timid in content, and occasionally even respectful in tone. But at the Twenty-second Congress a swelling chorus against Vyshinsky was initiated by then KGB chief A. N. Shelepin:

> . . . there has developed in jurisprudence a kind of cult of Vyshinsky, whose theoretical studies . . . were based on the well known and erroneous thesis that as we advanced to communism the class struggle would sharpen, which must entail intensification of measures of repression and other measures of coercion. Law as defined by Vyshinsky amounted to nothing more than coercion . . . the

> "theory" he developed that the confession of the accused was conclusive proof in cases of state crimes in effect justified the mass instances of arbitrariness in court and investigatory practice at the time. (Gruliow, 1962:182)[1]

From 1962 into the mid-1960s, a spate of explicitly critical and strident articles appeared in Soviet journals, followed by several specialized monographs; but the critical thrust of these was largely confined to Vyshinsky's "theoretical arbitrariness."[2] With Khrushchev's departure in 1964, a political silence descended around Vyshinsky; this applied both to his arbitrary and his constructive practices during the period of the cult of the personality of the 1930s. In two contemporary collections of essays on the history of the Soviet Procuracy—and these include bibliographical articles on all other major procurators—Vyshinsky is treated as a nonperson of Soviet legal history (*Na starzhe sovetskikh zakonov*, Moscow, 1972; *Sovetskaia Prokuratora: Istoriia sovremenost*, Moscow, 1977). Fragmentary images of Vyshinsky sitting at his desk and signing arrest warrants, for example for Procurator Ishov after the latter had complained in 1938 about the NKVD, have had to await the emergence of *samizdat* in the 1960s and 1970s (Medvedev, 1971:411–412; Antonov-Ovseyenko, 1981).

The account of Vyshinsky that follows is largely biographical and limited to his activities before 1938, the year he prosecuted Bukharin in the "great purge trial" (Tucker and Cohen, 1965). There are no standard biographical sources on Vyshinsky, past or present. We have therefore tried to reconstruct the fragments of his public life and work from diverse sources, many of which are so critical of Vyshinsky that wherever possible we have cross-checked them. Our account of Vyshinsky should be understood as a small contribution to a rather larger issue, namely, the specific manner in which Soviet legal theory was transformed from the open brilliance of Pashukanis's *General Theory of Law and Marxism* of 1924, to the dour and deadly pragmatism underlying the 1936 Stalinist Constitution. What was Vyshinsky's personal contribution to this transformation? An official obituary credited Vyshinsky both with "struggling for the strengthening of the Soviet legal order (and) the strict observance of socialist legality," and with "serving as the paragon of a Soviet prosecutor for his performances in the show trials of 1933–1938" (*SGiP*, 1954, 8:10). We believe this strange juxtaposition to be an accurate reflection of Vyshinsky's contribution to Soviet legal theory and an apt illustration of the dictum that the rule of law and organized terror are not always antithetical.

Vyshinsky: The Formative Years

Vyshinsky was born in Odessa, in December 1883, to a bourgeois family of Polish extraction. Nothing is known of his early life until he joined the Russian Social-Democratic Labor Party in 1903. He affiliated with the Mensheviks during the 1903 Congress, and then worked for the Mensheviks in Baku. He took an active part in the eruption of the 1905 revolution—forming Social Democratic fighting squads in the Caucasus, organizing a railway workers' strike, and serving as secretary of the Baku Soviet. He was reportedly arrested several times and exiled for these and other revolutionary activities. In 1906 he served a year in prison for his part in the rail strike of 1905 (Schulz, 1972:599); one of his fellow prisoners was apparently Joseph Stalin.[3] According to Uralov (the pseudonym of the Soviet historian Avtorkhanov, who later knew Vyshinsky) he apparently also had close ties with Caucasian nationalists who were hostile to the Bolsheviks during Vyshinsky's Baku period (1975:130). Later, in the early 1920s, Vyshinsky would exaggerate the length of his prison term in order to ingratiate himself with contemptuous Bolshevik colleagues (Orlov, 1953:331). Moreover, as a possible ex post facto confirmation of his prominent contribution to the 1905 revolution, Vyshinsky and his wife were reportedly wounded in a 1907 assassination attempt by a right-wing Russian terrorist group (Schulz, 1972:59).

Shortly after, within a year or so, Vyshinsky left the Caucasus and matriculated at the Law Faculty of Kiev University. After receiving his law degree in 1913, he apparently then intended to pursue an academic career in jurisprudence. As he later told a legal colleague, the arrangements made for him to stay on at Kiev University in pursuit of an academic vocation were aborted by the Imperial Ministry of Education, and he was expelled on political grounds (Orlov, 1953:333). Between 1915 and 1917, Vyshinsky practiced law as an assistant barrister in Moscow. Both friends and foes acknowledged his intelligence (Medvedev, 1971:304), although Lewin also describes his having at this time the political antennae of a perfect opportunist (Lewin, 1977:133–135). The Bolshevik Ostrovitianov (1967:218–219) remembered Vyshinsky as a fellow deputy and member of the Menshevik faction in one of the borough councils of Moscow after the February revolution. He reported that Vyshinsky alone caused the Bolshevik deputies more concern than the more numerous Kadets because of his great eloquence and talent as a polemicist. Foreshadowing the better-known Vyshinsky of later years, Ostrovitianov recalled:

> Debating with Vyshinsky was not easy. His speeches, though not very profound in content, were distinguished by their lively, witty form. In polemics he used extensively the subtle methods of juridical casuistry. At times it seemed to me that he was converting the argument into an end in itself, into a kind of authentic content. Therefore he did not rule out any means that would secure victory for him. (Ibid.)

We next find Vyshinsky as the head of the militia in a borough near the center of Moscow, under the aegis of the Provisional Government. In the summer of 1917 he signed orders for the arrests of Bolsheviks (Medvedev, 1971:312). This accords with other reports characterizing Vyshinsky as one of Lenin's most active Menshevik opponents during the 1917 revolution, one who denounced the Bolsheviks "in writing and in speech, as usurpers and the destroyers of liberty" (Uralov,

1975:130; compare Berger, 1971:134). In early 1918, possibly just after the outbreak of the Civil War, Vyshinsky was arrested by the Bolsheviks for his counterrevolutionary activity. Schulz (1972:599) also lists Red Army service and work in senior legal posts in 1919, but we have been unable to find independent confirmation of either. In any event, Vyshinsky was arrested on the order of Ter-Vaganyan, a Bolshevik who had been appointed chief of the Military Department of the Moscow Party Committee in late 1917. This temporary setback to his political career was recalled to Vyshinsky years later, in the offices of the NKVD, in very awkward circumstances. It was sometime during the summer of 1936 when Prosecutor Vyshinsky was briefly interviewing each of the defendants prior to the show trial of the "Trotskyite-Zinovievite Terrorist Center." Ter-Vaganyan was brought before Vyshinsky, who routinely asked if he confirmed his written testimony and received the brusque and contemptuous rejoinder "I had you arrested during the Civil War for genuine counter-revolution!" Vyshinsky apparently turned pale for some moments until the incident passed. His discomfort was a source of delight to the secret police present who, along with their chief Yagoda, treated Vyshinsky with the disdain befitting a former prisoner in the NKVD building on Lubianka Street (Orlov, 1953:327).

Vyshinsky could not have enjoyed the company of the NKVD for very long because he probably attended the inaugural meeting of the new law group of the Socialist Academy on September 9, 1918. This was convened by the Old Bolshevik jurist P. I. Stuchka, and both Pashukanis and Vyshinsky were listed as the junior charter members. Soviet archives apparently reveal little evidence of Vyshinsky's participation in this group, but he was nevertheless reappointed as a scientific associate in the spring of 1919 (Plotnieks, 1978:113 n.168, 118). By 1919, Vyshinsky had doubtless gained some favor with the Bolsheviks because the first shoots of his academic and administrative careers now appeared. A *rabfak* (workers' faculty) was opened in Moscow University for the fall term of 1919, with Vyshinsky a member of the teaching staff. He, who a decade hence would preside over the "cultural revolution" in higher education, later recalled the resistance to the *rabfak* and the contempt for it among some of the Moscow University professors and the old student body (Fitzpatrick:79–80). Simultaneously, Vyshinsky held an executive position in the Commissariat of Food; here he was directly involved with the organization of the rationing system in late 1919 (Carr, 1966, 2:234).

By 1920, as the Civil War neared its violent end, Vyshinsky had been placed in positions of trust and responsibility. His several careers were securely underway, and it was now expedient to discard his Menshevik affiliation. Vyshinsky sought admission into, and was accepted by, the Bolshevik party. His anti-Bolshevik past was taken in stride by some party members, but his very late and opportunistic crossing of the political lines—only after the Bolsheviks had decisively won the war—laid him open to the charge of careerism and was a political liability for him throughout the 1920s. As a Bolshevik colleague later put it, "Till 1920 he was making up his mind whether to grant recognition to the Soviets or not" (Nemstov, cited in Orlov, 1953:330).

Vyshinsky's career advanced steadily, but his party future was very uncertain during the first years of the New Economic Policy. He was purged twice in the next four years, the first time in 1921 after having been in the party only a year. He was eventually reinstated a year later, in 1922, but only after great difficulty. By the time of the next purge, in 1923, Vyshinsky had been appointed prosecutor on the staff of the RSFSR Supreme Court. His Old Bolshevik colleagues disliked him and generally ostracized him from their conversation during afternoon tea. Vyshinsky reluctantly accepted his isolation at the court, rarely speaking in the presence of his colleagues, even at party meetings and judicial conferences. However, he tried to cultivate the friendship and empathy of several colleagues, primarily by recounting to them selected episodes from his revolutionary past. It was in this context that he told a fellow prosecutor that he had been imprisoned for two years after the revolution of 1905, an early documented instance of his strong proclivity toward mendacity. The discrepancy was discovered when, with his comrades, he needed to compose his biography for the local Party Control Commission which was conducting the purge in the fall of 1923. All of his comrades had their party cards returned from the commission with dispatch; but after a long interview, Vyshinsky's was withheld and he was again expelled from the party. He was understandably distraught and took advantage of the merciful Solts, who presided over the Judicial Collegium of the Supreme Court and was then the leading member of the party's Central Control Commission. After much hysterical weeping by Vyshinsky, the kindhearted Solts (whose purge Vyshinsky would personally order some years later) agreed to intervene and secured his reinstatement in the party. Another judge (Galkin, president of the Collegium of Appeal) who found Vyshinsky "simply a disgusting careerist," upbraided his friend Solts for the intercession. In the mid-1930s, Judge Galkin himself fell victim to a personal denunciation by Vyshinsky (Orlov, 1952:331–35, 339; Medvedev, 1971:217–18; Berger, 1971:139, citing the Menshevik Bukhshtab).

After his early work with the *rabfak* of Moscow University, Vyshinsky taught at the Economic Faculty of the Marx Institute of National Economy; this was during the academic year of 1922–1923 (Vyshinsky, "Vmeste predisloviia" in *Ocherki*, part 1, 1924). One of his courses there was on the history of social doctrines, and on the basis of this course he published his first book, *Essays on the History of Communism* (Ocherki po istorii kommunizma) in early 1924. This was the first half of an introductory text that traced social thought from the ancient world to nineteenth-century utopian socialism; the second part appeared in 1925, and covered the period from Marx to Lenin. Both volumes were subject to devastating reviews in Ter-Vaganyan's journal of Marxist philosophy, *Pod znamenem marksizma*. Both reviews were by Zaidel′ (a specialist in the history of socialist ideas whose name was later mentioned throughout the 1936 show trial in connection with terrorist activity), and were published in 1925. These reviews are perhaps the earliest evidence both of Vyshinsky's casual attitude to historical accuracy and of his public identification with Stalin. Zaidel′, writing with a degree of restraint and always looking for something positive, nonetheless berated Vyshinsky for several stylistic faults and for substantive shortcomings that included vagueness and imprecision, wrong analogies, misdirected quotations, and misattribution and miscitations of Marx's writings. He specifically pointed to Vyshinsky's vulgarization of Marx's concept of class struggle and his simultaneous minimization of the role of ideas and maximization of the art of politics and maneuver in the success of the October revolution. Zaidel' concluded that Vyshinsky "either simply does not understand the authors he cites or was carried away by his own mistaken ideas and adduced them as clumsy proofs" (1925a:248–44). Years later, in 1937, Zaidel' was mentioned at the show trial (Conquest, 1968:113–114 and 318).

The second volume of Vyshinsky's text fared little better than the first. The same reviewer listed just a sampling of glaring factual errors, including the designation of Eugene Debs as a "*leading communist* activist in America." Indeed, throughout his two-volume text, Vyshinsky tended to blur the distinction between socialism and communism; no doubt this was a pragmatic position for a Menshevik with Bolshevik pretensions. The second volume bore evidence of the frequent misuse of quotations from Marx, Engels, and Lenin. About Lenin, Vyshinsky apparently attempted no analysis of his own but merely compiled quotations and offered an interpretation of Leninism "according to Stalin." Zaidel', who was associated with the Trotskyist faction in the intra-party debate of the 1920s, judiciously remarked that "there is no dispute that Stalin's book is the best book on Leninism; however, this does not mean that Comrade Stalin has exhausted the question."

Finally, in an effort to say something positive about Vyshinsky, Zaidel' observed that he was a lively writer, a good synthesizer of complex material, and undoubtedly well-versed in Marxism. However, he found a clear and unscholarly tendency in Vyshinsky to convert research in "citology"—ironically, a criticism Vyshinsky himself later leveled at his postwar juridical colleagues and one which was subsequently addressed to Vyshinsky's posthumous followers by Mikoyan in 1956. Zaidel' ended his second review by asserting flatly that Vyshinsky's work on political theory failed to meet scholarly standards and therefore could only be recommended to readers if thoroughly revised (1956b:311–15).[4]

In the fall of 1924, Vyshinsky applied to the personnel division of the Commissariat of Education for an appointment to the Law Faculty of Moscow University. On the questionnaire he completed for this purpose, Vyshinsky listed as evidence of his scholarship the first volume of his *Ocherki*, which had been published some months earlier. In processing the application, the personnel division routinely demanded an evaluation of the political and intellectual quality of Vyshinsky's book from the appropriate department of the Commissariat. Anticipating this procedure, however, Vyshinsky contacted an old friend and former Menshevik who served as consultant on jurisprudence in that office and arranged that he himself would "write a note on his work which his friend would sign" (Uralov, 1975:128). When Vyshinsky subsequently went for his interview, the personnel chief (whom he was to replace several years later) had before him the collusive, highly eulogistic self-reference on the applicant's scholarship. Vyshinsky delivered a paper to an important conference of legal personnel in 1924. Here he laid the basis for the subsequent transfer of the investigative function from the court to the procurator, thereby concomitantly strengthening the Procuracy at the expense of the judiciary (*Moskovskii universitet za 50 let sovetskoi vlasti*, Moscow, 1967:531).

Vyshinsky's academic and administrative careers accelerated rapidly barely a year after his joining the faculty, and he was appointed rector of Moscow University, probably with Stalin's patronage. This was at a time when the university was becoming more proletarianized, and when its curriculum and course content were being brought under tighter political control. Under Vyshinsky's administration, a new academic planning commission was created within the university structure. This included external representatives from the Presidium of the Supreme Council of National Economy, the RSFSR Commissariat of Justice, and the trade union of the Commissariat of Education. Meanwhile, Rector Vyshinsky taught fewer courses, and intensified his scholarly activity in the field of law. It is to Vyshinsky's legal scholarship that we now turn.

Vyshinsky and Soviet Jurisprudence

Vyshinsky played a visible, albeit secondary, role in the commodity exchange school of law, and his first appearance in it was his brief essay on the *Advokatura* (Vyshinsky, 1925). This was a minor entry in the school's first major collective publication, *Revoliutsiia prava* (Revolution of Law). The major essays in this volume (Stuchka, 1925) were by Bukharin, Stuchka (the editor), Pashukanis, and Razumovsky.[5] In an otherwise unremarkable article that contrasted the "bourgeois" bar with the Soviet colleges of defenders, Vyshinsky limited defenders' responsibility to their clients and declared the doctrine that "the defense in a Soviet court, as well as the prosecutor and the court itself, also serves the interests of truth and the state" (Vyshinsky, 1925:61). The implications of this doctrine were later made manifest in the severely weakened and politically compromised role of the defense attorney even in ordinary criminal cases. Indeed, Vyshinsky soon insisted that a defense counsel should present evidence not from the client's interest but from that of socialist construction and the state.

In another brief article in *Rabochii sud* (Workers' Court), directed to Soviet judges, Vyshinsky asserted that law was "merely an expression of economic relations," but avoided expressing any indication of his attitude toward Pashukanis's stress on the economic relations of commodity exchange as the source of law. However, he implicitly adopted Stuchka's position on a "Soviet law" of the transitional period against Pashukanis's radical insistence that the law of the transitional period was exclusively bourgeois; he suggested that "only recently has the proletariat succeeded in advancing *its own law* against bourgeois law" (emphasis added) (Vyshinsky, 1925a).[6] Vyshinsky's claim is of course remarkable because NEP law between 1921 and 1928 was explicitly directed to the retention of the capitalist mode of production in crucial segments of the Soviet economy. Moreover, this law was unabashedly based on an amalgam of foreign, bourgeois codes.

In 1925 Stuchka and the Communist Academy jurists published a comprehensive view of their jurisprudence with the first part of the three-volume *Entsiklopediia gosudarstva i prava* (1925–1927). Vyshinsky served as editor for articles on criminal procedure; he wrote a large number of the entries himself, though he delegated some of the more specialized topics to Roginsky (later one of his procuratorial deputies). Vyshinsky wrote on "Evidence," "Measures of Suppression," "The Procuracy," and "The Supreme Court"; in addition, he contributed essays on "The Paris Commune" and "The Commissariat of Food." Although Vyshinsky was one of a small group of editors among the 110 contributors, his own *Entsiklopediia* entries added nothing noteworthy or original to the Marxist critique of bourgeois jurisprudence. His essay on "Preliminary Investigation" was typical. Here, he made a brief historical comparison between medieval and modern investigatory practices, and went on to explicate just the then current concept, according to the provisions of the NEP criminal procedural codes of the different union republics (Vyshinsky, 1925b:450–456). Similarly, in his essay "Evidence" he warned "there is not yet and probably will not be for a long time a class theory of evidence, a revolutionary critique of this area of law" (Vyshinsky, 1925c:986). Therefore, he continued, he had to limit himself to a formal analysis of the extant concept and practice; anticipatorily, he stated both that evidence was the cynosure of procedural science (he was awarded a Stalin Prize in the 1940s for his book on the subject) and urged that reliance be placed on "social legal consciousness" to offset the gaps in legislation—a harbinger, perhaps, of his juridical licentiousness.

Something curious occurs in the second volume of the *Entsiklopediia*. Consider the juxtaposition of Vyshinsky's "The Paris Commune" and "Measures of Suppression" with an entry by Estrin (1925). In "The Paris Commune" Vyshinsky argued that the proletariat cannot achieve social emancipation without possessing state power, and that it cannot possess state power without destroying the bourgeois state and creating a new apparatus with quite special qualities. This was the historical lesson of the Commune. He then asserted that the Commune was the source of the historical form of the dictatorship of the proletariat—whose "most complete form is in the USSR in the present period" (Vyshinsky, 1925e:486)—because it was a worker's body that combined legislative and executive powers. But what, precisely, does this mean? None of Vyshinsky's comments here is at all exceptional, largely because they are so abstract that they say nothing concrete. We must add that the general tenor of Vyshinsky's commentary on the Commune embodies much of what was very soon to become the dominant problematic within Bolshevism. This included a mania for citology; the use of prose devoid of inspiration, specificity, and subtlety; and a technist view of the achievement of social emancipation in which means were held to be external to social relations, and in which social emancipation was either a pre-given object or conceived of simply in economistic terms. Vyshinsky's thoroughly conventional article "Measures of Suppression," which not only ignored the notion of *otmiranie prava* (the withering away of law) altogether but even implied its very opposite, was immediately followed by the unusually long "Measures of Social Defense," written by one of the more radical members of the commodity exchange school (Estrin, 1925). Indeed, Estrin consistently urged the simplification and eventual elimination of law, especially the traditional categories of criminal sanction that Vyshinsky had upheld in the previous pages! It seems, in retrospect, almost as if the general editor (Stuchka) sensed in Vyshinsky a reluctant adherent. We should add that nowhere in his procedural essays did Vyshinsky suggest the peculiar doctrine of confession which he would later assert with great vigor, and with which he would become irrevocably associated in the history of Soviet jurisprudence. Given Vyshinsky's general strength of clear exposition and formal analysis, and his relative lack of creative insight, we should ask whether the pernicious concept of confession was indeed his creation or whether he was merely the conceptual codifier of the preference of his predecessors and superiors (Dzerzhinsky, Krylenko, and Stalin). Whatever the answer might be, Vyshinsky should not be exculpated for his subsequent assiduous promulgation of the confession doctrine in Soviet political and criminal justice. Indeed, he has been described as "The great theorist of confession," with Stalin and Dzerzhinsky as sources of the doctrine and practice (Conquest, 1968:147, 550; Berman, 1972:66 n. 23).

Vyshinsky's scholarly contribution to the developing Marxist critique of bourgeois law was at best negligible in the 1920s. A debate soon emerged within the Marxist school of law between its radical and moderate wings, but Vyshinsky remained aloof to the issues in his own writings and adopted an impossible neutral posture toward the debate itself. Moreover, judging by what, with whom, and under what auspices he published, it is almost certain that from the very beginning Vyshinsky opposed the overall thrust of *otmiranie prava*.

By 1927, a clear gulf existed between Vyshinsky and the Communist Academy law group. He made only minor appearances in the latter's new journal *Revoliutsiia prava* which was launched that year and very much under the influence of Pashukanis. The growing intellectual cleavage between the radical Marxist jurists and Vyshinsky was now reflected in the mixed critical reception of his writings. In 1927 Vyshinsky published his lectures as a *Kurs* on criminal procedure and he also contributed a chapter to a collective volume of *Osnovy* (Principles) (Magerovsky, 1927) of Soviet law. The latter was published under the auspices of the rival Institute of Soviet Law, and contained writings by jurists hostile to the concept of *otmiranie prava*. In both of these publications Vyshinsky treated criminal procedure as a system of compulsory legal norms expressing definite economic, social, and class relations. This was a thinly veiled form of positivism antithetical to the Pashukanis-Krylenko view of procedure as "technical rules" bound to disappear. It was also a harbinger of Vyshinsky's official definition of law, in 1938, following the purge of his erstwhile radical rivals (see Hazard, 1957:336 for his initial, post-Pashukanis, definition of law; also Beirne and Sharlet, 1980:31–36). Vyshinsky's *Kurs* was favorably reviewed by a colleague (Strogovich, 1927) in the Supreme Court's journal, but received cool treatment in the pages of *Revoliutsiia prava* 1928, no. 2:168–170). The *Osnovy* received just as ambivalent a reception in the same two journals in 1928.[7] Subsequently, the careers of several of Vyshinsky's fellow contributors and those of his friendly reviewers were eclipsed by Pashukanis's increasing ascendancy over the Soviet legal profession; they only resurfaced after the latter's disappearance. Predictably, Vyshinsky referred to the jurists whom he later rehabilitated as "those honest jurists who, being educated in and penetrated by the old legal culture and science, were unable, just because of their weak Marxist-Leninist preparation, effectively to resist the saboteurs" (Berman, 1963:172).

Two years later Vyshinsky placed himself in direct opposition to the radical theorists with a short, popular essay ("Soviet Law") which was probably widely read at the time. In a period when the radical jurists were vigorously advocating the transition from "criminal law" to "criminal policy," and actively promoting *otmiranie prava*, Vyshinsky actually asserted that the "class proletarian principle" was the basis of every branch of Soviet law and that Soviet criminal law "was especially intended to defend the socialist state . . . and its legal order from all encroachments" (1930:90–91). Taking his lead from Stalin's 1929 theses on class struggle and the dictatorship of the proletariat, Vyshinsky wrote in his essay that

> arising from a particular system of social relations, standing under the influence of the *dictatorship of the proletariat*, fighting for the construction of socialism in our country, Soviet law is distinguished by its strongly pronounced class character. (Ibid.)

This view was completely at odds with that of leading radicals of the day such as Cheliapov (1928:811–812; Sharlet, 1978:169–188).

In early 1928, Vyshinsky resigned his rectorship at Moscow University to direct a special office of the USSR Supreme Court for the "Shakhty case." This case was a show trial involving a large group of Soviet and foreign engineers, and it inaugurated the cultural revolution of 1928–1931. Krylenko (who had been Chief Prosecutor at the 1922 trial of the Socialist Revolutionaries, and whose closing speech there Bukharin praised for its "really brilliant expressive power" and "exceptional revolutionary fervor," [cf. Jansen, 1982:119]) prosecuted the case; two years later, he and Vyshinsky would assume the same roles and perform the same functions in the better prepared and more polished performance of the "Industrial Party" trial. The landmark Shakhty trial was based solely on the confessions of the many defendants—with Judge Vyshinsky intimidating the defense counsel whenever necessary. It is interesting to note that, compared with Vyshinsky, Krylenko made a relatively poor impression in this trial. One can speculate about what import this would have had for the high-level public criticism of Krylenko on the eve of his arrest in the late 1930s. Apparently, Krylenko made "a striking, unscholarly appearance" at the Shakhty trial compared with the well-groomed, dandyish Vyshinsky. Prosecutor Krylenko occasionally lost control of the proceedings, and it was then necessary for presiding judge Vyshinsky to come to his rescue and to conduct the examination, especially when one of the German defendants digressed from the script and contradicted an allegation to which he had already confessed. Krylenko suffered further setbacks in the trial, including being taken to task in the open courtroom for his technical ignorance by the chief Russian defendant (Bailes, 1978:89–94).

In retrospect, the Shakhty trial was a rehearsal for later events and, as such, it was no doubt instructive for all the judicial and police personnel involved. One lesson that was very quickly learned—in time for the "Industrial Party" trial—was that there had been too many defendants. This made the actual courtroom handling of the case unwieldy at times, and occasionally unmanageable; it was perhaps partly responsible for Krylenko's less than effective performance. However, one could also infer (and Vyshinsky was certainly in the best position to do so) that Krylenko came to court ill-prepared and without mastery of the script for the trial. This impression is reinforced by the substance of the public criticism of Krylenko in 1938, just before he was dismissed as USSR Commissar of Justice and arrested several days later. The speaker in the Supreme Soviet was an associate of Beria's and, as Roy Medvedev has suggested, he could not have made such an "audacious" attack without "Stalin's prompting" (1977:217). However, the content of the criticism seemed to bear the imprint of Vyshinsky who, after all, had scores to settle with Krylenko and who had, a few years earlier, clashed with him in an acrimonious public debate over criminal procedure. Who, we might ask ourselves, would have been in a more ideal position to rehearse the speaker about Krylenko's "unserious attitude" toward his juridical responsibilities? (On Krylenko's fall see Conquest, 1968:551; Gruliow, 1957, 11:216–217; Medvedev, 1977:217.)

Vyshinsky published a short book and two articles about the Shakhty trial and, shortly after the trial, was appointed Commissar for the cultural revolution on the higher educational front. His book *Aspects and Lessons of the Shakhty Trial* (Vyshinsky, 1928a) offered a brief survey of the various methods of "wrecking," and was well reviewed in *Pravda* and *Izvestiia*. In one article, he discussed the political aspects of the trials, and in the other he treated it as a classic example of economic counterrevolution (Vyshinsky, 1928b, c). These exegetic glosses on the major political drama of the day, and his part in it, thrust Vyshinsky to national prominence. Stalin was his most important audience, of course, and he doubtless made a good impression in that quarter. Shortly after the trial, in the summer of 1928, Stalin criticized the Commissariat of Education for its political inefficacy—it was unable to produce the technical intelligentsia urgently needed both for the First Five-Year Plan and the long-term program of industrialization (Bailes, 1978:163, 170). Soon after Stalin's criticism, Vyshinsky replaced Khodorovsky (the man who had been so impressed with Vyshinsky's self-reference and who had him appointed to the Moscow University Law Faculty) as head of the technical education administration of the Commissariat of Education. Protesting this and other changes, Lunacharsky resigned as Commissar in 1929 and was replaced by Bubnov, an experienced Stalinist bureaucrat (Bailes, 1978:171; Fitzpatrick, 1978:15).

In his new office, Vyshinsky quickly moved to support Stalin's demand for the rapid production of a new technical elite. Beginning with the fall term of 1928, the party ordered that a detachment of a thousand Communists be enrolled in the higher schools without regard to academic qualifications. Vyshinsky at once responded with the directive that "military measures" designed to achieve "maximum results in the shortest time" were the only way rapidly to implement the new party policy on technical education (Joravsky, 1961:223). Vyshinsky presided over several aspects of educational reform, including the purge of bourgeois professors and the "reelection" of faculty by students in the reconstructed institutions (ibid., 234). There was irony in this as well: many of Vyshinsky's academic colleagues who advocated a developed and relatively stable Soviet legal system were purged by Pashukanis and his followers. This latter group assumed control over, and then radicalized, the Institute of Soviet Law (Sharlet, 1974:114). Vyshinsky was a kindred spirit of those purged academics who had opposed the radical theses on law, but he had the protection of his party card; so one might say that Vyshinsky left academe for the higher echelons of educational administration at a very opportune moment.

There is some evidence to suggest that Vyshinsky was not purely a passive instrument of Stalinist policy during the cultural revolution, but that he may have made some small contributions of his own. Vyshinsky temporarily returned to the legal front to preside over the trial of Professor Ramzin and the so-called Industrial Party in 1930, a case that involved "charging a number of experts formerly sympathetic to Narkompros's position on engineering training with 'wrecking' and citing a volume edited for Narkompros by Khodorovsky as one of the basic documents on which the prosecution had built its case" (Fitzpatrick, 1978:15). The convergence of Vyshinsky's several careers is suggested here, although other evidence indicates that he played a far less creative role in the subsequent and politically more significant show trials of the 1920s.

One more scene was to be played out at the very end of his formative years, a scene which perhaps aptly epitomizes the search for Vyshinsky. In 1931, the party bureau of Narkompros evaluated course syllabi prepared by Vyshinsky's department and discovered "a number of serious mistakes in the social science syllabi" for all educational levels; it then raised the question of imposing a party censure on Vyshinsky for the "careless" performance of his department in regard to the syllabi. One immediately wonders—were these mistakes of fact and interpretation (reminiscent of Vyshinsky's negatively reviewed 1924 *Ocherki*), or errors of inclusion or exclusion of materials (hence the subject of political and doctrinal differences within the Commissariat)? Was it indeed bureaucratic negligence, or rather "mistakes" of deliberate political omission or commission?

As befitting an *apparatchik* of his increasing stature, Vyshinsky remained offstage as the drama unfolded, allowing Bubnov (the People's Commissar) to ward off the censure. In retrospect, this tends to confirm that his alleged mistakes were actually Vyshinsky's conscious efforts to Stalinize the historiography of recent party history. The Stalinist Bubnov not only opposed the party bureau's proposal, but refused even to attend the meeting. Both of these moves had the effect of encouraging other senior cadres to go to all possible lengths to acquit Vyshinsky of the party charges. Only Krupskaia supported the charges against Vyshinsky and, suffering defeat, she even took the matter to the local party organization. Here she continued vigorously to press the case against Vyshinsky, although to no avail since by then he enjoyed Stalin's personal protection (Martirosian, 1966:211). Once again Vyshinsky eluded impending trouble by means of a career move at the critical moment. This time he moved, paradoxically, to the twin posts of Procurator of the Republic and RSFSR Deputy Commissar of Justice.

By 1931, therefore, Vyshinsky was ready for the final ascent to the Stalinist pantheon. It was Vyshinsky who would codify the draconian "jurisprudence of terror" (see Sharlet, 1977:163–168) and preside over its dual aspects of socialist legality and terror, dedicating himself with conviction to both, while constantly keeping in view the preeminence of revolutionary expedience should the two spheres ever collide (see Lewin, 1977:133–135).

From Jurisprudence to Terror

It is appropriate that Vyshinsky's primary medium of public expression now became his speeches. All of those who witnessed his career during the 1930s tend to credit him with strong performances in this respect. The remembrance of one individual who, as a boy, first heard Vyshinsky speak to a large public audience in Moscow, is typical. The place was a large open lecture hall in one of the Moscow parks and the audience was mainly workers who were impatiently awaiting a concert that was to follow Vyshinsky's remarks. However, as the account goes, Vyshinsky spoke so eloquently that his audience listened in respectful silence and appreciation.[8]

In his roles as procurator, commissar, and legal theorist, Vyshinsky was formally subordinate in the early 1930s to Krylenko, Akulov, and Pashukanis—all of whom he would soon eclipse. However, he was very soon to travel a path of inevitable conflict with Krylenko and Pashukanis. These two continued, despite politically necessary modifications to their theoretical positions, to represent the radical wing of Soviet jurisprudence. In contrast, Vyshinsky, in his speeches both in and out of court and in his new offices (the most important of which he would revise and publish as articles and even short monographs), began to conceptualize the Soviet state and law in harmony with Stalin's and the party's major policy statements. Increasingly, this conception was at variance with the academic theory and practice of that time.

Vyshinsky's publication of *Revolutionary Legality in the Contemporary Period* fortuitously coincided both with the Bolsheviks' decision to reemphasize legality (especially in rural areas after the main drive to collectivization) and the tenth anniversary of Lenin's restoration of the Procuracy. In this volume, as well as in other speeches and articles, Vyshinsky addressed and then transformed the prevailing notion of Soviet law in the early 1930s. We can summarize his position as follows. First, he strongly supported a "dual state" conception in which the dictatorship of the proletariat was the source of law, with *partiinost'* (party-mindedness) always superseding formal legality. Henceforth, Vyshinsky was adamant that *partiinost'* should revolve any collision between the formal commands of law and those of the proletarian revolution. Second, he stressed a derivative distinction between the adjudication of political and ordinary cases, the necessity of "socialist legal consciousness" in judicial decision making, and the need to maintain and enhance the prestige of legal institutions—including the then devalued status of defense counsel. Vyshinsky wrote of the need, in those tumultuous times, for a politically flexible approach to law as an instrument of policy, but at the same time for the restoration of legality in the countryside, better judicial discipline (especially on sentencing) and stronger courts, and the need to raise dramatically the standards for, and the qualifications of, legal cadres (see Vyshinsky, 1932; Gsovki, 1948; Kucherov, 1970). Third, and most ominously, Vyshinsky wished to put an end to the Bukharinite luxury of respect for legality. Legality, urged Vyshinsky, should always be dispensed with if it contradicted the interests of the "highest law," the proletarian revolution (see Towster, 1967:250).

During his first several years in office, it seems that Vyshinsky was intent on realizing Stalin's dictum that "revolutionary legality is not an empty phrase" (Vyshinsky, 1933:110). Implicit in his efforts was the notion of an affinity between revolutionary legality and "revolutionary arbitrariness," the latter to be subsumed by the former whenever conditions so dictated. In this spirit, the initial thrust of Vyshinsky's activities was to use the legal machinery at his disposal to support party policy on collectivization and related matters. For Vyshinsky, legal regulation was becoming increasingly synonymous with social regulation in general. By means of frequent speeches, he periodically contributed ad hoc addenda to his more systematic views on state and law under socialism. After each new party pronouncement—the Seventeenth Party Conference of early 1932, the decree on property of August 1932—Vyshinsky promptly lectured on the subject and then ordered his cadres, in the manner of a commander maneuvering troops, to swing into immediate action on the newly designated legal front. In 1933, the Procuracy was centralized and reestablished as an all-union agency, with Akulov as Procurator General of the USSR and Vyshinsky as his Deputy Procurator. Though nominally subordinate to Akulov, Vyshinsky seemed by 1934 to be the dominant figure in the Procuracy. By then, however, the general supervisory function of the Procuracy was in abeyance as local procurators scrambled to respond to the flow of party circulars on managing the economy. After the successful harvest of 1933, these day-to-day pressures on the

Procuracy diminished somewhat. Vyshinsky now began to redirect his subordinates' efforts away from indiscriminate prosecution of local officials for administrative failures and toward the concern for general supervision over administrative legality—especially to ensure that local party and state officials complied with central directives (see Vyshinsky, 1934:19–28). It was generally for this purpose that in 1934 the new all-union Procuracy acquired its own journal, *For Socialist Legality*, with Akulov and Vyshinsky as editor and deputy editor, respectively.

The new journal, which was soon dominated by Vyshinsky's presence as a frequent contributor (e.g., Vyshinsky, 1934a, b) as well as the effective managing editor, was dedicated to the discussion and implementation of party and state policy on the "strengthening of socialist legality and the protection of social property."[9] This provided Vyshinsky with a means both for self-promotion and for the projection of the authority of the new USSR Procuracy vis-à-vis Krylenko's power center in the RSFSR Commissariat of Justice with its influential journal *Soviet Justice*. From its inception, Vyshinsky used the Procuracy's journal to present his own legalist approach to the "pragmatic" role of law in socialist construction, and to criticize, without reference to names, the revised but still radical theoretical views of Pashukanis. In his report to the Seventeenth Party Congress in January 1934, Stalin himself observed that a section of the Institute of Red Professors continued to interpret the thesis of the construction of communism to mean that state power should be relaxed during the period of socialist transition. This section, warned Stalin, would be eliminated quickly and without unnecessary sacrifice if it did not recant its leftist prattle. Vyshinsky at once followed suit. In a speech before the Central Executive Committee (the all-union legislature), Vyshinsky attacked those who did not recognize the "absolute and fundamental" distinction between Soviet and bourgeois legality, and the unnamed persons who continued to underrate "the role of the Soviet statute as a powerful cultural force and a key factor for the state of the proletarian dictatorship" (1934c:6).

In another presentation at the Communist Academy, with Pashukanis himself in the audience, Vyshinsky was more direct in his criticism of the notion of *otmiranie prava*. On this occasion, while Vyshinsky was attacking the notion of procedural norms as mere "technical rules," Pashukanis challenged him with an interjection from the floor. To this Vyshinsky vigorously replied by sharpening the overall thrust of his critique and bluntly declaring that "the Party now demands of us the strengthening of the legal form, the court, and the procedural norm" (1934d:9, 11). The increasingly hostile debate among Soviet legal theorists now became public with Vyshinsky the sharpest and most conspicuous critic of Pashukanis and Krylenko. Against Pashukanis, and the ultimately untenable notion of "technical rules," Vyshinsky asserted the ubiquitous need for civil law, contract, and the legal enforcement of planning discipline. Against Krylenko, and the radicals' draft criminal code of 1934, Vyshinsky advocated the restoration of criminal procedure and the supremacy of the "Soviet socialist statute." By the end of the next year, Vyshinsky was able confidently to assert that Krylenko's efforts to advance the withering away of criminal law "are doomed to obvious failure in our time" (1935:4).

During the early 1930s, Vyshinsky also consolidated his position in the Procuracy, and used his office both to extend his influence over the administration of justice and to challenge, with increasing boldness, his theoretical and bureaucratic rivals, Krylenko and Pashukanis. Vyshinsky's trial work doubtless advanced his standing as a member of Stalin's entourage, but it remained for the Kirov affair to catapult him to the center of the political stage. On the morning following the assassination of Kirov (December 1, 1934), Stalin and other senior leaders arrived in Leningrad to oversee the investigation that had been immediately launched. Arriving with Stalin, or perhaps soon thereafter, Vyshinsky, Poskrebyshev, other Stalinist aides, and a team of senior secret police officials also began work on the investigation during that week in Leningrad. Vyshinsky was obviously under considerable pressure. He hastily presided over the framing of the cases and drafting of the indictments: first for the trial of former Zinovievites cast in the role of the "Leningrad Centre," which opened on December 27; second, for the related trial of Zinoviev himself, Kamenev, and others assigned to the "Moscow Centre" of the conspiracy. It was to this latter that Stalin and Vyshinsky assigned responsibility for organizing Kirov's assassination (Kerst n.d.:25, 49; Medvedev, 1971:161).

Vyshinsky prosecuted both trials, with the "Moscow Center" trial beginning two weeks later in mid-January 1935, while still finding time to dash off an editorial exhorting procurators vigilantly to execute *lex Kirov*, the draconic new procedural rules adopted in the wake of the assassination (Vyshinsky, 1834e:4–5).[10] For his exemplary service in the Kirov affair, Vyshinsky was subsequently awarded the Red Banner of Labor "for the fight against counter-revolution" (Dallin and Nicolaevsky, 1947:257). Very soon after, in 1935, Vyshinsky was appointed Procurator General of the USSR. In his new office, he simultaneously served on the party's "special security council" with Stalin, Yezhov, and other senior leaders (Uralov, 1975:29–30), and on the state's constitutional commission with Bukharin, both of which bodies were newly established in 1935. This dualism characterized all of Vyshinsky's major activities during the latter half of the 1930s, as he pursued his relentless practice at the political bar while steadily forging ahead on the legal front.

Conclusion

Vyshinsky is probably best known for his succession to Pashukanis in 1937. The exact details of Pashukanis's disappearance are still a mystery; no public trial was ever held, and the charges against him are not known. According to Hazard (1957:386), Vyshinsky later said that Pashukanis had violated an article of the criminal code requiring that "a person accused under its provisions be found guilty of criminal intent to overthrow the Soviet regime." Pashukanis was therefore purged lawfully. In a political pamphlet of 1937, Vyshinsky charged Pashukanis with the double political error of both leftism *and* rightism! "The pseudo-scientific positions of Pashukanis and his group in the field of law have been completely shaped by the counterrevolutionary 'theories' of Trotskyism and the rightists (in particular by the anti-Leninists views of Bukharin)'' (Vyshinsky, 1937:5).

While Vyshinsky presided over the downfall of Pashukanis and his school, he also rehabilitated the bourgeois law professors who had been ousted by the legal radicals during the cultural revolution (Berman, 1963:172). At the very moment when Vyshinsky ordered the revival of the general supervisory function of the procurator's apparatus (Morgan, 1962:91–92, 99–101), he ordered the removal and arrest of 90 percent of the provincial prosecutors (Conquest, 1968:199). According to an article in *SGiP* (1965, quoted in Conquest, 1968:199), with Vyshinsky's sanction ''many prominent workers in the prosecutor's office who had tried in one way or another to mitigate repressive measures and stop the lawlessness and arbitrariness were arrested and subsequently perished.''

Similarly, while Vyshinsky readily politicized ordinary criminal cases to meet purge quotas (e.g., by reclassifying accidents such as an infestation of ticks during the harvesting campaign of 1936–1937, as sabotage), he was also a sharp critic of the political abuse of Article 111 for such minor and unintentional mishaps as a cook failing to salt the food. Vyshinsky, the theorist of confession, maximum probability, and objective truth, paradoxically also led the way in restoring to Soviet law the formal juridical categories of intent, negligence, and other substantive characteristics of bourgeois criminal law. In 1937, Vyshinsky both ordered that designated percentages of the population in different parts of the country be arrested and purged (Avtorkhanov, 1959:223), and tried to foster the growth of new Soviet law schools (Kucherov, 1970:275). Finally, as the architect of an emerging fusion of law and terror, Vyshinsky prepared to prosecute the great purge trials while implementing the relegalization of Soviet society and its utmost juridicization.

Notes

1. For post-Congress criticism of Vyshinsky see *SGiP*, 1956, no. 2, pp. 6 and 8. For Procurator Rudenko's praise of Krylenko and indirect criticism of Vyshinsky see *SGiP*, 1956, no. 3, p. 18. For a particularly revealing criticism of Vyshinsky by a Deputy Procurator-Generator of the USSR, see *SGiP*, 1965, no. 3, pp. 22–31.

2. This phrase is taken from Il'chev, *Kommunist*, 1962, no. 1, as quoted in *Sots. zak.*, 1962, no. 2, pp. 56–62 and 62–66.

3. According to information provided by Professor Robert C. Tucker, Stalin and Vyshinsky were in the very same prison during the latter's Baku period.

4. For a reference to Vyshinsky's subsequent criticism of ''citology,'' see Jaworskyj (1967:279). A. I. Mikoyan in turn criticizes the practice in Gruliow (1957, 4:88–89).

5. Bukharin's essay in this volume was on the theory of the imperialist state. Vyshinsky's short piece was reprinted from *EGP*, 1925, 1, pp. 55–62.

6. This has been partially translated by Jaworskyj (1967:200–202).

7. The *Osnovy* was reviewed by Il'insky in *Vest. Verkh. Sud SSSR*, 1928, no. 3, pp. 47–48; and in *Rev. prava*, 1928, no. 1, pp. 158–64. A second edition was published in 1929.

8. Private communication, P. Rabinovich to R. Sharlet, December 20, 1979.

Vyshinsky's eloquence is confirmed by others, such as Davies (1941) and Medvedev (1971).

9. Quoted from an advertisement announcing the first issue of the journal for November 1933, and the first annual subscription for 1934.

10. This issue of the journal went to press on December 26, 1934, the day before the "Leningrad Center" indictment was published over Vyshinsky's name.

References

Antonov-Ovseyenko, Anton (1981). *The Time of Stalin*. New York: Harper & Row.

Avtorkhanov, Abdurakhman (1959). *Stalin and the Soviet Communist Party*. New York: Praeger.

Bailes, Kendall, E. (1978). *Technology and Society under Lenin and Stalin*. Princeton: Princeton University Press.

Beirne, Piers, and R. Sharlet (eds.) (1980). *Pashukanis: Selected Writings on Marxism and Law*. Trans. Peter B. Maggs. London: Academic Press.

Berger, Joseph (1971). *Nothing But the Truth*. New York: John Day.

Berman, Harold, J. (1949). "Review of Vyshinsky's *The Law of the Soviet State*." *University of Pennsylvania Law Review* 97:593–596.

——— (1963). *Justice in the USSR*. Revised edition. Cambridge, Mass.: Harvard University Press.

——— (1972). *Soviet Criminal Law and Procedure*. Cambridge, Mass.: Harvard University Press.

Carr, Edward H. (1966). *The Bolshevik Revolution 1917–1923*. 3 vols. London: Penguin.

Cheliapov. N. (1928). "Pravo." In *Malaia sovetskaia entsiklopedia*. Vol. 6. Pp. 811–812.

Conquest, Robert (1968). *The Great Terror: Stalin's Purge of the Thirties*. New York: Macmillan.

Dallin, David, J., and Boris I. Nicolaevsky (1947). *Forced Labor in Soviet Russia*. New Haven: Yale University Press.

Davies, Joseph, E. (1941). *Mission to Moscow*. New York: Pocket Books.

Estrin, A. (1925). "Mery sotsial'noi zashchity." *Entsiklopediiia gosudarstva i prava* II. Pp. 910–928.

Fitzpatrick, Sheila (1970). *The Commissariat of Enlightenment: Soviet Organization of Education and the Arts under Lunacharsky*. Cambridge: Cambridge University Press.

——— (ed). (1978). *Cultural Revolution in Russia, 1928–1931*. Bloomington: Indiana University Press.

Fuller, Lon, L. (1949). "Pashukanis and Vyshinsky: A Study in the Development of Marxian Legal Theory." *Michigan Law Review* 67:1157–1166.

Gouldner, Alvin, W. (1977). "Stalinism: A Study of Internal Colonialism." *Telos* 34:5–48.

Gruliow, Leo (ed.) (1957). *Current Soviet Policies* II. New York: Praeger.

——— (ed.) (1962). *Current Soviet Policies* IV. New York: Praeger.

Gsovki, Vladimir (1948). *Soviet Civil Law*. Vol. I. Ann Arbor: University of Michigan Law School.

Hazard, John N. (ed.) (1951). *Soviet Legal Philosophy*. Trans. Hugh W. Babb. Cambridge, Mass.: Harvard University Press.

——— (1957). "Pashukanis Is No Traitor." *American Journal of International Law* 51:385–388.

Jansen, Marc (1982). *A Show Trial under Lenin*. The Hague: Martinus Nijhoff.

Jaworskyj, Michael (1967). *Soviet Political Thought, 1917–1961*. Baltimore: Johns Hopkins University Press.

Joravsky, David (1961). *Soviet Marxism and Natural Science, 1917–1932*. New York: Columbia University Press.

Kerst, Kenneth A. (no date). "Leningrad: A Political History, 1934–1953." An occasional paper of the Kennan Institute for Advanced Russian Studies. Washington, D.C.
Kucherov, Samuel (1970). *The Organs of Soviet Administration of Justice*. Leiden, Holland: E. J. Brill.
Laski, Harold (1935). *Law and Justice in Soviet Russia*. London.
Lewin, Moshe (1974). *Political Undercurrents in Soviet Economic Debates*. Princeton: Princeton University Press.
——— (1977). "The Social Background of Stalinism." In *Stalinism: Essays in Historical Interpretation*. R. C. Tucker, ed. New York: Norton. Pp. 111–136.
Magerovsky, D. (ed.) (1927). *Osnovy sovetskogo prava*. Moscow.
Mandelstam, Nadezhda (1974). *Hope Abandoned*. Trans. Max Hayward. New York: Atheneum.
Martirosian, L. N. (1966). "Ei my obiazany mnogim." In *Vospominanie o Krupskoi*. Arsen'ev et al., eds. Prosveshchenie: Moscow.
Marx, Karl, and F. Engels (1973). "The Communist Manifesto." *Marx/Engels Selected Works*. Vol. 1. Moscow: Progress.
Medvedev, Roy A. (1971). *Let History Judge*. New York: Knopf.
——— (1977). "New Pages for the Political Biography of Stalin." In *Stalinism*. R. C. Tucker, ed. New York: Norton. Pp. 199–235.
Morgan, Glenn, G. (1961). *Soviet Administrative Legality*. Stanford: Stanford University Press.
Muggeridge, Malcolm (1973). *Chronicles of Wasted Time*. New York: Morrow.
Orlov, Alexander (1954). *The Secret History of Stalin's Crimes*. New York: Random House.
Ostrovitianov, K. V. (1967). *Dumy o proshlom*. Moscow: Nauka.
Plotnieks, A. A. (1978). *Stanovlenie i razvitie marksistsko-leninskoi obshchei teorii prava v SSSR, 1917–1936*. Riga, Latvia: Zinatie.
Schapiro, Leonard (1971). *The Communist Party of the Soviet Union*. New York: Vintage.
Schulz, Heinrich, E. et al. (1972). *Who Was Who in the USSR*. Metuchen, N.J.: Scarecrow Press.
Sharlet, Robert (1974). "Pashukanis and the Rise of Soviet Marxist Jurisprudence, 1924–1930." *Soviet Union* 1:102–121.
——— (1977). "Stalinism and Soviet Legal Culture." In *Stalinism*. R. C. Tucker, ed. New York: Norton. Pp. 155–179.
——— (1978). "Pashukanis and the Withering Away of the Law in the USSR." In *Cultural Revolution in Russia, 1928–1931*. S. Fitzpatrick, ed. Cambridge: Cambridge University Press. Pp. 169–288.
Strogovich, M. S. (1927). "Review of Vyshinsky." *Vest. Verkh. Suda SSSR* 4:50–52.
Stuchka, P. I. (ed.) (1925). *Revoliutsiia prava: sbornik* 1:158–161.
Terrar, Toby (1981). "Contemporary Bourgeois Legal Thought: A Marxist Evaluation of the Basic Concepts—Review." *National Lawyers' Guild Practitioner* 38:49–59.
Towster, Julian (1967). "Vyshinsky's Concept of Collectivity." In *Continuity and Change in Russian and Soviet Thought*. E. J. Simmons, ed. New York: Russell and Russell. Pp. 237–256.
Tucker, Robert, C. and Stepehen F. Cohen (eds.) (1965). *The Great Purge Trial*. New York: Grosset and Dunlap.
Uralov, A. (1975). *The Reign of Stalin*. Westport, Conn.: Hyperion.
Vyshinsky, A. Ia. *Ocherki po istorii kommunizma, I*. [Essays on the History of Communism, Part I]. Moscow: Krasnaia nov'.
——— (1925). "Advokatura." [The Bar]. *Entsiklopediia gosudarstva i prava, I*. Pp. 55–62
——— (1925II). *Ocherki po istorii kommunizma, II*. [Essays on the History of Communism, Part II]. Moscow: Gosudarstvennoe izdatel'stvo.

——— (1925a). "Eshche raz o sotsialisticheskom pravosozanni." *Rabochii sud* 5–6:196–200.
——— (1925b). "Predvaritel'noe sledstvie." [Preliminary Investigation]. *Entsiklopediia gusudarstava i prava, III*. Pp. 450–456.
——— (1925c). "Dokazatel'stvo." [Evidence]. *Entsiklopediia gosudarstva i prava. I*. Pp. 985–991.
——— (1925d). "Mery presecheniia." [Measures of Suppression]. *Entsiklopediia gosudarstva i prava, II*. Pp. 908–910.
——— (1925e). "Kommuna Parizhskaya." [The Paris Commune]. *Entsiklopediia gosudarstva i prava, II*. Pp. 483–487.
——— (1927). *Kurs ugolovnogo protsessa*. [Lectures on Criminal Procedure]. Moscow.
——— (1928a). *Itogi i uroki shaktinskogo dela*. [Aspects and Lessons of the Shakhty Case]. Moscow.
——— (1928b). "Itogi shaktinskogo dela." [Aspects of the Shakhty Case]. *Rev. prava* 5.
——— (1928c). "Klassicheskii primer ekonomicheskoi knotrrevoliutsii." [A Classic Example of Economic Counter-Revolution.] In *Ekonomicheskaia kontrrevoliutsiia v Donbase*. [Economic Counter-Revolution in the Don Region]. Pp. 17–37.
——— (1930). "Sovetskoe pravo." [Soviet Law]. *Malaia sovetskaia entsiklopediia 8*. Pp. 90–91.
——— (1932). *Revoliutsionnaia zakonnost' na sovremennom etape*. [Revolutionary Legality in the Contemporary Period]. Moscow.
——— (1933). *Revoliutsionnaia zakonnost' na sovremenom etape*. [Revolutionary Legality in the Contemporary Period]. 2nd ed. Sovetskoe Moscow: Zakonatel'stvo.
——— (1934). "Soiuznaia prokuratura i sotsialisticheskaia zakonnost'." [The All-Union Procuracy and Socialist Legality]. *Sovetskoe stroitel'stvo* 4:19–28.
Vyshinsky, A. Ia. (ed.) (1934a). "Dogovornaia kampaniia 1934 g.i. zadachi Prokuratury i suda." [The Campaign for Contract Discipline and the Tasks of the Procuracy and the Court]. *Za sots. zak.* 1:8–10.
——— (ed.) (1934b). "Bor'ba za distsiplinu—osnovnaia zadacha Prokuratury na transporte." [The Struggle for Discipline—the Basic Task of the Procuracy toward Transport]. *Za sots. zak.* 1:12–14.
——— (1934c). "Za vysokoe kachestvo nashei raboty." [For the Higher Quality of Our Work]. *Za sots. zak.* 1:5–8.
——— (1934d). "Reforma ugolovno-protsessual' nogo zakonodatel'stva." [The Reform of Criminal Procedural Legislation]. *Za sots. zak.* 11:6–13.
——— (1934e). "Za boevuiu raboty organov iustitsii." [For the Fighting Work of the Organs of Justice]. *Za sots. zak.* 12:4–5.
——— (1935). "Vopros deistvitel'no ischerpan." [The Question Is Settled]. *Sots. zak.* 12.
——— (1937). *K polozheniiu na fronte pravovoi teorii*. [The Situation on the Legal Theory Front]. Moscow.
——— (ed.) (1938). *The Law of the Soviet State*. (Translated by Hugh W. Babb. Edited by John N. Hazard). New York: Macmillan.
——— (1953). *Sudebnye rechi*. [Court Speeches]. 3rd ed. Moscow: Iuridicheskoi literatury.
Werth, Alexander (1971). *Russia: The Post-War Years*. New York: Taplinger.
Wolfe, Bertram, D. (1970). "Dress Rehearsals for the Great Terror." *Studies in Comparative Communism* 3:1–24.
Zaidel', G. (1925a). "Novye knigi po istorii sotsialisma." [New Books on the History of Socialism]. *Pod znamenem marksizma* 1–2:237–245.
——— (1925b). "Review of A. Vyshinsky, *Ocherki po istorii kommunizma*, Part II." *Pod znamenem marksizma* 8–9:311–315.

Chapter 7

Nikolai Vasil'evich Krylenko: A Reevaluation

Donald D. Barry

Among the leaders of the Soviet legal profession, Nikolai Vasil'evich Krylenko occupies a special place because of the multifaceted character of his career. His early adult years were devoted not to law but largely to the life of a professional revolutionary and then a political and military operative. He turned to law, the field in which he spent the last twenty years of his life, only in 1918, when he was in his thirty-third year. His work in law involved a breadth of experience not found among present-day Soviet jurists, and rare even in Krylenko's day: prosecutor in important political trials; Commissar of Justice at both the RSFSR and USSR levels; ardent legal reformer who wrote and published prolifically on legal issues of the day; editor and lecturer who, if numerous Soviet sources are to be credited, took seriously the need to disseminate "legal propaganda" among the populace.[1] In addition, Krylenko was well known for his interests outside of law, including chess, mountain-climbing, hunting, and tourism, all areas which he helped encourage and develop in the new Soviet state.[2]

One does not get the picture, then, of a closeted legal scholar, but of an active political operative who happened to work for a large portion of his life in the field of law. The superficialities of Krylenko's career are not difficult to trace and have been touched upon by numerous authors. A number of Krylenko's legal writings have been analyzed by specialists, both in the Soviet Union and in the West.[3] Despite this attention, however, the picture that emerges of Krylenko is contradictory and lacking in depth. Given the closed nature of the Soviet system and the practice of only guardedly releasing information about political personalities, this is not overly surprising. Particularly where a person has been purged and then rehabilitated, as was Krylenko, one is likely to find inconsistencies, contradictions, and a tendency to go to extremes: the "wrecker" and "enemy of the people" of

---

This chapter originally appeared in *Review of Socialist Law*, 1989, 15(2):131–147. Reprinted by permission of Kluwer Academic Publishers.

1938 may come close to being the person who could do no wrong after his rehabilitation, particularly when the chief hagiographer is a close relative, as has been the case with Krylenko.[4]

But numerous signs now point to an effort to deal more objectively with Soviet history. While this is directed in particular at the mass repressions of the late 1930s (the time when Krylenko was arrested and liquidated after a closed trial hardly worthy of the name), it has tentatively extended to other periods as well, including the phase of Krylenko's ascendancy in law. If this reexamination of history is carried to its logical conclusion, a reassessment of Krylenko as a legal functionary will be hard to avoid. There is evidence of an inclination among some Soviet writers to look more frankly at Krylenko's role in the development of the more negative aspects of Soviet law during his period in power. But there are also powerful reasons for reining in any such inquiry: if questions are asked about Krylenko's earlier years in legal administration, what about his superiors during that period, particularly Lenin? The treatment of Krylenko, then, represents yet another test case for the *glasnost'* period: will it be of the "damage control" variety, in which the veil is lifted slightly but is limited to the period when all can ultimately be blamed on Stalin; or will the full implications of the inquiry be allowed to emerge without limitation?

In this chapter the author seeks to provide perspective for the evaluation of Krylenko as a jurist by examining the way he has been treated over time, in Soviet and Western writings. This is not, then, primarily a biographical sketch, although it will be necessary to discuss some aspects of Krylenko's background and career. Nor is it intended to examine in any detail Krylenko's writings and speeches. The aim, rather, is to analyze how Krylenko has been perceived and regarded by those who came into contact with him or wrote about him, and the emphasis in this analysis will be on Krylenko's work as a prosecutor in a series of important political trials from the period just after the 1917 revolution until the early 1930s. In the context of the broader examination of Soviet legal history that is now under way, this analysis may provide the basis for a more balanced view of Krylenko.

Background and Early Career

As suggested above, the basic facts about Krylenko's life are well known.[5] Born May 14, 1885 in the village of Bekhteeva in Smolensk Province, he was one of six children of a tsarist official who had been exiled from Moscow for revolutionary activities. Nikolai Krylenko's personality and his revolutionary inclinations are said to have been strongly influenced by his father, Vasilii Abramovich.[6] What Soviet sources do not indicate, however, is that the elder Krylenko committed suicide during Nikolai's early adulthood.[7]

After completing the gymnasium in Lublin, where his father had later moved the family, Nikolai Krylenko enrolled in the History-Philology Faculty of St. Petersburg University in 1903. Student political activities soon followed, and he joined the Russian Social Democratic Labor Party in 1904. For his participation in the 1905 revolution he was forced to flee St. Petersburg. He went first to Moscow and then, in the first of several periods of exile abroad, to Belgium and France in 1906.

The next ten years were largely occupied with political activities, as a result of which Krylenko was arrested several times, spent more time in Western Europe, and served in the tsarist army. In exile he was in contact with numerous Bolshevik notables, including Lenin and Bukharin. Also during this ten-year period Krylenko was exiled to Lublin by the tsarist police, where he flirted with syndicalist ideas and the possibility of a nonviolent revolution, for which "vacillation" he earned the sharp criticism of Lenin.[8] While residing in Lublin he was able to return to St. Petersburg to take and pass the examinations for the diploma from the History-Philology Faculty.

While it seems established that Krylenko received a university degree in history and philology, the particulars of his legal education are less certain. He is widely referred to in both Western and Soviet writings as a jurist or lawyer. And given the significance of his work in the field of law over two decades, the question of the thoroughness of his legal training is not unimportant. The second edition of the *Great Soviet Encyclopedia* states that Krylenko completed both the Law Faculty and the History-Philology Faculty of St. Petersburg University.[9] The third edition indicates that he completed the History-Philology Faculty in St. Petersburg in 1909 and the Law Faculty of Kharkhov University in 1914.[10] But the timing of his various activities and travels during this period make it doubtful that he had time to complete law training in either of these universities.[11] It may well be, therefore, that the law training of one of the most eminent of the Bolshevik legal functionaries was virtually or completely nonexistent.

After another arrest by the tsarist authorities in 1915, Krylenko was again pressed into military service and sent to the front, where he remained until after the March 1917 revolution. Continuing political work in the army, he was elected to several soldiers' committees and sent as a delegate to the May 1917 congress of front-line soldiers in Petrograd. In June he returned to Petrograd for the First All-Russian Congress of Soviets. For his antiwar and antigovernment views he was again arrested, this time on the direct order of Kerensky, but was released shortly thereafter. He served on the Petrograd Revolutionary Military Committee with a small number of other Bolsheviks; there he supported Lenin's proposal of preparing for an armed uprising.

With the victory of the Bolshevik revolution, Krylenko joined the first Soviet government as one of three members of the Committee for Military and Naval Affairs. There were only thirteen other members of this first Council of People's Commissars, including Lenin as chairman.[12] Krylenko was soon called upon for further high responsibilities. When army Commander-in-Chief Dukhonin, a supporter of the Provisional Government, refused to obey instructions from the new government, he was replaced by Krylenko, who had only attained the military rank of *praporshchik* (ensign, the lowest rank of commissioned officer) in the tsarist army. For a short period of time Krylenko was Supreme Commander in Chief (*Verkhovnyi Glavkomanduiushchii*) and People's Commissar for Military Affairs.[13]

But these high positions lasted only a few months, and after the signing of the Brest-Litovsk Treaty in March 1918 the post of Supreme Commander-in-Chief was abolished, Trotsky took over as People's Commissar for Military Affairs, and Krylenko was sent off to work in the field of law.

Soviet sources avoid assessment of Krylenko as a high military official. His lack of command experience suggests that he may not have been up to the tasks that faced him, a conclusion endorsed by some Western writers.[14] Certainly the extremely short period that he remained on top indicates that he was not seen by Lenin and others as a great success. The breakdown of the army and the mass desertion of soldiers, which forced the Bolsheviks to accept the humiliating terms of the peace, may have been unavoidable regardless of who was in charge. In any case, Krylenko was never again as close to the center of power as he had been during these few months in 1917–18.

Legal Functionary, 1918–1938

Standard sources indicate that Krylenko was called to his new assignment to help develop law as a weapon against counterrevolutionary forces intent on overthrowing the Bolsheviks.[15] Thus he was named head of the revolutionary tribunals created early in 1918 to try enemies of the regime. From the start Krylenko played a principal role as prosecutor in these cases. Although he went on to occupy several other responsible posts in law, his early fame as a jurist came largely from his prosecutorial activity. He was the principal state attorney in most of the important cases from 1918 to the early 1930s, playing the part of the tough, relentless accuser, the kind of role for which Vyshinsky gained fame later in the 1930s. The purge trials of the late 1930s tend to overshadow the earlier trials because the defendants, such as Bukharin, Zinoviev, and Kamenev, were such prominent Bolsheviks. But a number of the trials that Krylenko was responsible for prosecuting were significant events in their own right, often covered thoroughly by the world press. Among the major trials prosecuted before revolutionary tribunals by Krylenko were the trial of Roman Malinovsky, the Bolshevik leader who secretly worked for the tsarist police (1918); the trial of the "Tactical Center," allegedly a loose-knit group of anti-Bolsheviks who wanted to bring Admiral Kolchak to power (1920); the trial of a group of "clergymen-counterrevolutionaries" led by the former High Procurator of the Holy Synod, Samarin (1920); the trial of the Right Social Revolutionaries, for organizing rebellion against Soviet power in several cities (1922). These trials took place during the Civil War and were held before revolutionary tribunals. Some of the post–Civil War proceedings received even more world attention. By this time Krylenko had become Deputy RSFSR Commissar of Justice and assistant to the RSFSR Procurator (he became RSFSR Procurator in 1929 and RSFSR Commissar of Justice in 1931). These later cases were tried in the regular courts. The important proceedings were the Shakhty trial in 1928, involving an allegedly counterrevolutionary group from the Donbass region whose aim was to disrupt the coal industry; the 1930 trial of the supposedly counterrevolutionary organization known as the "Industrial Party"; and the final major case where Krylenko appeared as state accuser—the 1931 case of the Menshevik "Union Bureau."[16]

Contemporary Soviet accounts, as well as those written in the years after Krylenko's rehabilitation, have been fulsome in their praise of his prosecutorial abilities. He has been described as a brilliant orator who, "with facts, invincible logic, and the power of Marxist analysis proved the groundlessness of the defense." His speeches were said to be based on exhaustive preparation, which allowed him to "provide a detailed psychological analysis of both the crime itself and the motives leading to its commission." Because of his preparation and his brilliant memory he virtually never used notes in his courtroom presentations. He was "implacable toward the foes of the revolution" and spoke "with ruthlessness and decisiveness" when the occasion demanded. But he was said to operate according to the principle that "a person may be convicted only when the fact of the crime and the guilt of the accused are established with absolute precision and certainty and without doubt."[17] It is difficult to imagine a statement more inaccurate in characterizing Krylenko's approach to his prosecutorial role than this last one. His reliance on confessions, many of them surely cruelly coerced, runs directly counter to the above ideal. This is a matter to which the discussion will return. These characteristics may be of some relevance in considering the views of outsiders who observed Krylenko's courtroom behavior, or those who stood before him as accused.

That Krylenko adopted the demeanor of the severe accuser is attested to by numerous commentators. Alexandra Tolstoy, a defendant in the early "Tactical Center" trial, said Krylenko reminded her of a "savage dog that needed to be kept muzzled."[18] The American journalist Eugene Lyons, in viewing Krylenko in later trials, described his "bullet head," his "Scythian features tensed in a cruel sneer." He saw Krylenko as "revolutionary vengeance incarnate." Lyons wondered about how Krylenko, "who sneered and snarled while the world looked on," would behave "when there were no witnesses and no public records."[19] The few Soviet writings that attempt to describe Krylenko out of the limelight are not much help on this matter. They assure the reader that he was a warm comrade and tender father, but provide little more than flat assertions.[20] Max Eastman, Krylenko's brother-in-law, saw some of these more human traits in Krylenko. However, he believed that they were overwhelmed by his intense commitment to the Bolshevik cause:

> I watched him in court demanding the death sentence for a counterrevolutionary conspirator. I saw him work himself up to the degree of histrionic fury that earned

> him the nickname in the Western press of "bloodthirsty Krylenko." But that was not his true nature. Like other ardent Bolsheviks of these early days, he was actuated in his "toughmindedness" by a "tender" idea. He was hard because he was convinced by Karl Marx and Lenin that it was necessary to be hard.[21]

While there may, then, have been another Krylenko persona besides that of Bolshevik henchman, the latter was the one observed by his victims and by Western commentators. And his fanaticism in fulfilling this role was seen by some as having gone well beyond the norm. Roy Medvedev suggests that different persons handled the virtually unlimited power available to them in these times in different ways. He singles out Krylenko (and Postyshev) as an example of "bureaucratic degeneration" reaching "criminal extremes," accompanied "by deeper moral and political degeneration."[22] No wonder, then, that Krylenko was described by his detractors with such terms as "universally despised"; the "embodiment of villainy";[23] an "epileptic degenerate . . . and the most repulsive type I came across in all my connections with the Bolsheviks."[24] Solzhenitsyn, in his analysis of the early trials, is scathingly sarcastic in describing "the glorious accuser" Krylenko, who dispensed with even the rudiments of objectivity in his courtroom behavior.[25]

For all of his fanaticism and cruelty, however, the question might be asked as to how effective Krylenko really was as a prosecutor. Convictions in most cases were achieved, but there were a few acquittals, and many of the sentences handed down by the courts were less severe than Krylenko demanded. Moreover, eyewitnesses have indicated that at times Krylenko appeared flustered,[26] or that his carefully prepared strategies appeared to backfire.

The foundation of Krylenko's prosecutorial strategy was the confession of the accused in open court, an approach carried further by prosecutor Vyshinsky in the more famous trials of the latter 1930s. This may not have been considered fully credible evidence by observers, but it had the advantage of making the proceedings relatively simple and directly buttressing the sentences the court meted out. But on those occasions when confessions were not achieved or were recanted and—after a recess called by the court—reasserted by the accused, the basis of Krylenko's case rested on even shakier grounds.[27]

Krylenko himself referred to these trials as "show trials" (*pokazatel'nye protsessy*),[28] and in the sense that they demonstrated to opponents of the regime, both real and imagined, that the authorities could exercise the power of life and death over them, it might be said that they were successful. But as believable examples of law in action, it is impossible to conclude that these proceedings, largely masterminded by Krylenko, reflected positively on his competence as a jurist. In several of these cases Vyshinsky served as presiding judge. Bailes, in his analysis of the Shakhty trial, comments that "at critical moments" Vyshinsky would take over the prosecution from Krylenko.[29] A few years later, when the show trials involving Stalin's Bolshevik opponents took place, it was Vyshinsky whom the Soviet leader called upon as prosecutor rather than Krylenko.

Numerous non-Soviet sources have long seen as groundless the charges against the defendants in several of the trials in which Krylenko served as principal accuser. Within the Soviet Union, at least in the dissident community, similar views have also long been expressed. Thus, for instance, the dissident Soviet historian Roy Medvedev has tried to sort out what he calls the "fakery" of the trials of 1928–1931. Regarding the records of the Industrial Party and the Menshevik Union Bureau trials, he concludes: "One has only to read them to perceive that a large part of these materials is fraudulent."[30] Medvedev quotes from the deposition of M. P. Iakubovich, one of the defendants in the Menshevik trial. The deposition was sent to the USSR Procurator General in 1967. Among other things this document states that no "Union Bureau of Mensheviks ever existed" and that Krylenko, in a pre-trial meeting with the defendant, asserted, "I have no doubt that you are not guilty of anything."[31]

While there are still Soviet writers who defend the legitimacy of the proceedings of this period,[32] the threads of supposed credibility that weave them together are beginning to unravel. Part of this process of unraveling derives from the numerous rehabilitations during 1988 of the purge victims of the late 1930s. The USSR Supreme Court has rescinded the sentences of the defendants in the three great trials of 1936, 1937, and 1938, and hundreds of less publicized victims of illegal repression during this period have also been cleared. Soviet publications now discuss the varieties of physical and moral torture used on these defendants, and the chief prosecutor of that era, Vyshinsky, is thoroughly condemned for the use of tactics pioneered by Krylenko.

Other phases of the Stalin era have been partially examined. The *Moscow News* noted in June 1988 that "judicial falsification" began long before the period of the present rehabilitations, "with the so-called Shakhty affair and the Industrial Party 'trial.' " Although Krylenko is not mentioned in this or other accounts critical of these trials, his role in "judicial falsification" is implicit.[33] In July 1987 the USSR Supreme Court rehabilitated fifteen agronomists convicted earlier in the 1930s in closed trials. The Working Peasants' Party (WPP), to which the defendants were alleged to have belonged, was found not to have existed, and their convictions were quashed "because their activities were found not to be criminal"; indeed, the sole documentary basis for the existence of the WPP was confessions obtained by Krylenko in the Union Menshevik trial. The *Moscow News* not only castigated Krylenko for regarding confessions as "the best clue in all circumstances," but cast doubt on the legitimacy of the whole series of show trials from the period 1929–1931.[34] At this point, however, one should not overestimate the significance of these revelations. Krylenko has been mentioned critically only in the *Moscow News*, and only with regard to the last series of trials in which he was accuser. Can the investigations be expected to go back further? Krylenko's prosecutorial tactics in the years right after the 1917 revolution seem to have differed little from those of the later period, although some of his first cases (e.g., against the tsarist police agent Malinovsky) may have had more substance to them. But the earlier trials took place with Lenin still in control of the machinery of state, and one can expect the authorities to protect the image of Lenin (and therefore of Krylenko in this earlier period) as much as possible.

A 1987 examination of Krylenko's contribution to the development of Soviet law appears to set the tone for what can be expected. This long article in *Izvestiia* was written by Yuri Feofanov, a frequent writer on legal issues. Part of Feofanov's purpose seems to be to draw a lesson from the past for the present: to show that even during Lenin's time, the commitment to the even-handed, fair administration of justice was opposed by some Soviet leaders, and that similar problems are faced during the perestroika period of the late 1980s. Feofanov's approach begs the question of Lenin's commitment to the rule of law in practice, but that is not a matter to be addressed here.[35] What is important to examine is his treatment of Krylenko. Essentially, Feofanov maintains that as long as Lenin was alive, Krylenko held to the Leninist precepts with regard to legality. But after Lenin's death Krylenko sided with those who favored narrowing the independence of the court and restricting the rights of the accused. Interestingly, however, Feofanov sees this position of Krylenko as a temporary one, which he later abandoned, admitting his errors in 1934. He quotes from the late Soviet jurist M. S. Strogovich, who claims that Krylenko's non-Leninist position at this time was a temporary aberration.[36] For Feofanov and others writing recently,[37] Krylenko remains the noble Bolshevik functionary who exhibited only a minor and brief divergence from the correct path.

A more likely explanation for Krylenko's change of views in 1934, however, is that by that time he had seen the handwriting on the wall: Soviet law, under the strong influence of Stalin and Vyshinsky, was going in a different direction. Not only his radical views but even his position as a high legal functionary were in danger of being eclipsed. At present, then, the dominant Soviet treatment of Krylenko leaves intact the mythology of the Lenin period, and it avoids making the linkage, recently put forward tentatively, between Krylenko's courtroom tactics and those used later by Vyshinsky. For Feofanov and others, Vyshinsky reached this point on his own.[38]

By 1931, Krylenko's career as a courtroom accuser had come to an end. While he retained high posts in the legal field (first as RSFSR Commissar of Justice and then, in 1936, as head of the newly created USSR Commissariat of Justice) and wrote extensively, his position and influence soon began to wane. In retrospect, it is clear that Krylenko was locked in a battle for supremacy in the law field with Vyshinsky, to whom he was gradually forced to yield. The battle was fought in part in the journals that these two men controlled—Krylenko in *Sovetskaia iustitsiia*, the organ of the Commissariat of Justice, and Vyshinsky in *Sotsialisticheskaia zakonnost'*, the journal of the USSR Procuracy (Vyshinsky had become Procurator General in 1935).[39] As Eugene Huskey has put it in his thorough analysis of the Vyshinsky-Krylenko rivalry, their "struggle for mastery over legal affairs in the 1930s" involved "personal, bureaucratic, and policy dimensions."[40]

Why was it that Krylenko lost? Three considerations seem most important. First, Krylenko had long advocated a radical, quasi-nihilistic approach to the law which was out of favor from the early 1930s on. While he later backed down from these extreme views, he never completely succeeded in shedding the image of a radical. Second, as suggested, he may well have been seen as less than effective in his previous prosecutorial work. The smoother Vyshinsky, well educated in law and with greater practical legal experience, could serve as a more effective legal spokesman for the tasks to come.[41] Related to this point is another aspect of the background of these two men: Krylenko was a genuine Old Bolshevik who had been close to the foremost Bolshevik leaders, including Lenin and Bukharin, since long before the revolution. Because Stalin was systematically eliminating Old Bolshevik opponents, he could hardly be expected to leave Krylenko as the leading law official in the country. The ex-Menshevik Vyshinsky was much more suitable for this position.

And so Krylenko had to go. Although he was not arrested until the end of January 1938, and continued to hold the position of Commissar of Justice until his arrest, it is clear that he was in serious trouble months before that time.

Purge and Rehabilitation

When Krylenko was at the height of his powers, many honors came his way. He was elected twice to the Party Central Committee and, in addition to regular membership on the All-Union Central Executive Committee, he also served on its presidium. He was the recipient of the Order of Lenin and the Red Banner Order. In 1932 the Leningrad Institute of Soviet Law was named for him. In line with his long interest in sport and outdoor activities, he headed the All-Union Chess Federation and the All-Union Society of Proletarian Tourism for many years. But as the standard formula has it, "in 1938 the life of N. V. Krylenko was tragically cut short."[42]

For a long time after his rehabilitation by the USSR Supreme Court, which is said to have taken place on August 10, 1955, no details of Krylenko's demise were published; he simply "fell victim to the illegal repressions of the period of the personality cult," as it was often phrased, or, in some Krylenko hagiographies, his fate was just not mentioned.[43] It was not until the Gorbachev period that further details of Krylenko's end were released.

Perusal of the pages of the leading Soviet law journals of the time provides some interesting insights about the period immediately prior to Krylenko's disappearance. Of the leading Soviet jurists arrested in the purges, Pashukanis was among the first to go, disappearing a full year before Krylenko in January 1937. Pashukanis and several others were immediately identified as wreckers and traitors. Shortly thereafter, Krylenko was openly criticized for not exposing Pashukanis. His reply to this criticism serves as an indication of the weakness of his position, even at this early time. At a meeting at the Commissariat of Justice in March 1937, Krylenko stated that the signs of the wrecking activity were clear and that he should have been aware: "in spite of this, neither our theoretical workers nor I personally could uncover the enemy in time."[44]

Krylenko was also criticized at the time as one of those who had followed the ideas of the wrecker Pashukanis. While Vyshinsky did not carry on this effort single-handedly,[45] he made a particular point in May 1937 of charging Krylenko with "the uncritical repeating of the 'ideas' of Pashukanis."[46] At this point, however, Vyshinsky still referred to his adversary as "comrade Krylenko," and the latter's disappearance was still some months away.

What must have been seen as an alarming development by anyone reading the legal literature took place toward the end of 1937. In the November 5 issue of *Sovetskaia iustitsiia* (Soviet Justice), USSR Supreme Court chairman A. N. Vinokurov published an article in celebration of the Twentieth Anniversary of the Bolshevik Revolution. Twice in the article Vinokurov referred to the "wrecking false theories of Pashukanis and K."[47] Although his enemies were not yet prepared to identify him by his full name, it is clear that for Krylenko the game was up.

The only thing left was the application of public ridicule, and this was done at a Supreme Soviet meeting (by, among others, Molotov)[48] in mid-January 1938, about ten days before Krylenko was supposed to have been arrested. At this meeting Krylenko was replaced as People's Commissar of Justice by N. M. Rychkov (who had been one of the judges in the 1937 Pyatakov trial). In public utterances Krylenko was thereafter invariably listed in the leading ranks of the wreckers.

Like many other victims of the purges, Krylenko disappeared essentially without a trace after his arrest, and for a long time the Soviet authorities released no details of the final period of his life. At the Twenty-second Party Congress in 1961, Shelepin had reported that in November 1937 Stalin, Molotov, and Kaganovich had signed a document sanctioning the trials of a large group of officials, including Krylenko.[49] And in the prison camp literature published in the West, an occasional mention of Krylenko was to be found.[50] But it was not until 1987 that the official Soviet press provided some details. The first discussion, in August 1987, came in the article on Krylenko by Yuri Feofanov quoted above. Fomichev's account published in 1988 agrees in most respects with Feofanov's.[51] The latter will be quoted in its entirety:

> I would like to say a few words about the fate of N. V. Krylenko himself.
>
> He was arrested on January 31, 1938 on orders from Yezhov. He was accused of ties with a right-wing anti-Soviet organization that was supposedly headed by Bukharin, of having created a wreckers' organization in agencies of the justice system and having carried out subversive activities, and of having personally recruited 30 people.
>
> It is now difficult to imagine what happened then, and how. In the official records of the case we read:
>
> On March 3, 1938, Nikolai Vasilyevich confessed that since 1930 he had been a member of an anti-Soviet organization and engaged in wrecking.

> On April 3 of that same year he went so far as to confess that even before the revolution he had been waging a fight against Lenin, and that immediately after the revolution he had plotted, with Bukharin, Pyatakov and Preobrazhensky, a fight against the Party.
>
> One can only guess at how these "confessions" were obtained.
>
> On July 29, 1938, N.V. Krylenko was sentenced to be shot.
>
> The record of his "trial" fit into 19 lines, and the trial itself lasted 20 minutes.
>
> In 1955 the Military Cases Collegium of the USSR Supreme Court overturned the conviction and rehabilitated N. V. Krylenko in full.[52]

There is no direct mention of Vyshinsky's participation in the events of Krylenko's final days. The names given in connection with his arrest and trial are Yezhov, Stalin, Molotov, and Kaganovich. Yet it is clear that the Krylenko-Vyshinsky rivalry went well beyond matters of policy and principle. There is reason to believe that a considerable animosity existed between them,[53] and that Vyshinsky might have wanted to settle old personal scores. Fomichev's account of Krylenko's trial refers to it as a "court session" (*sudebnoe zasedanie*), while Feofanov writes only of a "trial" (*protsess*). Both agree as to its extreme brevity, however, which suggests that rather than a regular court it was the extralegal body known as the "troika," which was so commonly used in those days.[54] A 1988 source now indicates that the troika often operated as a "dvoika" (i.e., a two-person panel), and that for the most important cases the two officials sitting in judgment were Yezhov (and later Beria) and Vyshinsky.[55] It may be, then, that his old adversary had the last word on Krylenko's fate after all.

Notes and References

1. Among the sources used in this paper, one of the more important is the writing about Krylenko by his daughter, Marina Nikolaevna Simonian. See, for instance, *Zhizn' dlia revoliutsii* (Moscow: Politicheskaia literatura, 1962); *Ego professiia—revoliutsiia*, 2nd ed. (Moscow: Znanie, 1985). One of her writings that particularly stresses Krylenko's work as a legal propagandist is "N. B. Krylenko—propagandist pravovykh znanii," *Sots. Zak.* 1987, no. 1:21–24.

Simonian's depiction of Krylenko's life is based in considerable part on a five-page autobiographical sketch by Krylenko that appeared in vol. 41 of *Entsiklopedicheskii slovar' Russkogo bibliograficheskogo instituta "Granat"*, 7th ed. (Moscow: Granat, 1933–1940), pp. 237–246. Hereafter referred to as "Autobiography," this source describes Krylenko's life up to 1922.

2. Many writings refer to these interests. A book devoted almost solely to these aspects of his life is E. D. Simonov, *Chelovek mnogikh vershin: Nikolai Vasil'evich Krylenko (1885–1938)* (Moscow: Fizkul'tura i sport, 1969).

3. See, for instance, Eugene Huskey, "Vyshinskii, Krylenko, and the Shaping of Soviet Legal Order," *Slavic Review* (1987) 46, no. 3/4:414–428. See also passim Huskey's *Russian Lawyers and the Soviet State: The Origins and Development of the Soviet Bar, 1917–1939* (Princeton, N.J.: Princeton University Press, 1986). I am indebted to Huskey for bringing several other important sources on Krylenko to my attention. See

also John N. Hazard, "The Abortive Codes of the Pashukanis School," in F. J. M. Feldbrugge, ed., *Codification in the Communist World*, no. 19; F. J. M. Feldbrugge, ed., *Law in Eastern Europe* (Leiden, The Netherlands: A. W. Sijthoff, 1975), pp. 145–175, esp. 158–170. Among numerous Soviet writings see M. S. Strogovich, "K voprosu o postanovke otdel'nykh problem prava v rabotakh P. I. Stuchki, N. V. Krylenko, E. B. Pashukanisa," in S. N. Bratus', ed., *Voprosy Obshchei teorii sovetskogo prava* (Moscow: Gosiurizdat, 1960), pp. 384–405.

4. See note 1.

5. Basic sources used include: *Bol'shaia Sovetskaia Entsiklopediia*, 3rd ed., vol. 13 (Moscow: Bol'shaia Sovetskaia Entsiklopediia, 1973), p. 505; *Who Was Who in the USSR* (Metuchen, New Jersey, 1972), p. 320; Borys Levytsky, comp., *The Stalinist Terror in the Thirties* (Stanford, Calif.: Hoover Institution, 1974), p. 404; and sources cited in note 1.

6. Simonian, *Ego Professiia*, note 1, p. 11.

7. Max Eastman, *Love and Revolution: My Journey Through an Epoch* (New York: Random House, 1964), p. 340. Eastman married Nikolai Krylenko's younger sister, Elena.

8. *Ego professiia*, note 1, pp. 29–30. See also Lenin, *Polnoe sobranie sochinenii*, 5th ed., vol. 15 (Moscow: Politicheskaia Literatura, 1961), p. 387.

9. Krylenko does not appear in the regular alphabetical volume (volume 23) of the second edition, which was published in 1953. But he is included in a supplementary volume, volume 51, published in 1958. *Bol'shaia Sovetskaia Entsiklopediia*, 2nd ed., vol. 51 (Moscow: Bol'shaia Sovetskaia Entsiklopediia, 1958), p. 167. Many other sources indicate that Krylenko was a graduate of the Petersburg Law Faculty. See, e.g., N. S. Alekseev, "150-letie Iuridicheskogo Fakul'teta Leningradskogo Universiteta," *Pravovedenie* 1969, no. 1, 8.

10. *Bol'shaia Sovetskaia Entsiklopediia*, 3rd ed., vol. 13 (Moscow, 1973), p. 505.

11. Krylenko's daughter, who has written the most thorough biographies of her father, confirms that he received the History-Philology degree from Petersburg University in 1909. She also indicates that, in the summer of 1912, he returned to Petersburg at the request of Lenin to participate in the election campaign for the Duma. Apparently while there he became convinced of the importance of legal training in his work with the Bolsheviks, and so he "again enrolls in the university and completes the law faculty" (*Ego professiia*, note 1, p. 35). This seems difficult to credit, because she immediately goes on to indicate that he only stayed in Petersburg for several months, when he was called into the military service. In another writing she states that Krylenko "enrolled" in the law faculty and simultaneously took the examinations for a degree (*Zhizn'*, note 1, pp. 19–20). As for having done his legal study in Kharkhov in 1914, his daughter places Krylenko in Kharkhov for several months in that year, but says nothing about his studying law or taking examinations.

An article in *Pravda* on the occasion of the one hundredth anniversary of Krylenko's birth has a somewhat different version. It states that after completing the Petersburg History-Philology Faculty, Krylenko "immediately enrolls in the law [faculty]. Exiled by the police to Kharkhov, here in 1914 he passes the state examinations of the testing commission of the university." *Pravda*, 14 May 1985, p. 6. Not only is this version inconsistent in several respects with that of Krylenko's daughter, but it also gives the impression of perhaps several years of legal study by Krylenko in Petersburg. This was clearly not the case. Krylenko's "Autobiography" (above, note 1, pp. 243–44) indicates that he enrolled in the Petersburg law faculty in 1912, but remained in that city only briefly, perhaps one or two months. Krylenko further states that in 1914, while briefly in Kharkhov, he "completed the state examinations for the law faculty." A thorough biographical article on Krylenko in *BVS SSSR* 1965, no. 3, 15–18 makes no mention of legal education. In a 1985 article based on archival sources only made available in 1980, an attempt is made to clear up some of these inconsistencies. The author's conclusion is tentative, however. He states "with a large degree of probability" that Krylenko took the law exams in Kharkhov in 1914. But he has no answer to the question of the time when it might have been possible for Krylenko to engage in the active *study* of law. This author also notes that for at least part of his early university days in Petersburg, Nikolai Vasil'evich used the traditional family name of Krylenkov rather than Krylenko. No light is shed on exactly when or why the name was changed. V. Chernous, "Obvinitel', Sud'ia, Prokuror, Narkom Iustitsiia," *Sots. Zak.* 1985, no. 6, 30.

It might be added that in 1934, at the height of his authority in Soviet law, Krylenko was among nine persons, including Vyshinsky, who received, without writing a dissertation, the academic degree Doctor of State and Legal Sciences (*Doktor gosudarstvennykh i pravovykh nauk*) from the Communist Academy. See *Sovetskoe gosudarstvo* 1936, no. 2:119. Some sources list the name of this degree as Doctor of State and Social Sciences (*Doktor gosudarstvennykh i obshchestvennykh nauk*). See, e.g., the article on Krylenko in *Izvestiia*, 14 May 1965, p. 3.

12. *Dekrety sovetskoi vlasty*, vol. 1, (Moscow: Politicheskaia Literatura, 1957), p. 20.

13. Krylenko signed official documents with both of these titles and is so identified by numerous sources. See, for example, *Ego professiia*, no. 1:80; also "Iz Istorii Sozdaniia Raboche-Krest'ianskoi Krasnoi Armii," *Voenno-istoricheskii zhurnal* 1988, no. 2:38.

14. John Erickson refers to the naming of the inexperienced Krylenko as commander-in-chief as a "crude jest": *The Soviet High Command: A Military-Political History 1918–1941* (Boulder, Colo.: Westview Press, 1984), p. 12. Isaac Deutscher states that the organization of the General Staff was "a task which had been quite beyond the ensign Krylenko." *The Prophet Armed: Trotsky: 1918–1921* (New York: Oxford University Press, 1954), p. 408. Krylenko, in "Autobiography" p. 246 (see note 1), says he left his military posts "because of fundamental disagreements on the question of the formation of the Red Army."

15. See, e.g., the introduction to *N. V. Krylenko: Sudebnye rechii (izbrannoe)* (Moscow: Gosiurizdat, 1964), p. 14.

16. The transcripts or detailed accounts of several of these trials were published. See, for instance, N. V. Krylenko, ed., *Ekonomicheskaia kontr-revoliutsiia v Donbasse (itogi shakhtinskogo dela): Stat'i i dokumenty* (Moscow: Sovetskoe zakonodatel'stvo, 1928); *Protsess "Prompartii" (25 Noiabria–7 Dekabria 1930 g.): Stenogramma sudebnogo protsessa i materialy priobshchennye k delu* (Moscow: Sovetskoe zakonodatel'stvo, 1931); *Protsess kontrrevolutsionnoi organizatsii Men'shevikov (1 Marta–9 Marta 1931 g.)* (Moscow: Sovetskoe zakonodatel'stvo, 1931). A book-length account in English of the 1922 trial of Social Revolutionaries is Marc Jansen, *A Show Trial under Lenin: The Trial of the Socialist Revolutionaries* (Moscow, 1922; The Hague: Martinus Nijhoff, 1982).

17. The quotations are from *N. V. Krylenko: Sudebnye rechi*, note 15, pp. 17–18. Further information was obtained from E. Adamov, "N. V. Krylenko kak Sudebnye Orator," *Sov. iust.*, 1965, no. 10:28. Also on Krylenko's courtroom style see A. I. Vaksberg, "Politik, Tribun, Uchenyi-Iurist," *SGiP* 1975, no. 5:116–119; E. Boboritskii and S. Bogunov, "Tribun Revoliutsii," *Sots. zak.* 1962, no. 5:31. A sampling of Krylenko's courtroom speeches may be found in *Sudebnye rechi*, note 15 and *Sudebnye rechii sovetskikh obvinitelei* (Moscow: Gosiurizdat, 1965), pp. 44–65.

18. Alexandra Tolstoy, *Out of the Past* (New York: Columbia University Press, 1981), p. 122.

19. Eugene Lyons, *Assignment in Utopia* (New York: Harcourt Brace, 1937). The quotations are from pages 116, 117, and 372.

20. See, e.g., *Ego professiia*, note 1, p. 125.
21. Eastman, *Love and Revolution*, p. 346.
22. Roy Medvedev, *Let History Judge: The Origins and Consequences of Stalinism* (New York: Alfred A. Knopf, 1972), p. 415.
23. R. V. Ivanov-Razumnik, *The Memoirs of Ivanov-Razumnik* (London: Oxford University Press, 1965), p. 312.
24. R. H. Bruce Lockhart, *Memoirs of a British Agent* (London: G. P. Putnam's Sons, 1932), p. 257. Lockhart was sent by the British government on a mission to the new Bolshevik government in 1918. Residing in Moscow during the Civil War, he was arrested and scheduled to be tried for counterrevolutionary activities. He was released before trial and expelled from the country.
25. Aleksandr I. Solzhenitsyn, *The Gulag Archipelago*, I-II (New York: Harper and Row, 1973), especially 306–310. Solzhenitsyn pictures Krylenko not as a "revolutionary ascetic," as some analysts have seen him (see, e.g., note 3, Huskey, *Russian Lawyers*, p. 170, note 82), but as a kind of paramilitary bully wearing "an unbuttoned civilian jacket, with a glimpse of a sailor's striped undershirt just visible at the open throat" (p. 309). Solzhenitsyn claims, p. 306, that Krylenko tried to have himself named "Tribune" during this period, but that this was vetoed by Lenin.
26. Tolstoy, *Out of the Past*, note 18, p. 125.
27. The best eyewitness accounts on these matters known to the author are those of Eugene Lyons and Louis Fischer. Both described events of this kind in the Shakhty trial and both commented negatively on Krylenko's performance as accuser. See Lyons, *Assignment*, note 19, pp. 124–131 and Fischer in Richard Crossman, ed., *The God That Failed* (London: Hamilton, 1950), pp. 211–212. For further comments on Krylenko's competence as a prosecutor, see this author's "Leaders of the Soviet Legal Profession: An Analysis of Biographical Data and Career Patterns," *Canadian-American Slavic Studies* (1972) 6, no. 1:81, and Lyons, note 19, pp. 81–82; see also Robert Sharlet and Piers Beirne, "In Search of Vyshinsky: The Paradox of Law and Terror," *supra*.
28. "Autobiography," note 1, p. 246.
29. Kendall E. Bailes, *Technology and Society under Lenin and Stalin: Origins of the Soviet Technical Intelligentsia, 1917–1941* (Princeton, N.J.: Princeton University Press, 1978), p. 92.
30. Medvedev, *Let History Judge*, pp. 117 and 124.
31. Ibid., pp. 125–130.
32. See, e.g., Simonian, on page 22 of the 1987 article cited note 1. An article that examines some of the matters treated in the present part of this paper is Julia Wishnevsky, "Socialist Legality and the Falsification of History," *Radio Liberty Research*, no. 348/87, August 20, 1987.
33. *Moskovskye novosti*, 19 June 1988, p. 10, *CDSP* (1988) 40, no. 24:6. See also Arkady Vaksberg's attack on Vyshinsky, in which the "show trials" of the late 1920s and thereafter are also criticized. "Tsaritsa dokazatel'stv," *Lit. gaz.*, 27 January 1988, p. 13, *CDSP* (1988) 40, no. 6:9. But Vaksberg distorts the picture by giving Vyshinsky the leading role and not mentioning Krylenko at all: "At the end of the 1920s the grandiose show trials that reached their culmination ten years later were already beginning to be staged. From the very beginning, no other than Vyshinsky was designated as their bloody director."
34. *Moscow News* (1987) no. 33:12.
35. But see Wishnevsky, note 32, who analyzes what she concludes to be Feofanov's distortion of Lenin's role.
36. Yuri Feofanov, "Stanovlenie Zakona," *Izvestiia*, 11 August 1987, p. 3; a condensed translation may be found in *CDSP* (1987) 39, no. 32:7.

37. An article that reflects Feofanov's views in most essentials is S. M. Fomichev, "Nikolai Vasil'evich Krylenko," *SGiP* 1988, no. 7:114.

38. Feofanov, note 36; accord Fomichev, note 37.

39. See Barry, note 27, p. 82; also Sharlet and Beirne, note 27, pp. 170–71.

40. Huskey, "Vyshinsky, Krylenko . . . ," p. 414. Huskey has thoroughly and accurately analyzed the details of the Vyshinsky-Krylenko clash. His article is recommended to those who wish to examine this matter further. Only one major point in Huskey's analysis seems open to question. He devotes considerable attention to demonstrating that Vyshinsky, in his writings up to the mid–1930s, objected to over-reliance on the sufficiency of the confession of the accused (see Huskey, pp. 421–422). While this seems to be true, it is worth pointing out that while sitting as presiding judge in the important political trials of the late 1920s and early 1930s Vyshinsky apparently made no objection to prosecutor Krylenko's heavy reliance on confessions as a prosecution tool. On the Vyshinsky-Krylenko debate see also Robert Sharlet, "Stalin and Soviet Legal Culture," in Robert C. Tucker, ed., *Stalinism: Essays in Historical Interpretation* (New York: W. W. Norton, 1977), pp. 172–73.

41. As a law student in Moscow in the 1930s, John Hazard attended lectures by many of the important legal personages of the day, including Krylenko and Vyshinsky. He described Krylenko as "the epitome of the hard-boiled revolutionary" but not "an intellectual heavyweight." Hazard saw Vyshinsky "as a man trying to save his own neck, an abject servant of his boss," but also as "a cultured man with a remarkably broad knowledge of Western law." John N. Hazard, *Recollections of a Pioneering Sovietologist* (New York: Oceana, 1984), pp. 23, 25. See also the comparisons of Krylenko and Vyshinsky as to their effectiveness in the courtroom by Robert Sharlet and Piers Beirne, note 27, p. 166.

42. The quotation is from Fomichev, note 37, p. 119, as are most of the facts in the paragraph. On the naming of the law institute see N. S. Alekseev, "Leningradskomu Universitetu 150 Let," *Pravovedenie* 1969, no. 1:9.

43. The quotation is from then Procurator General R. Rudenko, "Na strazhe zakona," *Izvestiia*, 14 May 1965, p. 3. This phrase is repeated more or less word for word in numerous other writings. Among the sources that don't mentioned Krylenko's demise are the two books by Krylenko's daughter cited in note 1, the two editions of the *Great Soviet Encyclopedia* mentioned in notes 9 and 10, and a *Pravda* article on the occasion of the hundredth anniversary of Krylenko's birth, 14 May 1985, p. 6.

44. "K Polozheniiu na pravovom teoreticheskom fronte," *Sov. iust.* 1937, no. 6:4. At this point, however, Krylenko had not completely given up the fight. The battle between him and Vyshinsky about the nature of Soviet law continued. On the question of the influence of bourgeois law on Soviet law (Krylenko acknowledged some bourgeois inheritances in Soviet law), he discussed "the errors of my opponents" and said that he awaited anxiously works from them that could be analyzed, "in particular from Vyshinsky, who long ago promised to produce a work on this theme. Unfortunately there is no such work yet, while the demand for it remains sharp" (p. 8).

45. Many law scholars participated in this activity, among them S. N. Bratus', later one of the most respected jurists of the post-Stalin period. Early in 1937 Bratus' published a long article "On the Status of Theoretical Work in Soviet Civil Law," in which he attacked the "enemy of the people E. Pashukanis" and numerous other scholars, including Stuchka, Venediktov, and Amfiteatrov. ("O Sostoianii teoreticheskoi raboty po sovetskomu grazhdanskomu pravu," *Sovetskoe gosudarstvo* 1937, no. 1–2:48–64.) Bratus' no doubt felt compelled to write in this way because he was under attack himself. In the next issue of this journal, Vyshinsky identified Bratus' as one of a number of jurists who had come under the influence of the erroneous ideas of Stuchka. A. Vyshinsky, "Polozhenie na pravovom fronte," *Sovetskoe gosudarstvo* 1937, no. 3–4:35.

46. "Polozhenie na pravovom fronte," *Sovetskoe gosudarstvo* 1937, no. 3–4:45.

47. "20-Letie Oktiabrskoi Revoliutsii i Sotsialisticheskogo Suda," *Sov. iust.* 1937, no. 21:14. This issue did not come out until early December 1937, by which time Krylenko was close to being arrested. It contained what may have been Krylenko's last article, "Oktiabr' i sud," pp. 5–10.

48. Deputy M. D. Bagirov began the attack with an extended discussion of Krylenko's interests in mountain-climbing, tourism, and chess and concluded: "We have to find out what we have in the person of comrade Krylenko—an alpinist or a People's Commissar of Justice (laughter). I don't know which comrade Krylenko considers himself more of, but as a People's Commissar of Justice he is undoubtedly poor." Molotov then endorsed Bagirov's view, raising laughter in the hall by saying that the positive side of Krylenko's activity was in mountain-climbing, tourism, and chess, but that Krylenko did not understand the need for a model Commissar of Justice. These Supreme Soviet speeches were widely published, including in *Sov. iust.* 1938, no. 2–3:7–9.

49. Charlotte Saikowski and Leo Gruliow, eds., *Current Soviet Policies IV: A Documentary Record of the 22nd Congress of the Communist Party of the Soviet Union* (New York: American Association for the Advancement of Slavic Studies, 1962), p. 181.

50. He was rumored to have been put in Butyrka prison under particularly strict conditions "to knock the conceit out of him." Ivanov-Razumnik, *Memoirs*, p. 313. Medvedev, *Let History Judge*, p. 268, gives this description of Krylenko in prison: "M. V. Ostrogorskii tells us that the former Commissar of Justice N. V. Krylenko gave in only after cruel tortures. He asked for some paper in his cell, and there, in the presence of his comrades in misfortune, he began to create his counterrevolutionary organization. He would mumble 'Ivanov? No, he's a good official and a man, I won't put him down. But Petrov, he's a louse; let's sign him up.' " In a 1977 article Medvedev adds further details on Krylenko's arrest, based on a 1964 Soviet source. According to Medvedev, after Krylenko was dismissed as Commissar of Justice, he went to his dacha outside Moscow. Stalin telephoned him there, telling Krylenko: "We have confidence in you. Continue the work you were assigned to on the new legal code." That night NKVD forces surrounded the dacha and arrested Krylenko. Roy Medvedev, "New Pages from the Political Biography of Stalin," in Tucker, ed., *Stalinism*, p. 217.

51. Fomichev, note 37.

52. Feofanov, note 36.

53. The defector Alexander Orlov tells of working with both Vyshinsky and Krylenko and of a 1923 meeting of the three of them and one other prosecutor at Krylenko's mansion in Moscow. Orlov explains how Krylenko went out of his way to embarrass and ridicule Vyshinsky in front of his colleagues and of Vyshinsky's fawning servility. *The Secret History of Stalin's Crimes* (New York: Random House, 1953), pp. 336–339. This interaction between Krylenko and Vyshinsky is told in greater detail by Robert Sharlet in "In Search of Vyshinsky: The Formative Years," a paper presented at the 1979 meeting of the American Association for the Advancement of Slavic Studies, October 12, 1979, New Haven, Conn., pp. 17–18.

54. On the troikas and their relationship to the "special boards" of the NKVD, see Robert Conquest, *The Great Terror* (New York: Macmillan, 1968), p. 313.

55. V. L. Kuritsyn, "1937 God i Istoriia Sovetskogo Gosudarstva," *SGiP* 1988, no. 2:117.

Chapter 8

Vyshinsky, Krylenko, and Soviet Penal Politics in the 1930s

Eugene Huskey

Students of the Soviet Union have been reassessing the rise of Stalinism in the 1930s.[1] By shifting the focus of research from high politics to the constituent parts of the political and social system, recent scholarship has exposed the confusion and conflicts that plagued the nascent Soviet bureaucracy as it struggled to put down roots in the country and to satisfy the enormous demands placed upon it by the center and periphery. This research has brought a new recognition of the extent to which the political leadership in the 1930s was bedeviled by local resistance to central directives, by poor communication and inadequate staffing in the bureaucracy, and by the low "cultural level" of those asked to implement policy.[2]

The rise of Stalinism through the early and mid-1930s settled the question of who would wield power, but not how. On many fundamental issues of public policy the general line of the party was still being formed. Although Stalin was intent on replacing politics with administration, he was unable in this period to transform government from an art of resolving competing claims to a science of bureaucratic management.[3] Frequently standing above the policy debates, Stalin allowed subordinates to engage in lengthy and occasionally bitter struggles over the way forward. This was especially evident in the legal system, where the 1930s witnessed a protracted conflict between those who sought to restore important elements of the bourgeois legal tradition[4] and those who favored a continuation of the radical, or nihilist, approach to law that reigned during the second revolution of 1928–1932.[5] I argue below that A. Vyshinsky championed the first position, N. Krylenko the second, and that an appreciation of the personal, bureaucratic, and policy dimensions of this struggle for mastery over legal affairs in the 1930s is essential to an understanding of

This chapter is an amended version of Eugene Huskey, "Vyshinsky, Krylenko, and the Shaping of the Soviet Legal Order," *Slavic Review* Fall/Winter 1987, 46(3/4):414–428. Reprinted by permission.

the institutionalization of the Soviet political and legal order.[6]

From 1932 to 1936 Vyshinsky and Krylenko regularly aired their policy differences at professional conferences and in the popular and legal press, usually over questions of criminal justice and legal theory. But the competition between the two also turned on questions of personal and bureaucratic power, and in particular on the relative prominence of the Procuracy and the People's Commissariat of Justice, which served as the institutional bases of Vyshinsky and Krylenko, respectively. At stake were the jurisdictional boundaries of the Procuracy and Justice Commissariat, their relations to other legal institutions, especially the courts, and the claim of their leaders to speak with the authoritative voice in Soviet legal affairs.

On one level, then, this chapter is a case study of bureaucratic politics that seeks to illuminate the linkage between power and policy in Soviet legal development in the 1930s. But it is also an assessment of the legal revival that accompanied the winding down of the revolution in Soviet Russia. As such it must consider another major axis of conflict, that between Vyshinsky at the center and the legal periphery. The campaign by Vyshinsky to introduce a stable, disciplined, and professionalized legal system encountered the hostility and backwardness of local legal officials and institutions. Localism, the scarcity and poor quality of cadres, and the widespread reliance in the periphery on revolutionary "instincts" provided perhaps the most serious challenge to Vyshinsky's attempts to define and introduce a Soviet legal culture.

In this study Vyshinsky emerges as the central figure in what might be labeled the moderate, or positivist, wing of the Soviet legal community. For those who know Vyshinsky primarily through his participation in the Great Purge trials, the association of his name with even a partial restoration of law and legality in the USSR may appear farcical, if not worse. However, in the policy debates of the day it was Vyshinsky who championed the rejection of the legal nihilism of the second revolution and the installation of a new order that accepted a substantial part of the bourgeois legal heritage.[7] Although Vyshinsky later became infamous in the West for his support of analogy and the special evidentiary force of confession as principles of Soviet law, he initially sought to restrict their use—a position that placed him in conflict with Krylenko and the radical wing of the legal community in the early and mid-1930s. This paper is in part, therefore, a reinterpretation of the role of Vyshinsky in Soviet history.

The Interregnum in Legal Affairs

During the second revolution the future of law under Soviet socialism was in doubt. The campaign for the simplification of the legal system launched by Krylenko in 1927–1928 was perceived by many to be the beginning of the running down of law, which, it was argued, was being made redundant by the plan, by *administrirovanie*, and by communist morality. As legal procedures gave way to administrative methods, legal theorists spoke of the imminent demise of law. Legal education went into decline and students abandoned the law for more promising professions, such as engineering.[8]

But radical experimentation in law was increasingly vulnerable to attack at the beginning of the 1930s. By encouraging flexible and simplified legal norms and procedures, and thus breaking down the relatively stable legal structures that had emerged during NEP, the nihilist approach to law facilitated the adaptation of the legal system to the drive for the rapid industrialization, collectivization, and proletarianization of Soviet society. However, once the social and economic foundations of state socialism had been laid, a new appreciation emerged of the costs of the leftward shift in legal policy and of the advantages that a legal revival might provide to a regime in search of order and legitimacy.

The signal for a reassessment of the role of law under Soviet socialism came in June 1932 with the issuance of a joint party-government decree "On Revolutionary Legality." The decree reminded legal personnel that the law had not been abandoned and that a strict observance of legality, and procedural norms in particular, was expected. Although the decree and the exegesis that followed did not prompt an immediate rejection of legal nihilism, it did provide an opening to those who had been fighting a rearguard action throughout the second revolution against the legal policies of Krylenko and the legal theories of Pashukanis.[9]

Vyshinsky emerged at once as the leading proponent and theorist of a legal revival. The essential elements of his critique of legal nihilism were evident in a *Pravda* article published a day after the decree "On Revolutionary Legality."[10] Rejecting the idea that law is capitalist in form, Vyshinsky argued that it in fact reaches its fullest expression only under socialism. This required, therefore, the elevation, not the running down, of the role of law in Soviet society. Where Krylenko had sought the simplification of legal norms and procedures, Vyshinsky desired a return to the stability and precision of detailed legal codes. Vyshinsky also favored a restoration of specialization and professionalization in the legal community. He understood, moreover, the advantage of law as a legitimating device in Soviet society. He strove to remystify the law, which had been left exposed by the legal nihilists as a naked weapon of state control. Finally, Vyshinsky was particularly sensitive to the educative role of law. "In the current conditions," he wrote, "revolutionary legality assumes special importance not only as a weapon of proletarian struggle against class enemies, but also as a school of educating and reeducating unstable elements in the laboring classes."[11]

For almost two years, however, the ideas of Vyshinsky had little impact on legal behavior. If the development of legal policy had a direction in the period from 1932 to 1934, it came not from legal officials or theorists but from periodic decrees mobilizing the law in the service of the national economy. These decrees, such as the infamous August 7, 1932 law on the theft of socialist property, were authoritative policy statements that bore the direct imprint of the party leadership.[12] With the legal system of NEP shattered by the nihilist onslaught of the second revolution, the new decrees were less amendments to existing laws than *mots d'ordre* enlisting legal institutions in the latest political campaign. According to one jurist, because the existing Code of Criminal Law was outdated and inadequate, the decrees were introduced "so that the requirements of the party could be given legal form (*oformleny v zakone*)."[13]

Government by decree clearly did not represent the reconstruction of the legal system that Vyshinsky had envisioned. The heavy reliance on administrative signals, rather than reworked legal codes, to inform legal behavior was in many respects a continuation of the approach favored by radical jurists like Krylenko. Yet Vyshinsky seemed undaunted by the reluctance of the political leadership to restore legal stability. Indeed, from 1932 to 1934 he took the offensive by holding himself out as the most faithful and vigorous supporter of the new decrees, either through public pronouncements or the mobilization of his institution, the Procuracy, behind the expansion of the role of criminal law in the economy.

Restricted to a supporting role in the development of legal affairs, Vyshinsky nonetheless enjoyed a steady increase in his personal standing and bureaucratic power from 1932 to 1934. After working under Krylenko for two years as Procurator and Deputy People's Commissar of Justice of the RSFSR, Vyshinsky became the first Deputy Procurator of the USSR at the formation of an all-union Procuracy in June 1933. This appointment granted Vyshinsky all-union status (not to be achieved by Krylenko until the creation of a USSR People's Commissariat of Justice in 1936) as well as institutional independence from the RSFSR Justice Commissar. Unlike the RSFSR Procuracy, which operated within the RSFSR Justice Commissariat, the USSR Procuracy was a freestanding bureaucracy answering only to the Central Committee of the Communist Party. And although Vyshinsky reported formally to the USSR Procurator Akulov, he appears to have overshadowed the Procurator General in the articulation of legal policy and the day-to-day operation of the Procuracy.

As Deputy USSR Procurator, Vyshinsky was well-placed to compete with Krylenko and other republican justice commissars for the loyalty of procuracy workers. With the formation of a USSR Procuracy, Vyshinsky could reasonably claim a share in the supervision of procurators throughout the country. It was soon evident, however, that he desired nothing less than the complete transfer of control over republican procuracy organizations from the justice commissariats to the USSR Procuracy. He also sought a larger role for the Procuracy in the supervision of the courts. A justice official from Armenia reported in early 1934 that "the all-union Procuracy has exerted great influence on the strengthening of revolutionary legality in the region. In a short period of time the organs of justice in Armenia have felt the strong and practical (*operativnoe*) leadership of the all-union Procuracy."[14]

Krylenko understood the seriousness of this challenge. The apparatus of the justice commissariats was only a rump without its two subordinate institutions—the courts and the Procuracy. In 1931 Krylenko had successfully "fended off attacks" from officials in the Procuracy and judiciary who sought to separate their institutions from the RSFSR Justice Commissariat.[15] But the organizational unity shored up during the second revolution was again under threat, this time with Krylenko in a more vulnerable theoretical and bureaucratic position. Krylenko still appeared to be the dominant figure in Soviet legal affairs, as indicated by his leading role at the April 1934 Congress of Justice Workers. However, after two years of sniping at the exposed flanks of Krylenko's power and policies, Vyshinsky was poised to launch a frontal assault on the RSFSR Justice Commissar.

The Rise of Vyshinsky

In the spring of 1934, shortly after the party's Congress of Victors, a new phase began in the struggle between Vyshinsky and Krylenko. Leftist tendencies in law came under attack at national legal conferences[16] and in the pages of a new legal publication edited by Vyshinsky, *Za sotsialisticheskuiu zakonnost'* (For Socialist Legality) (renamed *Sotsialisticheskaia zakonnost'* in 1935). The introduction of a Procuracy journal under the control of Vyshinsky expanded and intensified the public debate, which had been largely restricted to the pages of *Sovetskaia iustitsiia* (Soviet Justice), the organ of the RSFSR Justice Commissariat. Unlike Krylenko, for whom legal publishing appeared to be peripheral to his administrative concerns as Justice Commissar (he became chief editor of *Sovetskaia iustitsiia* only in April 1936), Vyshinsky put his personal imprint on the Procuracy journal through regular lead articles and detailed legal analyses.[17]

The assassination of Kirov in December 1934 provided the first serious political test of Vyshinsky's ability and orientation as an editor. In an article printed ten days before the death of the Leningrad party leader, Vyshinsky—clearly unaware of the impending crisis—emphasized the need to accept numerous bourgeois legal principles into Soviet law, much as Lenin had favored the introduction of Western production techniques (e.g., Taylorism) into the Soviet economy. He also advocated the adoption of a single code of criminal procedure that would be applied to all defendants.[18] Yet when TsIK issued the *lex Kirov* on December 1, Vyshinsky temporarily abandoned his earlier tone of moderation. Traveling to Leningrad to assist in the investigation of Kirov's murder, he rapidly mobilized procuracy personnel as well as *Sotsialisticheskaia zakonnost'* in support of the latest party campaign. Where *Sovetskaia iustitsiia* appeared uncertain and restrained in its response to the events of early December, the journal of the Procuracy wrote at length and with confidence about the "rapid and decisive reworking of the justice organs [required] for the struggle against this type of crime." In antiterrorist cases, Vyshinsky argued, the Procuracy and its investigative organs assumed a special responsibility.[19]

The paradoxical position of Vyshinsky—the proponent of a single, or "unified," criminal process—taking the lead in the implementation of a law that applied radically simplified procedures to certain criminal cases was not lost on Krylenko. The RSFSR Justice Commissar ridiculed Vyshinsky for his theoretical inconsistency and opportunism. But to Krylenko's claim that the law of December 1, 1934 bore out his own theories on the flexibility of law and procedure, Vyshinsky asserted that the act against terrorism was simply an exception to the general rule of procedural stability and unity.[20] In spite of his vulnerability to criticism on theoretical grounds, Vyshinsky emerged as a major beneficiary of the campaign of repression unleashed by the assassination of Kirov. The party leadership, apparently more impressed by his actions in the weeks that followed Kirov's death than by the restorationist themes contained in his writings, named Vyshinsky USSR Procurator General in March 1935.[21]

The first authoritative public criticism of Krylenko accompanied the elevation of Vyshinsky to the post of Procurator General. In articles that marked Krylenko's thirty years of revolutionary activity, tributes to the Old Bolshevik were qualified by references to his theoretical mistakes. One author complained that because Krylenko had an "insufficient appreciation of the Leninist inheritance and an inadequate understanding of the work of Stalin on questions of criminal policy and the class struggle," he had proposed legislation that misconstrued the relationship between persuasion and coercion and underestimated the legal form.[22] The critic recognized, however, that Krylenko had been able "in a Bolshevik manner to uncover and correct mistakes when they appeared in his works."[23] It was therefore a rebuke, but one limited to past mistakes and softened by generous praise for a distinguished revolutionary career.[24]

The public criticism of Krylenko was resumed in May 1935 with a personal attack by Vyshinsky on Krylenko's proposals for a new draft code of criminal law. At a joint meeting of the Communist Academy and the Institute of Criminal Policy, Vyshinsky accused Krylenko of sanctioning a system of criminal justice where laws did not bind but only oriented judges. Such a system, Vyshinsky argued, violated the intent of Stalin's May 4 speech on cadres, which the Procurator General interpreted as a call for strict adherence to law.[25]

The conflict between Vyshinsky and Krylenko was now in the open, and polemics were exchanged between the two men during the remainder of 1935. After noting with sarcasm Vyshinsky's self-proclaimed "reluctance" to raise areas of disagreement, Krylenko recognized that on the questions of principle involved they should "fight to the end" (*drat' sia do kontsa*). Krylenko was particularly scathing in his critique of Vyshinsky's support for the absolute stability of law. "Think of what you're saying," Krylenko wrote. "Any liberal would sign your proposal with both hands." He reminded Vyshinsky that his was a bourgeois formula that would complicate the issuance of administrative directives by the party.[26]

In the closing contribution to this exchange, Krylenko adopted more conciliatory language but did not soften his critique of Vyshinsky. He expressed frustration with Vyshinsky's method of argument, which he claimed led to obfuscation instead of clarity, and with his didactic style in attempting to instruct the entire legal community in the implications of Stalin's speeches. He also accused Vyshinsky of adhering to bourgeois principles, such as *nullem crimen, nulla poena sine lege.* In the final, and most telling, strike at the Procurator General, Krylenko charged him with "publicly articulating one principle and then opportunistically altering it in practice."[27] Krylenko clearly had in mind Vyshinsky's behavior in the wake of the Kirov assassination, though others would later apply the characterization to Vyshinsky's role in the Great Purges.

The Debate over Legal Policy

At the center of the policy differences between Vyshinsky and Krylenko lay a fundamental disagreement over the inheritability of law from the bourgeois order. Where Krylenko sought to distance the Soviet Union from the bourgeois legal heritage, Vyshinsky favored a return to certain ideas and practices found in the legal systems of capitalist states. In numerous speeches and articles from 1934 to 1936, Vyshinsky argued for the integration of capitalist achievements in criminal justice into socialist law. "If we borrow this or that from bourgeois systems of justice, it is not enough to condemn it by labelling it bourgeois." If it serves the proletariat, Vyshinsky contended, it should be accepted.[28]

In order to enhance the legitimacy and effectiveness of Soviet law, Vyshinsky advocated a restoration of elements of bourgeois legal ritual. As part of an effort to make court sessions more ceremonial (*torzhestvennye*), he suggested that those present should stand at the reading of the verdict. In an article that must have appeared heretical to many, Vyshinsky wrote, "We know of the authority enjoyed by the English justice of the peace among the population of his county. We must achieve not less but more authority for our own judges."[29] After a period in which the legal nihilists had attacked the sanctity of legal tradition, Vyshinsky began what Marxists might call a refetishization of the law.

The movement toward a legal revival was undoubtedly facilitated by the international climate, which had, since the beginning of 1934, encouraged an increasingly isolated and vulnerable USSR to seek diplomatic accommodation with the potential enemies of Nazism in the West. The *perelom* in Soviet foreign policy led to a temporary rejection of the idea of the unity of the capitalist world. One could now speak of progressive as well as reactionary capitalist forces. This enabled Vyshinsky to smear his opponents in the Soviet legal community by illustrating how close their own legal agenda was to that of the fascists. For example, as part of his campaign to restore the pre-trial judicial hearing (*rasporiaditel'noe zasedanie*), he reminded the legal nihilists that the English equivalent—the grand jury—was currently under attack by reactionary elements in the West.[30]

The differences between Vyshinsky and Krylenko over the inheritability of law emerged during policy debates that accompanied the drafting of new codes of criminal law and procedure. Although Vyshinsky was the head of the drafting commission on criminal procedure, he was apparently dissatisfied with the draft codes issued in late 1934, which he felt left in place some of the simplified procedure that had been advanced in Krylenko's abortive drafts of 1927, 1929, and 1931. Having failed to defeat thoroughly the legal nihilists in the private deliberations of the commission, he took his arguments to the broader legal community. Informing these arguments were concerns for, first, a single criminal process, regardless of the crime or the background of the accused; second, a more thorough criminal process, to be achieved by a greater reliance on the pre-trial judicial hearing and on expert testimony at trial; and, third, a more effective and legitimate criminal process, to be realized through a reintroduction of the principle of adversariness, which had occupied a respected place at the trial stage in both the post-1864 and NEP justice systems.

During the second revolution, adversarial elements in court proceedings had been largely abandoned. Prosecutors and defenders appeared in only a small minority of criminal trials, and even then judges possessed the right to dispense with the "debate between the sides" (*prenie storon*). Vyshinsky now sought not only a revival of adversarial elements in Soviet criminal procedure but a strengthening of the division of state prosecutors (located within the Procuracy) and of the Bar, both of which had gone into decline in the early 1930s.[31]

On the question of the evidentiary value of confession by the accused, Vyshinsky attacked the idea, which he attributed to the NKVD, that a personal confession was sufficient evidence to indict.[32] Responding to claims of some proceduralists that "objective evidence" is unnecessary once the confession is in hand, Vyshinsky retorted that "nothing could be more mistaken than such a point of view, which has nothing in common with a correct understanding of the tasks of the Soviet investigation, of Soviet procedure." An overemphasis on the confession of the accused reflected "procedural backwardness, which is reactionary, harmful, and dangerous for investigation based on the principles of proletarian democracy. It's not by chance that the martial law statute (*voennyi ustav*) of Peter the Great built its system of evidence precisely on the personal confession of the accused."[33] What a difference between the views of Vyshinsky in the mid-1930s and his later apologies for the special evidentiary weight of confessions!

Perhaps the most vigorous exchange between Vyshinsky and Krylenko occurred over issues raised in the 1934 draft code of criminal law, which was composed by a commission under the leadership of Krylenko. Vyshinsky's complaints here centered on the stability of criminal norms. The Procurator General favored the enactment of a new criminal code with a list of fixed elements of a crime (*tverdye sostavy*) that would direct judicial behavior into predictable channels. Krylenko, on the other hand, viewed the criminal code not as "unalterable dogma" but as a working instrument in the hands of the court. The dispute concerned, therefore, how much flexibility judges should enjoy in reaching legal decisions. The centralist logic of Vyshinsky's legal theory is evident here in his concern for stability, though the Procurator General legitimated his stance by an expression of concern for the individual. "We cannot allow a citizen to be brought to court for a crime that is not designated in law."[34]

On this point, of course, Vyshinsky's argument was vulnerable, since Soviet law had for some time recognized the principle of analogy. When an act satisfied the elements of a crime, but the specific offense was not covered under an existing article of the criminal code, judges were permitted to try the accused under an "analogous" article. Thus, Vyshinsky did not challenge the principle of analogy directly. To have done so would probably have been too damaging politically. Instead he sought to restrict its application by introducing fixed elements of a crime that would provide some uniformity in the judicial designation of criminal activity. In a clearly defensive reponse to Krylenko's suggestion that he was against analogy, Vyshinsky protested that

> he had never come out against analogy, though he had fought against the distortion of analogy. . . . Comrade Krylenko is not simply for analogy, but evidently for a broad application of analogy. I am against a broad application of analogy. I am for the application of analogy not in contrast to the meaning of the law but in correspondence to its exact meaning.[35]

Vyshinsky's reputation in the West as the champion of the principle of analogy in Soviet law is, therefore, not wholly deserved. In the mid-1930s Vyshinsky appears to have been a forceful advocate for limiting the effects of analogy in the criminal justice system.

The other major point of controversy between Vyshinsky and Krylenko in criminal law concerned the flexibility of criminal sanctions. The issue was whether judges should be able to select the appropriate punishment from a range of available sanctions or be bound to the imposition of a fixed sanction for a crime. Although generally in favor of limiting judicial discretion, Vyshinsky made an exception on this question by pushing for the inclusion in the criminal code of a range of possible punishments for each crime. This proposal, dubbed by the legal radicals as "punishment by doses" (*dozirovka*), drew heavy fire from Krylenko. He argued that not only did *dozirovka* depart from the fixed sanctions of Stalin's August 7, 1932 law and the other decrees of the 1932 to 1934 period, it represented a theoretical retreat to bourgeois principles of criminal justice. Instead of directing judges to impose punishment based on its deterrent value or some other "scientific" principle, Vyshinsky was encouraging a return to the vague and pedestrian idea of making the punishment fit the crime. In Krylenko's view this would signify a revival in Soviet law of the concept of retribution (*vozmezdie*), which "we had rejected because it was the goal of bourgeois punishment."[36] He regarded the restoration of retribution as a concession to a sense of popular justice. In this view he was probably correct. Vyshinsky was far more sensitive than the legal radicals to the image of the legal system among the masses. He was willing to trade the "rationalism" of radical legal theory for a legal policy that promised stability and legitimacy.

Whatever the theoretical merits of Krylenko's position, he recognized that on the question of *dozirovka*, as on most other questions of criminal law and procedure, his was an increasingly isolated voice in the Soviet legal community. In the spring of 1935 Krylenko admitted that he had been the only person on the drafting commission to remain opposed to the introduction of a sliding scale of sanctions into the code of criminal law. "My comrades on the commission outvoted me and restored fully 'punishment by doses.' " He continued to insist, however, that it was they who were mistaken.[37]

Bureaucratic Struggles at the Center and Periphery

Behind the policy debates between Vyshinsky and Krylenko lay a struggle for bureaucratic power between the USSR Procuracy and the RSFSR Justice Commissariat. Under the leadership of Vyshinsky, the USSR Procuracy in 1935 intensified its efforts to separate republican and local procuracy organs from the justice commissariats and to integrate them fully into a centralized all-union Procuracy. As it stood, republican procuracy organizations submitted to an awkward dual subordination—laterally to the republican Justice Commissariat and vertically to the USSR Procuracy. For Vyshinsky, the introduction of a single vertical subordination was not only desirable as a means of undermining Krylenko's institutional base, it was essential to the formation of a USSR Procuracy with reliable and disciplined local branches. Initially, however, the offensive against dual subordination enjoyed little success. The USSR Procuracy was still forced to work through independent-minded republican procuracy organizations in its supervision of local procuracy personnel. In the summer of 1935, Vyshinsky publicly criticized the RSFSR Procuracy for failing to transmit communications from the USSR Procuracy that were directed to local procurators.[38]

A resolution of the jurisdictional battle came only in July 1936 as part of a larger restructuring of the legal bureaucracy that anticipated the new constitution. At this time the Soviet government finally established a justice commissariat at the all-union level. Although Krylenko was appointed the first Justice Commissar of the USSR, his elevation to all-union status signaled a diminution in his bureaucratic power because the institutional reorganization reduced the jurisdiction of the justice commissariats. Henceforth, the functions of Krylenko's institution would be limited to legislative drafting, legal propaganda, and the administrative supervision of the courts. The responsibility for the oversight of the Procuracy hierarchy was transferred once and for all to the USSR Procuracy.[39]

This was one of many bureaucratic victories for Vyshinsky in 1936. The Constitution of 1936 confirmed the privileged position of the Procuracy in the Soviet governmental structure with the introduction of a fixed seven-year term for the Procurator General and the granting to the USSR Procuracy of supreme supervisory powers (*vysshii nadzor*) over the other all-union commissariats and agencies. Although political factors constrained the Procuracy from intrusion into the affairs of the more powerful commissariats, such as Narkomtiazhprom, it was less reluctant to investigate activities within the weaker commissariats. Sensing the vulnerability of his own institution to domination by the Procuracy, Krylenko had proposed to the Constitutional Commission that the word supreme (*vysshii*) be removed from the draft, thereby limiting Procuracy oversight to republican and local institutions. His amendment was rejected, however. The Constitutional Commission also refused to support an amendment that sought to reduce Vyshinsky's power as Procurator General by entrusting the selection of lower-level procuracy personnel to executive committees of republican soviets as well as the USSR Procuracy.[40]

Vyshinsky felt vindicated by the bureaucratic reforms of 1936. They confirmed, he wrote, "the thesis about the separation of the Procuracy from the justice commissariats [that] I have advanced [*propogandiroval*] in lectures and in the press for a number of years." Comparing his institution to the absolutist French state, Vyshinsky noted that the Procuracy was now *unie et indivisible*.[41] But the allusion, as he well knew, was not wholly apt. While the Procuracy had indeed expanded and stabilized its jurisdictional borders by 1936, it was as yet a fragmented and ill-disciplined organization. Therefore Vyshinsky launched a new offensive, this one directed toward the centralization of power within the Procuracy itself.

Vyshinsky faced two major obstacles in his campaign to transform the Procuracy into an efficient bureaucratic apparatus led from the center. The first was the localism of lower-level Procuracy officials, the second, the absence of a professional legal culture among ordinary Procuracy workers. As Peter Solomon has shown, local justice officials, including procurators, were bound to local networks of political power through the financial support received from local government and through the power of appointment enjoyed by local party organs.[42] In the early 1930s legal nihilism further heightened the tendencies toward localism in legal institutions by discouraging strict adherence to centrally issued legal norms. The result was the development of a tradition among local legal cadres of relative autonomy from the center.

In 1936, the RSFSR Procurator Antonov-Ovseenko attacked local procurators for their insubordination, claiming that they at times refused to implement specific instructions from his office.[43] At a meeting of 500 leading Procuracy workers in Moscow in March 1937, Vyshinsky made clear his concern that the Procuracy could not function as a single, disciplined organization as long as each procurator regarded himself as independent and autocratic in his own realm. "We have still not eliminated the old unhealthy order in which each local procurator considers himself a sovereign prince (*udel'nyi kniaz'*). Khan Borkov is now ruling in Western Siberia, Sovereign Prince Philippov in the Moscow Region, and the acting Justice Commissar in the RSFSR is Duchess Niurina."[44]

The assault on localism by the USSR Procuracy assumed two forms. First,

Vyshinsky attempted to undercut the influence of local government on the Procuracy by reducing the financial dependence of procuracy organs on supplements from the budgets of local soviets. In the Kursk region, for example, the local procurator complained that he had been receiving more funds from the regional executive committee than from the RSFSR Justice Commissariat.[45] With the resolution of the jurisdictional disputes between the justice commissariats and the Procuracy in the last half of 1936, procuracy organs were removed from the budgets of republican justice commissariats, which had been traditionally underfunded, and transferred to the unitary budget of the USSR Procuracy. Local procuracy officials welcomed this step, apparently recognizing the greater authority of Vyshinsky over Krylenko in governing circles.[46]

The second, and more important, tactic in the battle with localism involved the intimidation and purging of procuracy officials who refused to submit to the leadership of Vyshinsky. Although the terror in the Procuracy clearly had origins beyond Vyshinsky's own drive for power, the Procurator General exploited fully the weapon at hand. In early 1937 Vyshinsky joined forces with the Administrative-Political Department of the Central Committee to investigate the RSFSR Procuracy. The information gathered in the course of this revision was used to oust the acting RSFSR Justice Commissar, Niurina, who had long differed with Vyshinsky over the role of lay personnel in the administration of justice.[47] Purges followed in many regions and republics, including Belorussia, where the NKVD reportedly "exposed and destroyed enemies sitting in the procuracy organs." At the All-Union Procuracy Conference in late May 1938, Vyshinsky reported that a number of procurators had to be removed for "political passivity."[48]

A grim example of Vyshinsky's use of intimidation occurred during debate at the May 1938 Conference, where he singled out for criticism the procurator of the Omsk region, Busorgin. After an interrogation by Vyshinsky over the regional procurator's failure to read personally all terrorist cases, a broken Busorgin recanted: "I made a big mistake." In a display of power that symbolized his victory over the Procuracy, Vyshinsky continued, "It's clear that he is not a procurator . . . people like Busorgin are unworthy to occupy the post of procurator and to speak at our meeting. I think our next measure should be to suggest to Busorgin that he leave the conference (Voices—'Correct!')"[49]

With the resistance to central control broken among procuracy officials, Vyshinsky still faced the formidable task of imposing discipline on the mass of procuracy workers. Here the problem was not political, but professional, unreliability. Years of neglect in the training and supervision of rank-and-file justice personnel had left the Procuracy and other legal institutions with cadres lacking a professional tradition and a sense of legal culture. In 1935, 85 percent of people's court judges had no more than a primary education.[50] The figures were almost certainly higher for the investigative branch of the Procuracy, which served as a dumping ground for poorly trained legal cadres. The procurator of the Kalinin region reported in the summer of 1936 that of the sixty-nine investigators in his region, only three had more than a primary education.[51] Although legal training among investigators and other justice personnel became increasingly common in the mid-1930s, it was with few exceptions restricted to a six-month short course in law. Thus, unlike lawyers in more developed legal systems, Soviet legal personnel in the 1930s did not begin their careers possessing standardized professional knowledge and techniques inculcated during an extended period of formal training.

Rapid turnover of personnel, a heavy work load, and a rudimentary base of technical support also contributed to the professional unreliability of procuracy cadres. In 1935 the annual rate of personnel turnover in the Procuracy reached thirty-one percent in some republics.[52] Talented personnel in particular were likely to remain in jobs for short periods since competent cadres at the base were quickly identified and promoted into leading posts in political and legal institutions. Because of the lack of qualified personnel and a shortage of funds, the Procuracy never operated with a full staff in this period. It was common, for example, to have investigators doubling as procurators at the *raion* level.[53] The understaffing, taken together with the growing responsibilities claimed by Vyshinsky for the Procuracy—responsibilities that were not welcomed by some local procurators—and the abysmal work conditions, made the professional existence of procuracy personnel very difficult indeed. The problems were often quite mundane, as indicated by the hortatory title of an article in *Sovetskaia iustitsiia* in 1935—"A Bicycle for Every Investigator!"[54]

The backwardness of the Procuracy was more than an embarrassment to Vyshinsky; it was a potential restraint on his power and prominence in the political and legal community. As the head of an institution devoted to criminal investigation and prosecution and to the general supervision of legality, Vyshinsky was as accountable for the performance of the legal system as any jurist. He cannot have felt entirely comfortable making reports to the central party apparatus that detailed the high percentage of criminal cases dismissed after investigation or overturned on appeal or by way of extraordinary protest. Vyshinsky disclosed, for example, that only one-half of individuals prosecuted in 1935 under the decree of August 7, 1932 were found guilty by the court. And regional statistics from 1935 indicated that from 25 to 42 percent of all criminal cases were dismissed before a verdict was issued.[55]

The aggregate evidence of incompetence in the legal system was supported by anecdotal material, the collection of which appeared to be a favorite pastime of ranking legal officials in Moscow. Vyshinsky could amuse and shock legal audiences with stories of a cook prosecuted under Article 111 for failing to salt the food or of a procurator with ten years' experience who was unable on an examination to distinguish between a cassation appeal and an extraordinary protest.[56] But having identified what he viewed as the product of years of underestimating the law by the legal nihilists, it was now up to Vyshinsky to illustrate to the political authorities that he could develop a more efficient and legitimate legal system. Hence his concern for legal education, improvements in the conditions of work, and professionalism.

Localism and the Campaign for Legality

Vyshinsky's commitment to legality and to the creation of a Soviet legal culture must also be understood, however, in the context of his struggle with localism. Vyshinsky saw in legality—that is, a respect for legal norms by citizens and jurists—a means of transferring the loyalties of rank-and-file procuracy workers from local officials to the center. At the base of the legal system, centrally issued laws and directives competed with the personal commands of local party, soviet, and legal officials. At least until the mid-1930s the center was not winning this competition. A procurator from the Chechen-Ingush region was reported by Vyshinsky to have told his investigators: "Don't pay attention to the laws, just listen to me."[57] Similarly, *raikom* officials frequently intervened to derail the legal process. In such cases, Vyshinsky argued, judges and procurators should not serve as the *chinovnik* of a *raikom* secretary. "It's proper to keep the *raikom* informed, to present them with the facts. [But] one should in a party manner, and not bureaucratically, show them, convince them, insist on one's own point of view."[58]

This desire to replace local influence with central direction lies at the source of the campaign for legality undertaken by Vyshinsky. In encouraging legal personnel to "breathe deeply the atmosphere of Soviet law" and to establish their own professional culture and language, Vyshinsky was not attempting to erect a legal facade for the Great Terror but to further the development of a centralized bureaucratic order as well as his own rise to power.[59] Both these goals were in fact put in jeopardy by the Terror. Thus, although Vyshinsky favored vigorous state repression (once labeling it "cultured activity"),[60] he had reason to resist the launching of a mass terror campaign under the direction of the NKVD. It threatened him personally, as a former Menshevik with untold enemies among party and justice officials, and professionally, as the head of an institution whose powers of supervision over the courts and law enforcement were eroded by the expanding jurisdiction of the NKVD. The Terror also halted, albeit temporarily, the stabilization of the legal order begun by the Procurator General.

From Vyshinsky's perspective, then, law was less a supplement to the administrative repression of the NKVD than an alternative to it. In 1935, he had publicly attacked the secret, summary procedures of the NKVD because unlike open, exemplary show trials, they served no educative or legitimating functions.[61] Indeed they promised to reawaken the nihilist tendencies toward law held by many justice workers. An assessment of Vyshinsky's role in the formation of the Soviet legal tradition must consider, therefore, more than his brutality as chief prosecutor in the purge trials or his retreat from moderation in the late 1930s on issues like analogy or the evidentiary value of confessions. With an array of options available to the

Stalinist leadership to eliminate opposition and spontaneity in politics, Vyshinsky consistently promoted law as the most effective, legitimate, and stable means of imposing rigid discipline on the Soviet bureaucracy and society.

Notes and References

1. This paper benefitted from the comments of Peter Solomon and an anonymous reviewer, and from the financial support of the Bowdoin College Faculty Research Fund.

2. See, for example, Kendall Bailes, *Technology and Society under Lenin and Stalin: Origins of the Soviet Technical Intelligentsia, 1917–1941* (Princeton, N.J.: Princeton University Press 1978); J. Arch Getty, *Origins of the Great Purges: The Soviet Communist Party Reconsidered, 1933–1938* (Cambridge: Cambridge University Press, 1985); and Peter Solomon, "Local Political Power and Soviet Criminal Justice, 1922–1941," *Soviet Studies* 1985, 31(3):305–329.

3. On the tendency of Marxism-Leninism to "abolish politics as activity and replace it with politics as apparatus," see A. Polan, *Lenin and the End of Politics* (Berkeley: University of California Press, 1984).

4. By bourgeois legal tradition I refer to those elements of stability, precision, and professionalism in law that were found in the capitalist states of the West and in the cities of Russia and the Soviet Union during the late Imperial period and the NEP.

5. On the role of Vyshinsky in Soviet legal affairs from 1931–1934, see Sharlet and Beirne, *supra*, chapter 6.

6. Although the writings of the legal theorist E. B. Pashukanis gave rise to the legal nihilism of the second revolution, it was the legal bureaucrat Krylenko who took the lead in the legal policy debates and in the personal and institutional struggle for control of the legal system. While critical of law as a bourgeois vestige, Pashukanis seemed more reluctant than Krylenko to dispense with the legal form in the 1930s. On his attempt to moderate the radical position of Krylenko on the reform of criminal procedure during the second revolution, see Eugene Huskey, *Russian Lawyers and the Soviet State: The Origins and Development of the Soviet Bar, 1917–1939* (Princeton, N.J.: Princeton University Press, 1986), pp. 171–173.

7. Vyshinsky and the legal moderates were not seeking, of course, a return to bourgeois jurisprudence but the development of a Soviet law of the transition period that contained bourgeois admixtures. Vyshinsky's position in the 1930s recalled the critique leveled at the end of NEP by Stuchka, Piontkovskii, and others against Pashukanis's commodity exchange theory of law. On the moderate-nihilist debates on legal theory in the last half of the 1920s, see Robert Sharlet, "Pashukanis and the Commodity Exchange Theory of Law: A Study of Marxist Legal Thought" (1968), Ph.D. dissertation, Indiana University.

8. By the mid-1930s more than half of judicial cadres had no legal training whatsoever, and of the 220 persons registered to teach law only eight had a *kandidat* or doctoral degree. "Na soveshchanii sudebnykh rabotnikov RSFSR," *Sovetskaia iustitsiia* 1936, 24:13.

9. "O revoliutsionnoi zakonnosti," *Sobranie zakonov i rasporiazhenii raboche-krestianskogo pravitel'stva SSSR* (1932), art. 298, p. 50.

10. A. Vyshinsky, "Revoliutsionnaia zakonnost' i nashi zadachi," *Pravda* June 28, 1932, p. 2.

11. Ibid.; A. Vyshinsky, "Reforma ugolovno-protsessual'nogo zakonodatel'stva," *Za sotsialisticheskuiu zakonnost'* 1934, 11:10–11. To say that Vyshinsky favored a legal revival in the Soviet Union in the 1930s is not to suggest that he supported the rule of law.

In his view law obligated the bureaucracy and society but not the lawgivers.

12. Solomon, "Local Political Power and Soviet Criminal Justice," p. 327 (fn. 47).

13. F. Volkov, "O reforme ugolov'nogo zakonodatel'stva," *ZSZ* 1934, 7:16; Ia. Berman, "O peresmotre UK," *ZSZ* 1934, 11:13–15.

14. "Na pervom vsesoiuznom soveshchanii rabotnikov iustitsii," *SIu* 1934, 13:28.

15. N. Krylenko, "Ocherednye zadachi organov iustitsii," in *Organy iustitsii na novom etape* (Moscow, 1931), pp. 17–26.

16. "K pervomu vsesoiuznomu soveshchaniiu rabotnikov iustitsii," *ZSZ* 1934, 4:3; "Pervoe vsesoiuznoe soveshchanie sudebno-prokurorskikh rabotnikov," *ZSZ*, 1934, 5:7–32.

17. Vyshinsky oversaw the rapid growth of the journal's tirage. At the end of its first year of publishing, 8,600 copies of the monthly *Sotsialisticheskaia zakonnost'* were printed, compared with 19,500 of its bimonthly competitor *Sovetskaia iustitsiia*. By the time of Krylenko's arrest in 1938, the print run for the Procuracy journal reached 25,000 copies, only 5,000 shy of *Sovetskaia iustitsiia*, which had served since 1922 as the authoritative journal on Soviet legal affairs.

18. A. Vyshinsky, "Reforma ugolovno-protsessual'nogo zakonodatel'stva," pp. 6–13.

19. A. Vyshinsky, "Za boevuiu rabotu organov iustitsii," *ZSZ* 1934, 12:4.

20. A. Vyshinsky, "Rech' tov. Stalina 4 maia i zadachi organov iustitsii," *SIu* 1935, 18:8; A. Vyshinsky, "Nashi zadachi," *ZSZ* 1935, 5:14.

21. This appointment was part of a broader shakeup of leading personnel in the political and legal system triggered by the fall of Enukidze, the secretary of TsIK. Accused by Khrushchev and others of "rotten liberalism" for his attempts to shield coworkers from the effects of the post-Kirov purge, Enukidze was replaced as TsIK secretary by the Procurator General Akulov, thus enabling Vyshinsky to assume the highest post in the USSR Procuracy. "Doklad tov. Khrushcheva na sobranii moskovskogo partiinogo aktiva," *Pravda* June 16, 1935, p. 3.

22. S. Bulatov, "Bolshevik-teoretik," *SIu* 1935, 4:6.

23. "30 let na revoliutsionnom postu," *SIu* 1935, 4:4.

24. Krylenko's fiftieth birthday would be noted several weeks later without critical comment. Indeed it was an occasion that personnel in the RSFSR Justice Commissariat proposed to remember by giving the name *Krylenko* to the village outside Moscow that served as the retreat for the Justice Commissar. "Prisvoit' imia tov. Krylenko," *SIu* 1935, 15:4. The major tribute on this occasion came from Bukharin, who lauded Krylenko, "his old comrade and friend," as more than "a dry legalist" (*sukhoi zakonnik*). Bukharin, "Zhizn' dlia revoliutsii," *SIu*, 1935, 15:4.

25. A. Vyshinsky, "Rech' tov. Stalina . . . ," pp. 1–8.

26. Krylenko, "Otvet k Vyshinskomu," *SIu* 1935, 18:8–10.

27. N. Krylenko, "Tochki nad 'i'," *SIu* 1935, 33:8–11.

28. A. Vyshinsky, "Rech' tov. Stalina . . . ," p. 6; "V institute ugolovnoi politiki," *SZ* 1936, 6:82; A. Vyshinsky, "Problema otsenka dokazatel'stva v sovetskom ugolovnom protsesse," *SZ* 1936, 7:27.

29. "O nekotorykh vazhneishikh voprosakh nashei sudebnoi politiki i sudebnoi raboty," *SZ* 1936, 4:6.

30. Vyshinsky, "Rech' tov. Stalina . . . ," p. 6; A. Vyshinsky, "Rasshirenie sovetskoi demokratii i sud—o nekotorykh voprosakh organizatsii sovetskoi iustitsii," *SIu* 1936, 19:10–12.

31. A. Vyshinsky, "Nashi zadachi," p. 15; A. Vyshinsky, "Rol' protsessual'nogo zakona v sotsialisticheskom gosudarstve rabochikh i krestian," *SZ* 1937, 3:1–11.

32. A. Vyshinsky, "Nashi zadachi," pp. 13–14. In the mid-1930s the evidentiary

question exacerbated the already strained relations between the NKVD and the Procuracy, which in law possessed supervisory powers over investigations carried out by the NKVD. The criminal investigation wing of the NKVD resented the requests by supervising procurators for evidence beyond a personal confession. Vyshinsky in turn complained that NKVD officials often treated procurators with the same contempt that procurators reserved for criminal defenders (ibid., pp. 12–13).

33. Ibid., p. 13.

34. A. Vyshinsky, "Rech' tov. Stalina . . . ," p. 7.

35. A. Vyshinsky, "Otvet na otvet," *SZ* 1935, 10:29–30. See also Vyshinsky, "Rol' protsessual'nogo zakona . . . ," pp. 1–11.

36. N. Krylenko, "Proekt ugolovnogo kodeksa Soiuza SSR," *SIu*, 1935, 11:1–10.

37. Ibid., p. 10. The isolation of Krylenko was made more complete by the success of Vyshinsky in tying him to the nihilist policies of the second revolution, many of which the Justice Commissar had disavowed. Whether because of political expedience or the changed environment for legal development, Krylenko adopted a less radical approach to law in the mid-1930s. However, under constant attack from Vyshinsky for his mistakes during the second revolution, Krylenko was never able to shed the reputation of a legal nihilist.

38. V.[Vyshinsky], "Nel'zia li bez organizatsionnoi putanitsy, plodiashchei volokity," *ZSZ* 1935, 6:36.

39. Krylenko, "Narkomat iustitsii Soiuza SSR i ego zadachi," *SIu* 1936, 23:1–3.

40. A. Vyshinsky, "Stalinskaia konstitutsiia i zadachi organov iustitsii," *SZ* 1936, 8:6–23.

41. Ibid., p. 20. Vyshinsky, ever the formalist in dress and manners, liked to flaunt his knowledge of foreign languages and legal systems.

42. P. Solomon, "Local Political Power and Soviet Criminal Justice," pp. 305–329.

43. "Vsesoiuznoe prokurorskoe soveshchanie," *SZ* 1936, 8:56.

44. "Aktiv prokuratury," *SZ* 1937, 9:96–101.

45. "Vsesoiuznoe prokurorskoe soveshchanie," p. 58.

46. Ibid.

47. "Aktiv prokuratury Soiuza SSR," *SZ* 1937, 7:88–91.

48. "Vsesoiuznoe prokurorskoe soveshchanie," *SZ* 1938, 6:9.

49. Ibid., pp. 18–20.

50. Kozhevnikov, "Nashi kadry," *SIu* 1935, 35:5.

51. "Soveshchanie v prokurature Soiuza SSR i raionnye sledovateli," *SZ*, 1936, 7:73.

52. "Operativno-proizvodstvennoe soveshchanie v soiuznoi prokurature," *ZSZ* 1935, 8:49–50.

53. Ibid.

54. "Kazhdomu narodnomu sledovateliu—velosiped!" *SIu* 1935, 11:3.

55. A. Vyshinsky, "Trekhletie zakona 7/VIII 1932g. 'Ob okhrane obshchestvennoi (sotsialisticheskoi) sobstvennosti,' " *SIu* 1935, 28:8; A. Vyshinsky, "Rech' tov. Stalina . . . ," pp. 4–5; "Vsesoiuznoe prokurorskoe soveshchanie," 1936, p. 50.

56. A. Vyshinsky, "Rech' tov. Stalina . . . ," p. 3; "Vsesoiuznoe prokuroskoe soveshchanie," 1936, p. 46.

57. "Doklad t. Vyshinskego o merakh k uluchsheniiu kachestva sudebnoi i prokurorskoi raboty," *SIu* 1934, 13:20.

58. Vyshinsky, "Nashi zadachi," p. 6.

59. Ibid., p.5.

60. A. Vyshinsky, *Revoliutsionnaia zakonnost' i zadachi sovetskoi zashchity* (Moscow: Redaktsionno izdatel'skii sektor Mosoblispolkoma, 1934), p. 27.

61. A. Vyshinsky, "Nashi zadachi," pp. 12–15.

Index

About the Contributors

DONALD D. BARRY is University Professor of Government and co-director of the Center for International Studies at Lehigh University. He has frequently lived in and visited the Soviet Union. Among his many published books are *Contemporary Soviet Politics* and *The Legal Foundations of Public Administration.*

PIERS BEIRNE is Professor of Sociology and Legal Studies at the University of Southern Maine. His recent work has appeared in the *American Journal of Sociology*, the *British Journal of Criminology*, *Contemporary Crises*, *Criminology*, and the *Law & Society Review*.

SUSAN EVA HEUMAN completed a Ph.D. in history at Columbia University and studied international law at the Institut Universitaire des Hautes Études Internationales. She has taught at the City University of New York (CUNY) and the University of Zambia, and is currently teaching at Baruch College of the City University of New York. She is completing a book on B. A. Kistiakovsky.

ALAN HUNT is Professor of Law and Sociology at Carleton University, Ottawa. His research interests include jurisprudence, critical legal studies, and Soviet legal theory.

EUGENE HUSKEY is Associate Professor of Political Science at Stetson University in DeLand, Florida. He was educated at Vanderbilt, Essex, and the London School of Economics. Among his works are *Russian Lawyers and the Soviet State: The Origins and Development of the Soviet Bar* and articles on Soviet law and politics in *Soviet Studies*, *Slavic Review*, *Russian Review*, and the *American Journal of Comparative Law*.

PETER B. MAGGS is Corman Professor of Law at the University of Illinois at Urbana-Champaign. He graduated from Harvard College and Harvard Law School and did postgraduate work at Leningrad State University. He has taught as a Fulbright lecturer at Moscow State University, and has written extensively on Soviet law.

ROBERT SHARLET is Professor of Political Science at Union College, Schenectady. His most recent book is *P. I. Stuchka: Selected Writings on Soviet Law and Marxism* (M. E. Sharpe, 1988), co-edited and translated with Piers Beirne and Peter B. Maggs. His present research is on Soviet constitutionalism from Brezhnev to Gorbachev.